Y0-DYO-504

The Mexican American

The Mexican American

Advisory Editor
Carlos E. Cortés

Editorial Board
Rodolfo Acuña
Juan Gómez-Quiñones
George Fred Rivera, Jr.

Latin Americans in Texas

Pauline R. Kibbe

ARNO PRESS
A New York Times Company
New York — 1974

Reprint Edition 1974 by Arno Press Inc.

Copyright, 1946, by The University of
  New Mexico Press
Reprinted by permission of The University
  of New Mexico Press

THE MEXICAN AMERICAN
ISBN for complete set: 0-405-05670-2
See last pages of this volume for titles.

Manufactured in the United States of America

Library of Congress Cataloging in Publication Data

Kibbe, Pauline Rochester, 1909-
    Latin Americans in Texas.

    (The Mexican American)
    Reprint of the ed. published by the University of
New Mexico Press, Albuquerque, which was issued as New
Mexico. University. School of Inter-American Affairs.
Inter-Americana series. Studies, 3.
    Bibliography: p.
    1. Mexican Americans--Texas. I. Title.
II. Series. III. Series: New Mexico. University.
School of Inter-American Affairs. Inter-Americana
series. Studies, 3.
F395.M5K52 1974   301.45'16'8720764   73-14205
ISBN 0-405-05679-6

LATIN AMERICANS IN TEXAS

This is a publication of
The School of Inter-American Affairs
The University of New Mexico
Inter-Americana Studies III

The financial assistance of the Division of Spanish-Speaking Peoples in the United States of The Institute of Ethnic Affairs, Inc., Washington, D. C., made possible the publication of this edition in English. Arrangements have been completed whereby the National University of Mexico will sponsor an edition in the Spanish language.

Latin Americans in Texas

Pauline R. Kibbe

THE UNIVERSITY OF NEW MEXICO PRESS

ALBUQUERQUE : : 1946

DEDICATED

to

The People of Texas — All of Them

and to the

People of Mexico

Preface

THOSE WHO WOULD acquaint themselves with the problems of Latin Americans everywhere, especially their problems in getting along with Anglo Americans within the State of Texas, are confronted immediately with the complete absence of any one source book which might serve as a guide. It is to fill this need, in an admittedly inadequate but nevertheless comprehensive fashion, that the present text has been prepared.

I make no pretense that this is an exhaustive study. On the contrary, it is an attempt to sketch clearly, logically, and humanly, as a basis for understanding and action, the historical and economic background of our people of Mexican extraction, as I have understood it from extensive reading; the important bearing of conditions in Texas upon relations between the United States and the other American republics; the problems of Latin Americans in the State, as I have encountered them in actual experience; and a sound, workable approach to the solution of those problems, with a view to furthering mutual understanding among the people of Texas and a solemn appreciation of Texas' role in the maintenance of unity in the American Hemisphere.

The bibliography aims to be as complete as possible, insofar as the Texas situation is concerned, including some unpublished materials. Reference is made to pamphlets and bulletins relative to specific phases of problems in Texas which have been prepared by various State and Federal agencies. Some of these publications are still available; others are already out of print. It is hoped that realization of the paucity of reliable information in published form will stimulate research in the various fields discussed.

It would be utterly futile to attempt to acknowledge, by name, all those whose invaluable contributions have made this volume possible. It would be necessary to begin more than six years ago and recall the many cherished friends and casual acquaintances, not only in Texas, but throughout the United States and Mexico, who have added, consciously or unconsciously, to my knowledge and understanding of the subject.

The actual labor involved in the collection of data and the conduct of personal investigations has been made possible chiefly by three agencies. The first of these is the Office of Inter-American Affairs, Washington, D. C., which by a substantial grant of funds to the University of Texas, in February, 1943, gave the initial impetus to constructive work in the inter-American field in Texas. The group that administered these funds was composed of eight professors, with Dr. Robert L. Sutherland as chairman, and was known as the Executive Committee on Inter-American Relations in Texas. I was engaged as Field Associate to the Committee until August, 1943, when the Good Neighbor Commission of Texas was created by Governor Coke R. Stevenson. Thereupon I became Executive Secretary to the Commission, in which capacity I still serve.

It must be clearly understood, however, that this is a personal document and not an official statement on the part of the State of Texas or any agency thereof.

In addition to those individuals and organizations mentioned in the book, the unselfish assistance of others in supplying specific data, in giving unstinted inspiration and encouragement, and in reading and making constructive criticism of the manuscript, must be publicly acknowledged. Among them are Francisco Alatorre, Father John J. Birch, E. Marion Bonnell, Victor Borella, Connie Garza Brockette, Harry Benge Crozier, Father Paul J. Ehlinger, Mary Nan Gamble, M. C. Gonzales, June Hyer, Hall Logan, John L. McMahon, Jane and Michel Pijoan, Belle Rosenbaum, George I. Sánchez, Henry Nash Smith, Robert E. Smith, Thomas S. Sutherland, and Stanley Walker.

To Virginia Prewett, author of the excellent book, *The Americas and Tomorrow*, I wish to express my heartfelt thanks for a large part of the material incorporated into Chapter III; and to Joaquín Ortega my profound gratitude and appreciation for his painstaking criticism of the entire manuscript—without which I would have been guilty of several inaccuracies and lapses.

To Robert C. Eckhardt I am deeply grateful for much of the background material contained in Chapter XI, relative to the development of the cotton industry in Texas. His collaboration on many phases of the book has been indispensable.

For his keen analysis of the book as a whole, particularly those chapters relating to Mexico, for his many constructive suggestions on content and approach, and for his genuine interest in and enthusiasm for the work, I shall be forever indebted to Gustavo Ortiz Hernán.

PAULINE R. KIBBE

Austin, Texas
July 1st, 1946

TABLE OF CONTENTS

LIST OF ILLUSTRATIONS

Foreword

In November, 1945, when I was about to start work in the
new position to which I had been assigned and which I still
hold, I went to Washington to try to find some reliable information on "that problem" whose faint echoes had reached me
during my stay in the East. I thought at the time that the
ugly word "discrimination," which our Spanish purists decline
to translate into that language, meant mainly that somebody
could not get a cup of coffee or a glass of beer when he most
needed it, because, as soon as the owner of the place detected
in his accent or his personal appearance that he was a Mexican
or Latin American, the proprietor would feel it beneath his
station to render a service even in exchange for an odorless
and raceless dollar. My search in Washington was not fruitful.
The shelves of the Library of Congress and other institutions
are quite well provided with books on the relationships of
many different cultural groups to the North American life;
they bulge with studies of all types about the agencies and
forces that have created that mystic entity "the melting-pot of
the world." Perhaps the Ibero-Americans of the Southwestern
United States rate only a frying pan; but as a matter of fact,
very little has been written about them one way or the other.
Several months later, when I settled in San Antonio and
was more familiar with the environment and with the requirements of my work, I held a very interesting conference with a
beautiful blonde lady. She is an artist, a true and proven friend
of Mexico and the Mexicans. Out of pure love she has consistently devoted an important part of her time to the promotion of a good international relationship between our two

neighboring countries. She told me, and I had to agree with her, that there is a type of discrimination that every restaurant or cabaret or "speak-easy" owner practices in all regions of this vast earth. It seems that the right to accept or reject customers is as sacred as the right of mixing cocktails or of pouring cheap whiskey from one bottle into another with a more impressive label on it. An unshaven man or a stockingless woman would not be allowed at Ciro's or Ambassadeur's in Mexico City. To her mind everything was really sweet and orderly, and the whole problem of intercultural strife could be solved with a few more barbershops in the proper places, and with some cheap clothing stores established, to sell goods on the installment plan.

But I happened to have in my pocket the manuscript of the last chapter of this book, which I was to criticize. All I had to do was to let the lady read it—and she was convinced that the problem was deeper and wider than she had suspected and that, after all, not being able to get a cup of coffee or a glass of beer at the desired time and place was by no means the full measure of the problem of the Latin American in the United States—not even the most important aspect of the problem.

It serves no useful purpose to conceal any longer that I am at present serving as Consul General of Mexico for seven states in the South and Southwest, with headquarters in San Antonio. It is possible that this confession represents indulgence in the old Latin love for titles. In our countries, once you receive your diploma from the university, you are a "doctor," a "licenciado," or an "ingeniero" forever and ever after. At the same time it is often very difficult to divorce the skin from the uniform, and sooner or later you find that "el hábito sí hace al monje." I must make it clear, then, that I am not writing these lines as an official representative of my government. I am writing as a person, hoping to exercise my old right as a newspaperman to say what I think, and say it without trying too hard to be diplomatic.

In quoting two instances from my own professional experience, I hoped to illustrate how extensive the void has been in our knowledge of the conditions under which Latin Americans have lived in the Southwestern part of the United States. I hoped to show also how prone is everybody to look at certain surface disturbances, the dramatic "incidents," the mere symptoms of trouble and maladjustment, and to ignore the fundamental, underlying causes. The need of an intensive study and critical analysis of all questions arising from "race" prejudice was proclaimed by Professor Henry Pratt Fairchild in a recent article in *The Saturday Review of Literature*. He said: "It is certainly true that most of us, including even some that rank as experts in the field, have made very little effort to understand the real nature of group feeling, to differentiate among the various types of groups of which society is composed and the diverse emotions and sentiments that are associated with those groups, or to use conventional words and phrases with care and precision. Yet exactly this kind of care and study is indispensable if the grave and urgent problems that arise from group relations are to be dealt with efficiently and constructively, not to say scientifically."

Now, the chief virtue of this book by Mrs. Pauline R. Kibbe, to borrow some more words from Professor Fairchild, is that it makes "a plea for . . . an immeasurably wider grasp of the truth in this vast field, and for a readiness to face the truth, when established, squarely and courageously, and to use it intelligently in the interests of the brotherhood of all mankind." Where she does not know the answers, she puts the problem clearly. Above all, she states the problems, along with an excellent compilation of opinions and facts, so that the totally uninformed reader can find his way in a situation about which, in Texas and the Southwest particularly, he is confused by propaganda and incomplete information in the newspapers and by the false starts that have been made by well-intentioned but not too well-informed persons. The book will elicit the interest also of plain good citizens, people who have not yet recognized their important role in the solution of problems of discrimination through amicable adjustment in this part of the country—people who, in short, need only the unbiased information that such a book as this can give, to set them operating as good citizens in a wider and better sense.

Besides, Mrs. Kibbe's book, I think, is an important *political* document, a kind of political symptom, so to speak. In no sense an official statement coming from any formally authorized political source, the book is nevertheless the work of one who has occupied an executive position. That position has brought the author into contact with everyday realities, definite problems, concrete and specific situations fraught with difficulties. This book, then, unofficial as it is, represents a recognition from *within Texas,* from experiences within the area of "trouble," that a problem or a set of problems exists. No "do-gooder" from the outside speaks here. A citizen of Texas speaks out of her own mind and heart and experiences.

Some of the analyses of problems and some of the suggested solutions will undoubtedly stir controversy. It is well that a book should stir up controversy if the arguments and disputes send everybody looking for more illumination, if the specialists get busy to ascertain facts more clearly and to bring theories more closely into accord with facts and realities. If a book leaves anybody unsatisfied and sends him on to ascertain specific facts more clearly, it is a good book and will have served a great purpose.

But it would be a tragedy if a book like this should make any reader, because of disagreement over some detail, some explanation, some suggested solution, grow angry and resent the entire performance. Unfortunately, among the various groups and the outstanding individuals who concern themselves with any fight for human justice, it often happens that their ardor for a good cause is equalled only by their fervent distrust of, and growing enmity towards, other groups and individuals interested in precisely the same questions, the same ends, the same results. Political Leftists are notoriously given to this error. Members of closely related political faiths hate each other more fervently and violently than they hate the avowed common enemy. It is not inconceivable that this kind of resentment could crop up among groups ardently devoted to an improvement in the conditions of Latin Americans in Texas and the Southwest.

I now divulge a little backstage secret. The publishers of this book have sought to avoid such a situation in this instance. They put the author to no end of effort and put themselves to a great deal of trouble in an attempt to get the large objections to this work out of the way beforehand. Instead of risking futile critical wrangling after publication, they sought a kind of highest common denominator of agreement *in advance,* not because they are afraid of controversy, but because they wanted this book to serve a good cause in the best possible way. They called upon a number of people of varying slants upon the problems to make suggestions to the author. I know that all suggestions were made in good faith and that the author accepted all that she conscientiously could accept, in like good faith. And so I should like to plead with all new readers that they too adopt a constructive attitude towards it now that it is in print. For, let us make no mistake about it, the enemies of tolerance, reasonableness, and good will are enemies enough for all of those who are seriously devoted to the cause of improved intercultural relations.

These considerations prompt me to express earnest and unqualified praise for the University of New Mexico, and in particular for its Director of Publications, Dr. Dudley Wynn, and for that seasoned champion of the best intellectual causes, Dr. Joaquín Ortega, Director of the School of Inter-American Affairs. Both are fully aware of the problem of discrimination in the Southwest and its many implications as they translate themselves in terms of personalities . . . and of personal clashes. It was their untiring devotion and their tact which made this book, in its present form, a vertex of good will and enlightened opinions.

The problem of discrimination against a minority! It is, to my mind, at the same time a cause and an effect: a cause when a deep-rooted social prejudice—or antipathy—asserts itself with no other excuse or pretext, creating a wide variety of reactions among the offenders and the victims, an effect when it appears only as a symptom of economic, educational, and general level-of-living evils.

For the correction of the wrongs, there are people who believe in coercion by law and in punishment; there are others who believe in education. This argument is, to a great extent, futile. Education, of course, is ultimately the only cure. But we must not fall back into the rudimentary error that, while waiting for later generations to benefit from the teaching and preaching of good will, we now have nothing to do but to relax and enjoy this most perfect of all worlds. That nothing can be solved except by education is a deep truth—and a dangerous one when used as the final answer by those who wish to do nothing *now*. Lectures, work with groups, social and labor organization, wage improvements, sanitation, tribunals and fines, and even corporal punishment, all are, in the last analysis, educational measures. Dissent should not exist about this essential principle, but only about the means and the rate of speed of a really serious and profound educational campaign comprehending all the elements of the population of Texas and the whole Southwestern tip of the nation.

In the attack upon discrimination, the enactment of certain legal measures is no doubt necessary. (I regard as particularly intelligent the proposal of the author that a constitutional amendment be adopted embodying a primary principle that will avoid many of the technical difficulties that lawyers have already quibbled about.) But "timing" is important. You cannot legislate people into humane brotherliness. Adopt every measure so rightly advocated by Mrs. Kibbe and throw in stiff doses of coercion and punishment—and the eradication of prejudice and discrimination will still be a long, long task. That is why I find it so idle to reject blindly one measure which somebody advocates, while advocating another in its stead. All of them may be necessary; none of them will automatically solve all the problems. To work wisely and co-operatively, to improve constantly our knowledge of the problems, to trust in the good will of others, to discuss and to debate, to cling to the principle that hard work and good sense will accomplish more than angry shouting—these are the important things. It would be paradoxical indeed if we set out to combat prejudice with prejudice, intolerance with intolerance.

The Southwest of the United States is the point of confluence of two great peoples. Their history is common. Their Spanish and Anglo-Saxon names intertwine in every significant event of the past. Their labor, their sacrifice, their blood have always been mixed in every great enterprise for the common welfare. True, the present development of the Southwest and of the whole country could never have been possible without the geographical bases provided by former Mexican territories, and this consideration constitutes now not a material but a moral indebtedness, which just statesmen and thinkers are prone to acknowledge even if it is only by implication. But, as the author says, of greater importance has been the loyal toil of countless generations of workers of Mexican extraction in the building of the great country that the United States is today. The seemingly endless railway tracks, the highways, the orchards, the product of the cotton fields year after year, the cornucopia of produce emptying onto the tables of the whole nation—all these blessings of bounty could not have been and still would not be possible without their help. More dramatically, the lists of casualties in Bataan or Corregidor, the Far East, and many a shore of the Old Continent read like a telephone directory in any town in the Republic of Mexico. There are also the many important facets of the cultural contribution of this group which, in its immense variety, is a keeper of old and worthy traditions.

And so we have here no question of superficial politics, something to vote for or against and then forget. Nor is it a question of doing the right thing, endorsing an obviously wise policy such as the Good Neighbor Policy, and then promptly forgetting it too. It is a matter of establishing fundamental human rights which are universally recognized in theory but which need to be translated into the realities of life—every day, right in the world around us.

The wastage of human resources has been and is appalling. Segregation, discrimination, hatred, lack of even the will to understand other kinds of people have made our life narrower instead of richer. These failures keep idle the best capital of any nation, her own men. Why can't we think of prosperous communities in which two great modes of life come together like the arms of two mighty rivers? Why can't we work for a bilingual culture, the like of which has not been seen thus far in the world? Why are we depriving ouselves voluntarily and foolishly of access to the wealthiest treasures of the world, and why can't we share our glories and our achievements in the same way that we have always shared our struggles? Without contradiction, we could easily bury under the same monument the ashes of all our national heroes. Still, we are afraid of building our homes side by side.

This is the challenge for all of Texas, for the whole Southwest. This is the shining opportunity which seems at each turn to be slipping away in a stream of mud. The right path would be so much easier, and Texas and the Southwest could be proportionately greater. The beautiful words that we read every day in the editorials of the papers, that we hear from the pulpits, that are enunciated over and over again by the leaders, could then come to have a meaning.

I realize now, perhaps too late, that after all I am not the author and should not go on writing as if I were the owner of the place. I was not invited to come for dinner.

This is a good book; courageous, muscular, it is a call for immediate action. It is an extremely important event that a long, deadly silence on this matter is finally broken with an articulate exposition of facts and with a full schedule of proposed remedies. "Speech," said Thomas Mann beautifully, "is civilization itself. The word, even the most contradictory word, preserves contact—it is silence which isolates."

Independently of how many opinions could be advanced in regard to the many questions brought to the public mind by the following pages, and as I come to the end of my remarks, I cannot but acknowledge a general feeling which lingers in my memory. It is, I would say, like recalling the essential features in the physiognomy of a friend, when, maybe, some particulars are overlooked, but the essence, the character, stand out. In thinking about the book now, I have forgotten many details; but, foremost in my mind, is the attitude of sympathy, understanding, almost tenderness toward Mexico and Mexicans, which permeates the context and which expresses what really is the intention and the soul of the author. From the very first chapter, with its dramatic presentation of contrast and injustice, and throughout the other chapters, there is a continuous effort to comprehend and to explain, to overlook difficulties, and to call generously for admiration of the virtues of the Mexican nation by the people of the United States. And no matter how many opposite viewpoints could be presented in regard to concrete proposals or even the abstract opinions of the author, it is only too clear that her protest against the evils we suffer is unmistakable and vigorous.

She has fulfilled that commandment of Kahlil Gibran to his good people:

> "When you meet your friend on the roadside or in the market place, let the spirit in you move your lips and direct your tongue.
> For his soul will keep the truth of your heart as the taste of wine is remembered
> When the colour is forgotten and the vessel is no more."

GUSTAVO ORTIZ HERNÁN

xxi

Part 1

The Challenge

Chapter 1

What's the Matter With Texas?

H E WAS A little thin, this boy who joined the group in the room behind the grocery store; and he moved rather slowly, like one who has recently spent long, weary weeks in a hospital bed. He still wore the uniform of the United States Army, and on his chest were displayed five ribbons, including the Purple Heart, and the coveted blue and silver badge of the combat infantryman.

He was an American hero, and his face and neck offered mute testimony of the sacrifice he had made for his country. The shrapnel that caught him in Germany had shattered his left cheekbone, drawing up his mouth in a set grimace. He was blind in his left eye, deaf in his left ear, and was just regaining the power of speech. He had been unable to utter a sound for forty days after the shrapnel hit him. Around his neck ran a long, angry welt, like a saber cut.

He was an American hero—but his name was Arturo Músquiz, and his home was a little town in West Texas.

He had just come home eight days previously, and was awaiting the call to return to the hospital for plastic surgery. He should have been happy, this young soldier on the verge of being honorably discharged from the Army after more than three years of active service. He should have been happy, but he wasn't. He was bewildered.

He spoke only occasionally, leaving the burden of conversation to the other men. There were five of them altogether, Texans of Mexican descent. For all of them that little West Texas ranching center was home. It was the only home they knew. It was the only home Arturo had ever known, but somehow he no longer felt at home there.

It wasn't that he was suffering from wanderlust or a desire to get back into action and help finish off the Japs. That wasn't it. He knew he was incapacitated for further military service, and there wasn't any place he really wanted to be except right where he was—at home with the family. His unhappiness sprang from another source.

It wasn't that the town had changed while he was gone. The town was about the same, but Arturo was seeing it in a different light—as well as he could see it, that is, with one eye.

His friends did his talking for him, at first, and the things they had to say weren't pretty. They didn't seem a fitting welcome, somehow, for a boy who had all but died in the service of his country. They didn't seem to belong in the picture of what an American hero has a right to expect when he comes home, triumphant, from the wars.

After the first few days with the family, Arturo had wandered down town to take in the sights and do a little gossiping with friends over a cup of coffee or a beer, and maybe go to a movie. That was the day of his disillusionment. That was the day he learned that a uniform and service ribbons—even obvious wounds—didn't affect his status among the townspeople. To them he was a "Mexican," and Mexicans weren't served in the cafes or restaurants. Mexicans wanting a shave or a haircut were directed to one certain barbershop on the edge of town. Mexicans wishing to see a movie were told there were seats in the balcony only.

No, things hadn't changed in his home town. But Arturo had changed. During the long years he had been away— going through training, sharing bunks and fox holes and K-rations with other soldiers, advancing, fighting, advancing, and fighting again—he had forgotten what things were like in his home town. He had even forgotten the bitterness that he carried with him when he went off to war; bitterness toward the invisible but nonetheless impregnable walls that had separated him from those called "Anglo Americans." For in the Army those walls had ceased to exist. He had been accepted on equal terms. He had done his job as well as or better than the next man. He had become simply an American among Americans.

Now, as he sat slumped in his chair, he was groping for an explanation. He wasn't bitter again—not yet; he didn't have the strength to be bitter. He was puzzled, and he was very unhappy.

But his friends were bitter. They were older men, and they hadn't been away. They were accustomed to suffer the town's pettiness. It was an old story to them, but suddenly they had found a new resentment against it. Conditions to which they had long ago resigned themselves were now spotlighted and magnified by their effect on Arturo. And Arturo was only the first of many who would soon be returning to the home town; only one of the dozens of Latin Americans whose names were printed boldly on the town's honor roll in the lobby of the court house. Some of those boys wouldn't be coming back, for there were gold stars beside their names.

Finally, Arturo roused himself and broke in on the conversation of the older men. He spoke haltingly, for speech was still difficult.

"It was different over there, see. I was just 'Mex'—and no questions asked. And we played baseball, all of us."

The words were slurred, and the thoughts expressed were not always logical in sequence. But their meaning was clear, and the hurt they betrayed was naked and quivering.

"Villegas and I and Johnson—we did not like the Sarge. Anyway, he was a good guy. And all of us were against the Nazis, but good."

Briefly he was silent, remembering. Then abruptly, passionately:

"I don't know anything now! Now I am 'different,' and other people are 'better.' Mother, what's the matter with Texas?"

What's the matter with Texas?

A great many people, in and out of Texas, have asked that question—and will continue to ask it. There is an answer, but it isn't a simple one. In fact, the answer is so complex, and its implications so ramified, that we must begin at a point seemingly far removed from the immediate situation in Texas.

Part 2

The American Neighborhood

Chapter 2

Americas United

"IN THE FIELD of world policy, I would dedicate this nation to the policy of the good neighbor; the neighbor who respects himself and because he does, respects the rights of others; the neighbor who respects his obligations and respects the sanctity of his agreements in and with a world of neighbors."

So spoke Franklin Delano Roosevelt on March 4, 1933, and thus was born a new era in international relations within the Western Hemisphere.

The policy of the good neighbor reached its maturity at the Inter-American Conference on Problems of War and Peace, held in Mexico City during February and March, 1945. There the Act of Chapultepec was promulgated, and resolutions of paramount importance to each and all of the American nations were adopted. These resolutions pertained to the continued prosecution of the war. They set forth an agreement upon the punishment of war crimes and the elimination of underground Axis operations. They provided for the creation of a permanent military agency and for the control of armaments. They reaffirmed the principles and purposes of the Atlantic Charter. They looked forward to the renewed participation of Argentina in hemisphere affairs.

In anticipation of the World Security Conference, scheduled to be held three months later at San Francisco, the American republics agreed to insist upon the desirability of solving controversies and questions of an inter-American character in accordance with established inter-American methods and procedures, and the necessity for Latin American representation in the proposed Security Council.

With an eye to strengthening the inter-American system, the delegates at Mexico City declared that an international conference of American states shall meet regularly at four-year intervals, and ordinary meetings of the Ministers of Foreign Affairs shall be held annually upon call by the governing board of the Pan American Union.

In order to draw the peoples of the Americas ever closer together, the representatives of the American republics recognized their essential obligation to guarantee to their people free and impartial access to sources of information. To that end, they agreed, upon the conclusion of the war, to abandon, at the earliest possible date, those measures of censorship and control over the services of the press and radio which were necessary in wartime.

Getting down to practical means of assuring the enjoyment of "the American way of life" to all the peoples of the Americas, the delegates concurred in numerous sound, farsighted principles with regard to economic, social, and cultural conditions and relations within the hemisphere.

In the Economic Charter of the Americas, adopted at the Mexico City meeting, it was set forth that the American republics collaborating in the war effort were determined to continue the mobilization of their economic resources until the achievement of final victory. At the same time, they would work together to assure an orderly transition of the economic life of the Americas from war to peacetime conditions, with joint action aimed at maintaining the economic stability of the American republics during the transition period.

They declared it to be their firm purpose to evolve "a constructive basis for the sound economic development of the Americas through development of natural resources, industrialization, improvement of transportation, modernization of agriculture, development of power facilities and public works, and encouragement of investment of private capital, managerial capacity and technical skill, and the improvement of labor standards and working conditions, including collective bargaining, all leading to a rising level of living and increased consumption."

The Economic Charter concluded with the declaration of ten principles which will govern the policies of the American states in the attainment of these ends, in co-operation with like-minded nations, recognizing that these objectives form a fundamental aspiration of peoples everywhere. The principles include access "on equal terms to the trade and raw materials of the world"; elimination of economic nationalism; restriction of private business arrangements that obstruct international trade; just and equitable treatment for foreign enterprises and capital; and the promotion of the system of private enterprise.

In their Declaration of Social Principles, the representatives of the American republics pledged themselves to consider of international public interest the enactment by all the American states of social legislation that will protect the working class and that will embody guarantees as well as rights on a scale not inferior to the one recommended by the International Labor Organization.

They resolved, furthermore, to establish in all countries of the Hemisphere a minimum living wage, computed in accordance with the living conditions pertaining to the geography and economy of each American country. They agreed that this minimum salary should be elastic and related to the increase in prices, so that its remunerative capacity will protect and increase the purchasing power of the worker.

They voted, also, to expand the existing provisions for social insurance for illness, old age, disablement, death, maternity, and unemployment; and to provide for services of preventive medicine, protection of women and children, nutrition, and the enactment of necessary legislation to establish adequate means of hygiene and industrial insurance. Every aspect of social welfare was pondered.

The matter of racial and religious discrimination within the hemisphere likewise received the consideration of the Mexico City conferees. In order to eliminate these un-American practices, they reaffirmed the principle recognized by each of the American states of equality of rights and opportunities for all men, regardless of race or religion. They recommended, further, that the governments of the respective American republics, without prejudicing the freedom of the spoken or written word, make every effort to prevent all acts which tend to provoke discrimination between individuals by reason of their race or religion.

It was on March 3, 1945, just six days before the conference ended, and almost twelve years to the day after President Roosevelt's historic pronouncement of the Good Neighbor Policy, that the delegates of twenty of the American nations agreed unanimously to the Act of Chapultepec.

By its terms, the republics of the Western Hemisphere, with the exception of Argentina, pledged themselves, effective immediately, to the mutual protection of the territory and political independence of American nations during the war, and to the drafting of a lasting treaty afterwards, consistent with the purposes and principles of the general international organization, when established. The Act states specifically that the security and solidarity of the continent are affected to the same extent by an act of aggression against an American state by a non-American country as by one within the hemisphere.

In a speech officially interpreting the Act, Senator Tom Connally of Texas, chairman of the Senate Foreign Relations Committee, stated that the Act of Chapultepec is "one of the greatest state papers in the world."

In recognizing the mutual responsibility of the American nations to preserve the peace of the hemisphere, a milestone in political progress was passed. The Act of Chapultepec, as a firm pact of regional security, represents a significant advance over the recommendations that came out of Dumbarton Oaks; and, as was expected, the delegates of the United Nations in San Francisco were influenced by the conclusions of the Act of Chapultepec in their difficult task of creating machinery to protect the economic and political integrity of all the peoples of the world.

At eleven o'clock on the morning of April 9, 1945, the United States, in conjunction with the other American republics, resumed "normal diplomatic relations" with Argentina, following that country's declaration of war on the Axis powers immediately after the close of the Mexico City conference, and her adherence to the resolutions there adopted.

During the World Security Conference at San Francisco, which closed on June 26, 1945, the American nations achieved complete victory on the two points agreed upon at Mexico City, namely, the right to solve controversies and questions of an inter-American character in accordance with methods and procedures already established within the hemisphere; and Latin American representation in the Security Council.

After much heated debate, the conferees at San Francisco voiced their approval of regional security systems, operating within the new world organization. By the terms of the agreement, any country or group of countries may offer immediate resistance to armed attack without waiting on the world organization and its peace-enforcing agency, the Security Council, to act.

As to representation on the eleven-member Security Council, the United States has a permanent membership as one of the "Big Five," and Mexico and Brazil were elected to two of the six non-permanent memberships.

The perfect accord and unanimity of purpose now existing among the American nations did not come about accidentally or by easy stages. On the contrary, the singleness of mind and spirit evidenced by the delegates to the Inter-American Conference on Problems of War and Peace signifies the fruition of seeds patiently and tenderly nurtured through long, tense years.

Chapter 3

Development of American Unity

L UIS QUINTANILLA, formerly attached as Minister to the Mexican Embassy in Washington, wrote a book in 1942 which he called *A Latin American Speaks.* In it he expresses himself clearly, logically, and disinterestedly as an American in the broadest sense of the word, but, naturally, with the viewpoint of a Mexican, a Latin American.

Upon the mighty stage of the Western Hemisphere, he tells us, a drama is taking place, a drama in which every man and woman of America, North, Central, and South—plays a part. The first act, Independence, is long since finished. The second, Good Neighborliness, has run its course and somewhat overlapped the third act, Inter-Americanism. After an interlude which the gravity of the hour undoubtedly will cut short, our hemisphere will be called upon to play the final act in the organization of a Civilized World Order.[1]

If we accept Quintanilla's thesis, the accomplishments of the Inter-American Conference on Problems of War and Peace and the World Security Conference indicate that now the climax of the third act has been reached and that the Americas

[1] Luis Quintanilla, *A Latin American Speaks* (New York: The Macmillan Company, 1943), p. 237.

have emerged upon a stage set for the fourth and final act—an act in which there must be no fumbling of lines.

The first act, Independence, was a rather lengthy one. Actually, within a fifty-year period, dating from 1776, practically all of the American colonies of England and Spain achieved their freedom from the mother countries. But in the years that followed, each new republic was too much involved with internal problems to think constructively or objectively about the American neighborhood.

This was despite the fact that even during the struggle for independence, Simón Bolívar, the Liberator of South America, had been able to foresee the advantages to be gained from close co-operation among the republics, to which end he called the first Pan American Conference in Panama in 1826. The results of that first meeting were unsatisfactory. The American nations were not yet prepared to extend their interests beyond their national boundaries.

It was not until October 2, 1889, that the first International Conference of the American States met in Washington. The deliberations upon that occasion did not result in a plan of arbitration to settle disputes that might arise among the American countries, as had been hoped for; but they did bring about the creation of the International Union of the American Republics and the Commercial Bureau of the American Republics, the purpose of each of which was to further, by various means, commercial relations between the Americas. The Pan American Union was the direct outgrowth of these agencies.

The second inter-American conference was held at Mexico City in 1901; the third, at Río de Janeiro in 1906; and the fourth in Buenos Aires in 1910.

Between 1901 and 1910, the other American republics found ample reason to doubt the sincerity of our participation in hemisphere conferences. Early in that decade, Theodore Roosevelt employed his "Big Stick" policy to obtain the concession for the Panama Canal. During this ten-year period, we sent Marines into the Dominican Republic to collect customs duties with which to pay European creditors of that nation; we intervened in Cuba and imposed a resident governor; we landed troops to supervise elections in Nicaragua and Panama. The first four inter-American conferences failed to accomplish a union of the American republics for defensive purposes; to agree upon a method of arbitrating disputes within the hemisphere; and to establish the doctrine that armed force should not be resorted to for the collection of international contract debts. But through them a system of international diplomatic round-table discussion was set up, and instruments were created through which the agreements reached at these meetings could be put into effect.

Co-operative action loomed as the potential keynote of international dealings in the New World.

Gradually there had developed the idea that Latin America was ripe for United States commercial and industrial expansion, and as a result, our interventions swerved from the original purpose of "protecting" our neighbors from powerful European nations and took on instead the new and selfish purpose of attempting to impose order so that United States financial interests might flourish. By 1910, our financial investment in Mexico alone amounted to $800,000,000, and represented 42 per cent of all the direct foreign investments United States citizens then owned.[2]

The year 1910 saw the beginning of the Mexican Revolution, a social phenomenon of utmost importance to the entire hemisphere (discussed in detail in Chapter V). In 1914 World War I began. Between 1910 and 1920, particularly while World War I was going on, we not only fought a campaign in Mexico, but we also intervened in Haiti, the Dominican Republic, Panama, Nicaragua, and Cuba—all for the protection of United States financial interests.

The policy of the good neighbor was yet a long way off. When, in 1923, the Fifth Inter-American Conference met

2 Virginia Prewett, *The Americas and Tomorrow* (New York: E. P. Dutton & Company, 1944), p. 65.

in Santiago, Chile, thirteen years had elapsed since the last meeting, and in the meantime the United States had become branded as the "Colossus of the North." The United States delegates at Santiago were received in chilly silence. In Mexico, the social revolution was in full sway. The new liberal Constitution of 1917 was being applied in furtherance of Mexico's revolutionary aims, and we were withholding recognition from President Alvaro Obregón's government until he should guarantee that United States oil properties would not be molested in any way. The Latin American nations, led by Mexico, with the Dominican Republic, Panama, Colombia, and Nicaragua as strong seconds, were demanding that something be done to eliminate the threat of force from international relations in the New World.

The result of the Fifth Conference was the Gondra Treaty, officially entitled "A Treaty to Avoid or Prevent Conflicts between the American States." While the Gondra Treaty was in the nature of a gesture, providing only for a "procedure of investigation," it was nevertheless the first one the United States had ever made toward converting into action our words regarding peace and peaceful settlements.

By 1928, when the Sixth Inter-American Conference met at Havana, Cuba, there existed a painfully obvious disparity between the avowedly non-imperialistic aims of the United States and the course of action we were pursuing. We continued to interfere in Cuba, in Haiti, in the Dominican Republic, and in Nicaragua.

Herbert Hoover was elected President of the United States in 1928. Realizing that something had to be done to change our policy toward Latin America, he began withdrawing the Marines from Haiti and Nicaragua. But meanwhile the "Big Depression" came in 1929; the United States withdrew into a shell of economic as well as political isolationism; and the trade barriers raised during Hoover's administration increased Latin America's resentment against us.

During the depression years, 1930-1933, there were strikes,

uprisings, and revolutions that brought about violent changes in government in Argentina, El Salvador, Brazil, Costa Rica, Chile, Peru, Ecuador, Panama, Honduras, and the Dominican Republic. Sandino defied the United States with force in Nicaragua in 1931. Haitians were stoning customs houses controlled by United States Marines in 1929, and the situation grew worse as the economic crisis became more acute.

By 1932, when the Seventh International Conference of American States was scheduled to convene in Montevideo, Uruguay, the peace of the world was gone again, for in Asia, Japan had occupied Manchuria. On March 5, 1933, the National Socialists came into power in Germany, and Adolf Hitler became Chancellor.

As we look back upon it now, we can see that it was perhaps fortunate for our generation, fortunate for the cause of American unity and for the future of all the democratic nations of the world, that the Seventh Inter-American Conference was postponed until 1933, until an administration in the United States had formulated a clear-cut concept of good neighborliness.

On March 4, 1933, the day before the National Socialists rose to power in Germany and assumed control of the *Reichstag,* Franklin D. Roosevelt rang up the curtain on the second act of the hemisphere play—that of good neighborliness—by proclaiming the Good Neighbor Policy in his first inaugural address. Little more than a month later, in his Pan American Day address to the governing board of the Pan American Union, the President said:

Never before has the word "good neighbor" been so significant in international relations. Never have the need and benefit of neighborly co-operation in every form of human activity been so evident as they are today.

Friendship among nations, as among individuals, calls for constructive efforts to master the forces of humanity in order that an atmosphere of close understanding and co-operation may be cultivated. It involves mutual obligations and responsibilities.

The essential qualities of a true Pan-Americanism must be the same as those which constitute a good neighbor, namely, mutual understanding, and through such understanding, a sympathetic appreciation of the other's point of view. It is only in this manner that we can hope to build up a system of which confidence, friendship and good will are the cornerstones.

These were, indeed, strange words to emanate from the Colossus of the North. Skeptical Latin Americans were not prepared to accept them at their face value, and with good cause. Nevertheless, we may remember with satisfaction that the Good Neighbor Policy was proclaimed in a year when the United States was not involved in any international difficulty and when no one could reasonably foretell that, in less than ten years, the United States would desperately need the friendship and co-operation of the other American countries, not only for the protection of the hemisphere, but for its own safety.[3]

When the Seventh Conference of American States finally met in Montevideo late in 1933, Secretary of State Cordell Hull was faced with a definite challenge, although no one voiced it publicly. That challenge was to "put up or shut up" on Pan Americanism.

Hull courageously accepted the position in which he found himself, and proved, to the full satisfaction of the Latin American delegates, that the United States was honest and sincere in its newly adopted policy. Above everything else, he assured the conference that "no government need fear any intervention on the part of the United States under the Roosevelt administration." Furthermore, he proposed a general reduction in tariff barriers, thus striking at the thorny core of troubles in the American hemisphere.

From that moment, American unity began to assume a tangible shape.

Immediately following the history-making conference at Montevideo, our government set to work to demonstrate that it was in earnest. In May, 1934, the Platt Amendment was abrogated, and we formally relinquished our right to interfere

[3] Quintanilla, *op. cit.,* p. 239.

in Cuban affairs. In August, 1934, we ceased our meddling in Haiti. In June, 1934, the Reciprocal Trade Agreements Act was passed by Congress, and that same year a trade agreement was signed with Cuba; in 1935, with Haiti, Brazil, Colombia, and Honduras; in 1936, with Guatemala, Nicaragua, and Costa Rica; in 1937, with El Salvador; in 1938 with Ecuador; and in 1939, with Venezuela.

Lázaro Cárdenas became President of Mexico in 1934. Of chief concern to him were agrarian reforms and universal education. But in carrying out to the letter the liberal Constitution of 1917, the matter of taking over from the capitalists, both native and foreign, the principal economic resources of the nation assumed increasing importance—so much so that British and United States oil interests in Mexico became decidedly uneasy.

The third act of the hemisphere drama, that of Inter-Americanism, might be said to have gone into rehearsal about the time of the Inter-American Conference for the Maintenance of Peace, which was held in Buenos Aires in 1936. Inter-Americanism, advancing beyond mere good neighborliness, implies definite commitments. By the time the meeting opened, the League of Nations was completely discredited, for in Europe, the Spanish Civil War—actually the opening European engagement of World War II—was raging; in Africa, Italian troops had invaded Ethiopia; and in Asia, Japan was going ruthlessly on her way, unchecked.

It was at this conference, which was attended by President Roosevelt, that the statesmen of the American republics recognized the fact that a threat to one was a threat to all, and unanimously agreed that in event of war between American states, or in event of an international war outside America that might menace the peace of the American republics, the governments of the American states should consult together for their mutual protection.

At long last, the principle of inter-American co-operation first advanced by Simón Bolívar received unanimous approval—a union of American nations operating within a conference system.

In 1938, Mexico expropriated foreign-owned oil properties. 1938 was also the year of Munich. It was there, in September of that year, that Chamberlain, to assure "peace in our time," acquiesced in the occupation of Czechoslovakia by Germany. Japan was wreaking havoc in China, and the United States, with a one-ocean navy and a standing army that ranked eighteenth in the world, appealed again and again, to both Europe and Asia, for peace; but the peace was definitely and irretrievably gone.

In December, 1938, when the Mexican oil question was still pending, the Eighth International Conference of American States met at Lima, Peru. The result was the Declaration of Lima:

> The governments of the American states declare:
>
> 1st, that they affirm their continental solidarity and their purpose to collaborate in the maintenance of the principles upon which said solidarity is based.
>
> 2nd, that faithful to the above-mentioned principles and to their absolute sovereignty, they reaffirm their decision to maintain them and to defend them against all foreign intervention or activity that may threaten them.
>
> 3rd, and in case the peace, security or territorial integrity of any American republic is thus threatened by acts of any nature that may impair them, they proclaim their determination to make effective their solidarity by means of the procedure of consultation.
>
> 4th, that in order to facilitate the consultations the ministers of foreign affairs of the American republics, when deemed desirable and at the initiative of any one of them, will meet in their several capitals.

Also, at Lima, the inter-American question that had been pending since 1889 was finally settled, when the American republics agreed, as a principle of the international law of the Americas, that no nation should "employ armed force or resort to diplomatic intervention for the collection of public or contractual debts or to support claims of an exclusively pecuniary origin."

Mexico endorsed our proposal of co-operative action to meet threats from the outside, thus reaffirming hemisphere solidarity. We concurred in the agreement not to use arms or diplomatic intervention to support financial claims. Therefore, it was obvious, after Lima, that the United States could not, and would not, protect by force the interests of United States oil companies in Mexico. The warning was clear that, from then on, United States financial interests operating in Latin America were on their own; they could not look for armed protection from this government.

Confidence in the Good Neighbor Policy increased enormously throughout Latin America after this final evidence of our good faith. By September 25, 1939, when the First Conference of American Foreign Ministers convened in Panama, as a result of the declaration of war on Germany by Great Britain and France, the American republics were more nearly in accord than ever before in history.

The principal achievement of that conference was the Declaration of Panama, signed by the twenty-one republics, which established a line around the New World three hundred miles off shore, to provide a "zone of security," which would be free from action by any belligerent nation.

The war in Europe went on. Although "it wasn't our war," the American republics were drawn increasingly close together.

Things were happening throughout the continent. Nazi and Fascist plots and subversive agents were uncovered in many of the countries and were quickly dealt with by the respective governments. Great unrest was caused by the European war's dislocation of trade. On June 17, 1940, France fell, and the Second Conference of American Foreign Ministers was called to meet in Havana on July 21. Perhaps nothing in the whole sequence of events between 1938 and 1941 more deeply disturbed the Latin American countries than the fall of France, for France, even more than Spain, had been the spiritual mother of democratic-minded Latin Americans for many decades.

The chief concern of the delegates was the fate of European

possessions in this hemisphere, and an agreement was finally reached under which any American nation was empowered to seize European colonies within the hemisphere when it appeared that their control was about to pass to another European power, and providing that a provisional government would then be set up by the American republics.

In August, 1940, the Office of the Coordinator of Commercial and Cultural Relations between the American Republics, which eventually became the Office of the Coordinator of Inter-American Affairs, was created for the purpose of promoting cultural and economic relations, and to fight by all legitimate means the inroads of Fascism in Latin America.   Also, the Export-Import Bank's lending power was increased from $200,000,000 to $700,000,000, and it was given authority to work toward the economic defense of the hemisphere.

Activities in the realm of inter-American relations during the remainder of 1940 and 1941 were greatly intensified.   New government agencies, such as the Inter-American Development Commission, were created.   Our purchases from Latin America were sharply increased.   As our zone of security proved to be not so secure and American ships began to go down with tragic regularity, the Pan American Highway System became a pressing necessity, and work on it was pushed to the limit.

Diversification of crops was encouraged in the Latin American countries, and the United States offered assistance, when needed, both in money and in technical advice.   Lend-lease was extended to include military equipment for Latin America. Airports were built in Venezuela and Brazil, air bases and artillery defenses in Panama, and an air base in Guatemala. Military bases were established in Ecuador, both on the mainland and on the highly strategic Galapagos Islands.   Arrangements were made to improve airport and harbor facilities in Mexico, and United States flying instructors started training courses in Brazil, Chile, Peru, Ecuador, and Colombia.   All of these enterprises were carried on with the consent and co-operation of the other American governments.

Our good intentions had been thoroughly tested by Mexico's expropriation of oil properties. The test of Latin America's good faith came on December 7, 1941.

Virginia Prewett points out that in evaluating Latin America's role in the second World War, and also in appraising the United States policy that led it to play that role, it should be remembered that circumstances made the other Americas far more important to us on December 8, 1941, than they had been on December the sixth.

In the first place, Latin America was not only the actual producer of vital supplies—copper, zinc, manganese, aluminum, iron, mica, iodine, quartz crystal, and other metals, oils, and foodstuffs too numerous to mention—which we needed and were going to need in enormously increased quantities to build and maintain a war machine powerful enough to defeat our two enemies. Latin America was also our only hope for recouping in part, at least, the inevitable loss of such strategic commodities as tin, rubber, manila hemp, quinine, and other products from the Southwest Pacific.

In the second place, after the near death-blow dealt to our Pacific Fleet at Pearl Harbor, our most vulnerable single point was the Panama Canal. The crippling of the Canal, on top of Pearl Harbor, would have been disastrous. An attack on the Canal could have come from the sea, or from some secret airfield in one of the Latin American countries in the neighborhood of the Canal.[4]

But we need not have worried. The republics of Latin America lost no time in proving that they, too, meant what they said with regard to the policy of the good neighbor. Costa Rica declared war on Japan before we did. On the same day, December 8, El Salvador, Guatemala, Honduras, Nicaragua, Panama, Cuba, the Dominican Republic, and Haiti declared war on Japan, and Mexico and Colombia broke off diplomatic relations.

These were not empty gestures. They were accompanied

4 Prewett, op. cit., pp. 196-197.

by immediate clamp-downs everywhere on Japanese nationals and subversive activities. All of these nations gave their whole-hearted co-operation in establishing and maintaining an alert defense in the area of the Canal.

When Germany and Italy declared war on the United States on December 11, the Central American and Caribbean island republics promptly declared war on them and restricted the activities of their nationals also. Mexico broke relations with Germany and Italy on December 11; Colombia broke relations on December 19. On December 31, Venezuela broke relations with all three Axis powers. By January 1, 1942, the vital Panama Canal was protected by a solid ring of American nations at war.

Nor were the other American republics slow in aligning themselves with the United States. Within a few days after Pearl Harbor, each of them had declared war, broken relations, or declared the United States a non-belligerent.

Chile set the machinery in motion, just two days after the attack on Pearl Harbor, for the Third Conference of American Foreign Ministers, called to meet in Río de Janeiro on January 15, 1942.

It was there that Mexico rightfully and dramatically assumed a position of leadership among the Latin American nations. The Mexican delegation, led by the eloquent Ezequiel Padilla, then Foreign Minister of the Republic of Mexico, rendered the United States a service of the greatest magnitude by marshalling the forces of the entire hemisphere behind this country's war effort. It was Padilla who said at Río: "The men who have fallen at Wake and the Philippines have not fallen only to defend the honor of the United States; they have fallen also to defend the human liberties, and the common destiny of America."

Out of the Río conference came concrete plans for the defense and security of the New World. To meet the immediate emergencies of war, ways and means were agreed upon to produce an adequate supply of basic and strategic materials in the shortest possible time; to maintain the internal economies of the American countries; to mobilize transportation facilities; and to sever all commercial and financial relations with the Axis.

As longer-term hemisphere objectives, it was agreed to broaden the scope of the Inter-American Development Commission; to develop basic production; to proceed with the formation of an Inter-American Bank; to devise ways and means of facilitating the flow of capital among the American republics; to raise the standard of living of the people through industrialization, at the same time improving continental economic co-ordination through international agreements; to work together to improve health and sanitation conditions; and to hold a special conference of ministers of finance in order to work out ways and means for greater economic stabilization within the hemisphere.[5]

With regard to manpower for military purposes, the United States did not request the other American nations to give such aid. We possessed sufficient manpower within this country, and our most urgent need was for raw materials with which to equip our army and navy. Nevertheless, the other Americas were eager to lend military assistance. Eventually, Brazil sent a contingent to take part in the Italian campaign, and Mexico sent her United States-trained 201st Aerial Squadron to the Pacific. In addition, numerous pilots and other military personnel from many American republics came to this country for intensive training under United States instructors, as part of the total program for hemisphere defense.

Unconsciously, perhaps, we in the Americas have been working toward the final act in the drama of our common destiny—the part that, as a united continent, America must play in the shaping of a world society. What we are building in the Americas is a zone of security, not only for the United States, but for every American republic.

5 *Ibid.*, p. 202.

As Miss Prewett expresses it:

Security in this hemisphere makes it possible for us to stand steady and firm as we deal with our complex involvements with the rest of the world. It gives us a solid home base, something we must have whether the world is at war or at peace. Without it, we can neither wage a war successfully, nor deal adequately with the difficult problems of a world-wide, co-operative peace.[6]

"Building this zone of security," she says, "has been one of the most urgent tasks of our time. Preserving it will be one of the requisite tasks of our future."[7]

Luis Quintanilla voices the same thought when he says: "We are responsible for our present only in part. But we are wholly responsible for the future. We inherit conditions from the past, but *we* are the makers of tomorrow."[8]

And that tomorrow is now upon us. The sudden end of hostilities with Japan plunged the world—and the Americas— into a peace for which nobody was prepared. Yet the fact remains that we *are* the makers of this today, and of tomorrow. The war is over. The peace is here. What will we do with the opportunities and responsibilities that are ours? Will we profit by past experience? Will we capitalize upon our gains? Will we fulfill the tremendous obligations we have assumed? How shall we go about it?

[6] *Ibid.*, p. 248. Quoted by permission of the publishers in the United States, E. P. Dutton & Co., Inc., Copyright, 1944 by the author.

[7] *Ibid.*, p. 282.

[8] Quintanilla, *op. cit.*, p. 242.

Chapter 4

Texas: Its Strategic Position in Inter-American Relations

WITH THE accomplishments of the Inter-American Conference on Problems of War and Peace and the World Security Conference fresh in our minds, there is every reason to hope that, in the Western Hemisphere at least, statesmen have learned the value of co-operation and arbitration. Certainly we in the Americas are entitled to this hope of continued collaboration, for in no other region of the world has international co-operation of all kinds enjoyed a longer duration or a more practical test.

But what of the human front—the man-to-man relationship among the individual citizens of the Americas?

Unfortunately, co-operation and understanding between governments does not necessarily imply mutual respect, confidence, and understanding among the peoples those governments represent. The "Good Neighbor Policy," by its very terminology, is a human policy. The close friendship of the governments of this hemisphere, indispensable as it is to the perpetuation of American unity, is not enough. The peoples of the Americas, as human beings, must, through personal contact, through travel and reading, through business relations, through every other means at their disposal, come to know each other.

In contrast with the linguistic chaos of Europe, this hemisphere is blessed with but three principal tongues—English, Spanish, and Portuguese—with relatively small areas where French or Dutch are the official languages.

It is to our advantage that these three languages have many similar roots, in Greek and Latin; that many words in English and Spanish are spelled exactly the same, the only difference being in pronunciation, e.g., "municipal," which in Spanish is accented on the final syllable; that many, many others differ only slightly in spelling, e. g., "president" and "presidente," but have identical meanings. It is generally conceded that, of all foreign languages which English-speaking Americans try to learn, Spanish comes most easily.

The history of the development of the countries of the Western Hemisphere into independent nations has sometimes taken divergent paths, but has run more often along parallel lines. At all times, in all our countries, we Americans have fought and died for identical principles and ideals. We have much in common, yet we have remained strangely isolated from each other. Even where we have been brought together in constant, daily contact we have failed to develop the necessary qualities of mutual respect, confidence, and understanding.

But, you will ask, what relation does all this have to Texas?

The answer may be simply stated: Texas is the chief connecting link between the United States and Mexico, and therefore, between the United States and all of Latin America. Yet by its very simplicity, that statement belies the complexity and significance of its implications. The United States-Mexico border is the most extensive geographical area in which two of the principal cultures of this hemisphere actually meet. More than half of that border, approximately one thousand miles, is also the southern boundary of Texas.

Mexico is not only our nearest Latin American neighbor, but was one of our staunchest allies in the war just ended. According to the Mexican Foreign Office, more than 15,000 citizens of the Republic of Mexico were enrolled in the armed forces of the United States, many of whom were high-ranking officers, and many of whom were killed, wounded, or decorated for valor in the service of this country.

On February 22, 1945, the 201st Mexican Aerial Squadron, composed of three hundred of Mexico's finest young aviators, and commanded by Colonel Antonio Cárdenas, completed its advanced training at Majors Field, Greenville, Texas, and was assigned to combat duty in the Pacific. Based on Luzon in the Philippines, this Mexican contingent gave valuable and effective support to United States forces in the final liquidation of Japanese fighting strength.

Aside from such military assistance, the mines and forests and fields of Mexico, from the beginning of the conflict, furnished United States war plants with vital materials unavailable from any other source. (See Chapter VI).

At the present time, according to the best estimates obtainable, one out of every six persons in the State of Texas is of Mexican descent—more than one million of our people. A sizable number of our Mexican-American citizens are of the fourth, fifth, or sixth generation to be born in Texas, and they and their families have long since established themselves in positions of leadership in various fields of endeavor throughout the State; however, the majority of them have come or have been brought to Texas since 1900, as laborers. Of the total, perhaps 80 per cent are citizens of the United States, either by birth or naturalization.

Texas enjoys a unique position, historically speaking, in the relations between the United States and Mexico. Indeed, until 1836, the history of Texas was the history of Mexico.

When the original builders of this nation, smarting under the injustices of English despots, proclaimed their freedom by means of the stirring Declaration of Independence, there was no United States of America; only thirteen sparsely settled colonies on the eastern seaboard, far removed from, and certainly with little knowledge of, or interest in, the vast territory that was to become Texas.

The rebellion of the thirteen colonies was the spark that ignited a worldwide conflagration and set in motion the revolt against tyranny that was to topple the King of France from his throne and free the Western Hemisphere of European domination forever. The fifty-year period that followed the Declaration of Independence has gone down in history as America's heroic age, for during that time, the American colonies of Spain, likewise, one by one, with the exception of Cuba and Puerto Rico, struck off their shackles and cut the ties that had bound them to Europe for three hundred years.

Moved by the success of the rebellion in the thirteen colonies, by Thomas Paine's essay "The Rights of Man," and by the writings of the French philosophers, the leaders of Latin America realized that they, too, could survive only as free men. Those patriots were motivated by the same democratic principles of "liberty, justice, and equality" expressed in the Declaration of Independence, and as each Spanish American colony became a republic, it adopted a constitution inspired by that of the United States.

When Mexico's bid for freedom from Spain was made on September 16, 1810, thirty-four years after the Liberty Bell had sounded the death knell of English rule in the thirteen colonies, the territory known as Texas was still a Mexican province and subject to the King of Spain. The Spanish conquerors, during the period of the Conquest, had penetrated what is now western United States as far north as Washington and Oregon; on the east, into Georgia and Florida; and had left the indelible imprint of their culture, their customs, their language, and their religion upon California, Arizona, New Mexico, Southern Colorado, and Texas.

Before 1550, Cabeza de Vaca was shipwrecked near the present city of Galveston, and spent eight years wandering among the Indian tribes of the Southwest. Likewise before 1550, Coronado had traveled through a part of the region now known as Texas.

It was in 1650, just thirty years after the Pilgrims landed

on Plymouth Rock, that the Spaniards sent troops into Texas for the immediate purpose of subduing hostile Indian tribes. Settlement by Spaniards and Mexicans followed, and for almost two hundred years Texas was governed by the Spanish Viceroy at Mexico City.

During this period, adventurers from the infant republic of the United States gradually found their way into Texas, and finally, about the beginning of the nineteenth century, wagon caravans of colonists began to arrive, the newcomers settling peaceably in or near the small outposts of civilization previously established by the Mexicans, and some of them taking out Mexican citizenship.

In 1821, the independence of Mexico from Spain was achieved, and fifteen years later, on March 2, 1836, at Washington-on-the-Brazos, the Texas Convention decided upon separation from Mexico as a protest against the tyranny of Santa Anna, who was then President of the Mexican republic. A new republic began its struggle for existence.

Together, the people of Texas, Mexicans and Anglo Americans, fought for a common cause; and many are the Mexicans who rank equally in glory with Bowie, Travis, Crockett, Austin, and Houston. It was the Mexican flag which flew bravely over the Alamo on that historic day, March 6, 1836, when seven Mexicans were included in the small company that fell in its defense.

Among those prominent in the conflict and in the moulding of the Texas Republic was Lorenzo de Zavala, Sr., one of the signers of the Declaration of Independence, and first Vice-President of the Republic. Another whose signature appears on that document was José Antonio Navarro, who later served as Senator to the Congress of the Republic of Texas. Upon the entrance of Texas into the Union, Navarro was elected to the first Texas State Senate, where he served three terms.

Erasmo Seguín acted as co-commissioner with Stephen F. Austin in the colonists' overtures to the Mexican government in an effort to prevent war. He was the father of Colonel Juan

N. Seguín, who organized the 2nd Regiment of Texas Volunteers, an all-Mexican regiment, to fight with Travis.

On October 18, 1836, Captain Plácido Benavides, then mayor of Victoria, organized a company of thirty Mexican rancheros, and joined forces with Austin. It is estimated that one third of those who opposed the troops of Santa Anna were Mexicans, and considerable weight is given to this claim by the great number of Spanish names engraved upon the San Jacinto Monument at Houston.[1]

Title to lands was awarded in recognition of military service, and including those families who held original land grants from the king of Spain, the Mexican landholders in Texas, at the beginning of its statehood, comprised a large and influential group.

Aside from participation in the Texas Revolution, Mexicans have contributed materially in other ways to the welfare and culture of Texas. As Manuel C. Gonzales of San Antonio said, in an address to a conference of the 128th District of Rotary International, "through the centuries, Texas has been blessed with two cultures: the Latin and the Anglo-American, interwoven in some respects, yet, at the same time, keeping their distances, true to the traditions of their respective mother countries."

It was from Mexico that Spanish friars and priests came to introduce Christianity and lay the foundations of civilization. The lasting Spanish and Mexican influence upon architecture in those towns and cities which were originally Mexican settlements gives to Texas a distinctive atmosphere. Through the years, it has been largely Mexican labor that built our highways and railroads, herded our cattle and sheep, cultivated and harvested our cotton, rice, citrus fruit, and vegetable crops.

J. M. Woods, attorney, and member of the Texas Legislature from San Antonio, has made an exhaustive study of the debt which Texas owes to Mexican jurisprudence. He states

[1] Rubén Rendón Lozano, *Viva Tejas* (San Antonio: Southern Literary Institute, 1936).

that four of the most just laws on Texas statute books were derived from Spain via Mexico.

One of these, the law of descent and distribution, or "the
law of entails and primogenital succession," was abolished by
the Cortes of Spain in 1820. Yet it was adopted by the young
Republic of Mexico in 1823, and its benefits extended to the
Mexican State of Texas. After Texas secured its independence
in 1836, the law was incorporated into Texas statutes.

Texas was the first state in the Union to guarantee to a
married woman the property which belonged to her at the date
of her marriage, or which came into her possession afterward
by "gift, devise or descent." This "separate property" law, also,
was of Spanish origin, and all subsequent legislative bodies in
Texas have continued it in effect.

Likewise, Texas law which protects the community interest
of married women in property acquired during marriage (except that acquired by either spouse by gift, devise or descent,
or that purchased with the separate funds of either) is a direct
legacy from Spain, passed on by Mexico.

By means of its "homestead law," passed on January 26,
1839, Texas again was first in providing security for families.
The Texas law was an outgrowth of Decree No. 70 enacted by
the Congress of Coahuila and Texas on January 13, 1829, which
read as follows:

Art. 1. The lands acquired by colonization law, whether general
laws of the Republic or private laws of the state, by native or foreign
colonists and by empresarios shall not be subject to the payment of debts
contracted previous to the acquisition of said lands from whatever source
the debts originated or proceed.

Art. 2. Until after the expiration of twelve years from having held
legal possession the colonists and empresarios cannot be sued or in-
commodated by the judges on account of said debts.

Art. 3. After the expiration of the term prefixed in the foregoing
article, although they may be sued for said debts, they shall not be
obliged to pay them in lands, implements of husbandry, or tools of their
trade or machines, but expressly in fruits or money in a manner not to

affect their attention to their families, to their husbandry or art they possess.[2]

After Texas became a state in the Union, much of this enlightened legislation was adopted by other states, and thus the entire country became indebted to Mexican jurisprudence.

Spanish is not now, and has never been, a foreign language in Texas, and in many ways Spanish has influenced the English vocabulary of Texas people. Such words as lariat, rodeo, reata, frijoles, tamales, patio, enchiladas, tortillas, fiesta, siesta, piñata, pinto, hombre, sombrero, hacienda, rancho, loco, sarape, huaraches, borracho, and many others have been incorporated into our everyday speech to the extent that we sometimes forget they are not actually English terms.

Yet, despite all these many factors which, it might logically be assumed, would tend to amalgamate the people of Texas, Latin and Anglo American, into one harmonious whole, a yawning chasm gradually developed between the two groups.

This cleavage came about through a multiplicity of causes, and is fraught with multiple dangers—dangers of local, state, national, and international import. The problems involved, and the methods to be followed in solving those problems, constitute of Texas a living laboratory experiment in American unity, and are causing the eyes of the Americas to be focused upon Texas as the proving ground of all the agreements and treaties entered into during the past twelve years by the governments of the American republics; a test case, if you like, to prove or disprove the validity of the Good Neighbor Policy. It is in Texas, on the human front, that we must demonstrate to the satisfaction of the hemisphere that Americans can live together in an atmosphere of mutual understanding and progress.

Most Texans of Mexican descent who were citizens of the State prior to 1900 and many of those who have entered the country since 1900, by virtue of their personal qualities, education, and business or professional ability, have had little diffi-

[2] Gammel's *Laws of Texas*, I, 110.

culty in adjusting themselves to our way of life, and have received, on the whole, due consideration and fair treatment in our society.

It is not with this group of Mexican-Americans and their descendants that we are chiefly concerned. Rather, it is with that larger group—some 600,000 in number—composed of those who have come into Texas since 1900 as common laborers, and their Texas-born children. Many of them were driven across the Rio Grande ahead of revolutionary armies. Many crossed the river voluntarily to escape the peonage under which they had suffered so long in Mexico. Many were recruited in Mexico by labor agents for employment in agriculture, on the railroads, and elsewhere. Whatever their reason for coming, their lot, and that of their children, has been the same.

In order to understand and appreciate fully the problems faced by this segment of our Latin American population, let us review the history of Mexico, the conditions which prevailed in our neighbor republic before and during the Mexican Revolution of 1910, and the tremendous gains along all lines that have been realized through the Revolution.

Part 3

Background In Mexico

Chapter 5

The Social Revolution and the Common Man[1]

MANUEL GAMIO, one of Mexico's outstanding sociologists and anthropologists, said some years ago, in a lecture to an American audience, that the real American people are not consciously hostile to the Mexican. They are merely ignorant of his antecedents, his social characteristics, his economic needs, and his spiritual tendencies.

Generally speaking, in the minds of most of us, Mexico is represented by a question mark. Oh, we have toured the country—done it up brown, in fact—marveling at everything: the strange, hideous carved heads on the façade of the Temple of Quetzalcoatl; the blue perfection of the sea at Acapulco; the patient, white-clad peasant plodding behind his patient ox, as together they turn a straight furrow in the little field that clings at an impossible angle to the slope of the mountain. We think that the Mexicans have a delightful country, picturesque and magnificent, but primitive and barbarous, very backward socially.

[1] The specific citation of sources in this chapter is made only for those references that may prove of special interest to the reader. The sources of the other authoritative information and interpretations in this chapter are listed in the bibliography.

We have heard all about their revolutions, and know that Mexico is a turbulent, disorderly country. We have been told, too, that Mexico is being propelled rapidly into communism; just witness the policy of taking land away from the rich and giving it to the poor.

In the final analysis, Mexico is surrounded by an air of romantic mystery, as befits any unknown quantity. There is also an element of distrust, for we are prone to look askance at anything strange or different. Our general attitude is one of amused contempt and condescension, for we insist on judging our neighbors to the south by our own social and economic standards, with complete lack of understanding and total disregard of the great differences in the geography, the resources, the culture, and the national aspirations of the two countries. Mexico is consistent only with itself. It cannot be judged by standards other than those of Mexico.

Confusion and Contrast

As has so often been said, Mexico is a land of contrasts and confusion in every conceivable respect. Geographically, economically, socially, and culturally, Mexico offers extremes of good and bad, rich and poor, with a negligible proportion of middle ground. Only racially does the vast middle ground far exceed the extremes.

Since pre-Cortesian days, there has been a fiction prevalent to the effect that Mexico is a fabulously wealthy country, and a favorite legend is that of the lazy Mexican who leans against a horn of plenty but will not even take the trouble to stretch out his hands for its fruits.

Enormous riches have been extracted from the soil of Mexico, but they were obtained only because the standard of living of the population was so very low. Sweat and blood and hunger have always been the producers of wealth in Mexico.

The greed of the Spaniards caused the rapid dissipation of existing gold mines, and today Mexican silver, though fairly plentiful, has relatively little value in the world economy. It is, however, true that in the mountains, cliffs, and gorges which constitute more than half its total area, Mexico has a number of unexploited deposits of vitally important minerals, including manganese, placer tin, chrome, mercury, and molybdenum; but until now, the very nature of the terrain has precluded exploitation on any large scale, because of the prohibitive cost of constructing highways and railroads.

Due to the fact that vast deserts spread themselves over the northern states, no more than approximately 14 per cent of the country's area is even potentially arable, and differences in altitude, combined with differences in latitude, temperature, rainfall, and topography, have helped to form many distinct climatic regions, different types of plant and animal life, and different biological characteristics in the inhabitants.

Roughly, the arable land may be classified as tropical and non-tropical, the tropical area consisting of slopes and coasts on which tropical vegetation flourishes. These regions are the richest and most fertile in the Republic, and should not only supply domestic needs but also leave a large surplus for export. However, there is a joker in the deck. Because of the high temperature and extreme humidity, the poor living conditions, the tropical diseases, such as malaria, amoebic dysentry, and erysipelas, and the fact that extraordinary energy and perseverance are required to achieve what would be merely a normal amount of work elsewhere, production in the tropical regions is actually very small.

The non-tropical area consists largely of the central plateau, in which is located the City of Mexico and on which a great portion of the population of the country is concentrated. Here tropical diseases are unknown, the climate is agreeable and much more healthful, and labor is plentiful and efficient. In proportion to the great extent of this non-tropical region, however, its productivity is extremely limited by insufficient rainfall and inadequate water supply for irrigation. All the important sources of irrigation are located, paradoxically, in the tropics, where there is abundant rainfall.

The result is that, prior to agricultural advances of the past few years, the Mexican people lived mainly upon products which they could obtain only from the seven and one-half million acres of irrigated land and twenty-eight and one-half million acres of dry-farming land. In other words, for numerous and varied good reasons, less than 8 per cent of the total area of Mexico was under cultivation, to feed and clothe its twenty-two million people.

And these twenty-two million people—what sort of people are they? Where do they live, and how? They are just about as heterogeneous as the citizens of the United States, with this difference: the people of the United States are the result of the fusion of many bloods, and many nationalities, while the population of Mexico may be loosely divided into three main classifications, Spanish, Mestizo, and Indian. But the Mestizo group, by far the largest, is composed of many varying proportions of Spanish and Indian blood. Conservative estimates set the number of Mestizos in Mexico at between twelve and fifteen million, those of Spanish or other European blood at approximately one million, and the remainder, Indian, though such division is no longer attempted by the government census—a fact which contributes to national unity.

Mexico is all too frequently represented in the American mind by the metropolis of Mexico City; and Mexico City, until the Revolution of 1910, regarded itself as Mexico and the balance of the country as contributing territory. Nothing could be farther from the truth.

The capital is a cosmopolitan city of two million people, many of whom are foreigners. All the other large cities in the country combined have no more population than the City of Mexico. The remainder of the population, approximately eighteen millions, is scattered in some 80,000 little villages, many of them with less than 100 inhabitants. Their average population is about three hundred. Only three per cent of the rural communities have between 3,000 and 4,000 inhabitants. Thus we see that Mexico is overwhelmingly rural, and in the years to come, it will be the rural population that will form the Mexican nation.[2]

There are many differences other than size which distinguish the urban and rural communities. Mexico City, for example, culturally, architecturally, and historically, is a pleasing conglomeration of the Spanish, plus French, German, English, and other European influences, with a strong "Yankee" tinge, and with the Indian foundation showing through only occasionally. The villages, on the other hand, are faithful to their Indian crafts, festivals, and mode of life, upon all of which the superimposed culture of the conquerors, in those regions where it has penetrated, rests lightly as a decorative veneer.

Although Mexico is conceded to be a Catholic country, the Indians, in becoming Christian, did not cease to be pagan[3] and, as Anita Brenner points out in her *Idols Behind Altars,* in many localities their pagan idols receive homage side by side with the Christian images. Of course, the fact is not that the Indians are pagan but that the church was wise enough from the beginning to adapt itself to circumstances, and did not insist that the indigenous peoples give up completely their old ways.

The city is modern; the country is primitive. The city is living in the present; life in the country has made no perceptible change in centuries. The city has broad boulevards, automobiles, radios, electric lights, night clubs, palaces, museums, opera, and fine residential sections. Besides Spanish, one hears English, French, and German. The country has nothing; no lights, no roads, no elaborate buildings; is as apt to speak one of many Indian dialects as Spanish.[4] Despite all these tremendous handicaps, it is rural Mexico which holds the future of the Mexican nation in its hands.

[2] Frank Tannenbaum, *Peace by Revolution* (New York: Columbia University Press, 1933), p. 122.
[3] Henry Bamford Parkes, *A History of Mexico* (Boston: Houghton Mifflin Company, 1938), p. 107.
[4] Tannenbaum, *op. cit.,* p. 122.

History to 1910

There are solid, substantial reasons why the awakened Mexico of 1910 found itself in this deplorably backward state in a modern industrialized world. The governments since that date, and notably the administrations of Lázaro Cárdenas and Manuel Avila Camacho, have made great progress in the solution of their country's problems, but the revolution still continues, with the goal not yet in sight.

To be exact, there have been three revolutions which profoundly altered the structure of Mexican political and social life. The first, in 1810, was the struggle for independence from Spain, a conflict set off by one of the many sparks of greatness which have, from time to time, illuminated, if but briefly, the darkness of Mexican history. It was Father Miguel Hidalgo y Costilla, a Creole priest, in the little town of Dolores, who first made articulate the longings of a subjugated people by his call to arms, popularly known as the "Grito" or "Shout of Dolores."

The second revolution, called the War of the Reform, lasted for a dozen years, during the eighteen-fifties and -sixties, coinciding with our Civil War period. This was a war for the destruction of the most outstanding characteristics of the feudal colonial system derived from Spain, and specifically for the separation of Church and State. This crisis likewise produced its man of the hour, Benito Juárez, a Zapotec Indian of Oaxaca, who displayed a moral grandeur perhaps unsurpassed by any other Mexican before or since. In speaking of Juárez and his contemporary, Abraham Lincoln, Victor Hugo said: "America has two heroes, Lincoln and you, Juárez; Lincoln who gave death to Slavery, and you who have given life to Liberty."

But it is with the third revolution, the one that is referred to when THE revolution is mentioned, that we are most concerned. This bloody conflict, which attempted to uproot the plantation system and to free Mexico from foreign economic domination, broke out in 1910 and continues to this day, with far-reaching social, economic, and political consequences.

The year 1910 was a significant one in Mexican history.

For thirty-five years one man, Don Porfirio Díaz, had ruled with the iron hand of a dictator. Theoretically, Mexico under Díaz was not only a democracy, but an advanced democracy. Actually, it was an oligarchy in which an extraordinary man was allowed to perpetuate himself interminably in office in exchange for privileges and powers granted to a chosen few. The rich, the powerful, the well-connected, the foreigner did as they pleased, obeyed such laws as suited them. Where the law interfered, it was disregarded, violated, forgotten. It was a personal government with the consent of, and for the benefit of, a small group of natives and foreigners who held claims of family, politics, power, and foreign influence.[5]

All that was indigenous was ridiculed, looked upon with contempt. The great bulk of the population, the masses of the Mexican people, had no rights that must be respected, no influence that made itself felt. Resistance was met by force, by the "ley de fuga," which legalized the murder of supposedly escaping prisoners, by forced levy into the army, by forced migration from place to place, by forced labor in the henequen plantations of Yucatan. In the eyes of the world, Mexico was at peace for the first time in a century, but it was peace purchased at the price of tyranny, humiliation, oppression, and foreign approval.[6]

The date of September 16, 1910, marked the first century of independence from Spain. Because the aged dictator's eightieth birthday almost coincided with the anniversary of independence, a lavish celebration was planned, to which every civilized country in the world sent special representatives. No expense was spared, and in the capital there was great rejoicing.

But just as the surface of the skin may not at first give evidence of a deep-seated infection in the flesh, so Mexican life in 1910 gave no surface indication of the forces and evils that were seething and surging underneath. All the wrongs and abuses under which the Mexican people had silently agonized for centuries were at last coming to a head, and the costly spectacle

[5] *Ibid*, pp. 100-101.
[6] *Ibid.*, p. 101.

of the centennial had the effect of gasoline poured on a smouldering blaze.

Landholding and Peonage

Since the days of the Conquest, the lot of the masses had become steadily worse, until by 1910 the common people were stagnating in a hopeless morass of poverty, filth, disease, and ignorance. Although peonage, virtual slavery, was well established when the Spanish conquerors arrived in 1518, the importation of European feudalism and methods of exploitation caused living conditions among the peons to become infinitely worse.

As aforementioned, the arable land of the Republic is scarce, and what there is of it is concentrated more or less in the central plateau. In ancient times, the productive land was sufficient for the number of people living thereon, who were governed by a form of patriarchal communism. Under this system, the largest social and political unit was the tribe, formed of a number of kinship groups or clans, each of which was made up of many households. Several clans would settle together and form a village.

Each clan was assigned a definite part of the town land, certain sections of which were for cultivation, while others served to provide firewood, timber, grass for roofing and mats, and a place for hunting and fishing. A third portion of land was set aside for special public purposes, such as production of supplies for maintenance of the village chief, entertainment of visiting officials, payment of tribute to higher chieftains, carrying on wars, and for the support of religious institutions and the priesthood. This land was worked communally.[7]

Even before the advent of the Spaniards, however, this system of landholding was in process of change. The chief of the village gradually acquired a larger portion of land, cultivated by serfs, title to which, in time, became hereditary. A

[7] Eyler N. Simpson, *The Ejido: Mexico's Way Out* (Chapel Hill: The University of North Carolina Press, 1937), p. 4.

second class of privately owned and slave-exploited property developed out of warfare and conquest. Title to land was given as a reward for valor in war or other notable service. In some cases, a noble or chief would be granted by the king an overlordship embracing a number of villages under a system of feudal tribute. These fiefs involved jurisdiction over land and people and were heritable. The temple lands were greatly increased also, and a special class of serfs had to be dedicated to their exploitation.[8]

Eyler N. Simpson, in his exhaustive study of Mexico's agrarian problem, writes:

. . . by the time of the conquest, the nobles, overlords, chiefs, priests and other privileged persons were a large and growing group. The landholding village was still the dominant unit in the agrarian system of central Mexico, but the landless peon was a definitely established social class. The large landed estate of the Aztec noble is the great-grandfather of the Mexican hacienda, and the "macehuale" of pre-Conquest days is blood-brother to the peon of Colonial and later times. Debt slavery, the poverty of the disinherited, and the arrogance of the privileged were known in Mexico before the coming of the Spaniards; abjectness, humility and servility were not lessons which the masses of the Mexican people learned for the first time at the knee of Cortez and his successors.[9]

Needless to say, the primary purpose of the Conquerors was to garner the fabled wealth of Mexico in the shortest possible time and return to Spain. But when they began to see that their dreams of gold and precious stones were not to be realized, at least not in the measure which they had hoped for, they reluctantly but studiously turned their attention to the true riches which were theirs—the free labor of the Indians.

Enormous grants of land were made to Cortés and his lieutenants, known as *encomiendas*. The King of Spain's deed of encomienda read in part: "Unto you . . . are given in trust . . . so many Indians for you to make use of in your farm and

[8] *Ibid.*, p. 6.
[9] *Ibid.* Quoted by permission of the publisher. Copyright, 1937, by the University of North Carolina Press.

mines; and you are to teach them the things of the holy Catholic faith."

Cortés himself received an estate of twenty-two towns, each with its surrounding lands, with a total population of 23,000 head of families. The whole grant embraced an area of perhaps 25,000 square miles. This and other properties acquired by Cortés formed one vast family estate, which remained intact as late as the beginning of the nineteenth century. The town and district of Xochimilco, now famous as the Floating Gardens, which contained rich lands and some 30,000 Indians, were given to Pedro de Alvarado. Another lieutenant received 10,000 square miles in what is now the State of Guanajuato.

Before the close of the first half-century of occupation, a large part of the inhabited region of Mexico was held in encomiendas, instead of free villages. The larger villages, however, were not included in encomiendas, but their form of organization was accepted and their legal status recognized. They paid tribute directly to the crown. Their communal holding of land was respected, and each village was insured in its possession of a plot of land whereon to construct houses and public buildings. "In addition, every village was to have at least one square league, and more if necessary, made up of crop land, pasture and woodland. This was the 'ejido' . . ."—[10] the agricultural unit which is at the bottom of Mexico's problem of land for the landless. Of course, this system of encomiendas and ejidos which the Spaniards established in Mexico was an adaptation to the New World of the system followed in Spain itself during the long years of the struggle against the Moors. The king gave privileges to the nobles and other privileges to the communities, thus keeping something of a "balance of power," with himself in the center.

Thus the die was cast for the struggle which was to endure for more than 400 years: the struggle between the feudalism of the hacienda and the collective, communal operation of the ejido, with the hacienda winning every round of the battle until

[10] *Ibid.*, p. 13.

the second decade of the present century. By the end of the Díaz regime, Mexico had become a nation of peonage and poverty, a country in which the great majority of the population were not only "forgotten men," but men so long abandoned to misery and affliction that manhood itself had all but vanished from the land.

The Mexican historian, Luis Orozco, says that by 1910 the hacienda peon was like a beast of burden, destitute of illusion and hope. "The son receives at an early age the chains which bound his father and passes them along in turn to his sons. The 'tiendas de raya,' or payroll stores . . . are permanent agencies of robbery, and factories of slaves. There the liberty of the worker is traded for salt, soap and shoddy cloth—sold at fabulous prices. The peon almost never holds in his hand a piece of silver money." The payroll store always paid wages in worthless merchandise; the "four pesos and ration," the monthly salary of the workers, was converted into a series of marks in a book, none of which the peon could understand. "The landlords, and especially the administrators of the haciendas, were still the despots who, whip in hand, were allowed to perpetrate every class of infamy against the workers, their daughters and wives."[11]

These are the conditions which caused the agricultural economy of Mexico to be one of the most backward in the world. The majority of the large haciendas were owned by wealthy hacendados who lived either in Mexico City or Paris, and who returned to the site of their holdings only occasionally. The administrators, left thus undisturbed, drove the peons to maximum production at minimum cost. Farming methods were primitive beyond belief, the most common implements being crude versions of the ancient Egyptian wooden plow. There was no rotation or diversification of crops, no fertilizing, nothing scientific.

One of the principal aims of Benito Juárez had been a

[11] *Ibid.*, pp. 39-40. Quoted by permission of the publisher. Copyright 1937 by the University of North Carolina Press.

redivision of land among the landless, by confiscating from the large landowners the ejidos upon which they had encroached. But Juárez, unfortunately, did not live long enough to accomplish this end, and his successor, Porfirio Díaz, was a man with different ideas. By the year 1910, less than one per cent of the rural families owned about 85 per cent of all the rural land.[12]

Pre-Revolutionary Education

Throughout his long reign, Díaz had steadfastly refused to appropriate any money for the education of the masses. This had been the cause closest to the heart of Juárez, who said, in 1871: "The desire to learn and to acquire an education is innate in the heart of man. Strike off the fetters that misery and despotism impose upon him, and he will seek an education naturally, even when no direct guidance is given him."[13] The expressed attitude of Díaz was that education was dangerous, and that the Indians were much more easily controlled in a state of complete ignorance.

Universal education has never existed in Mexico. Even before the Conquest, only the children of nobles and military leaders were educated. After the Conquest, the children of native leaders were pushed back into the same position that the majority of the children had always occupied. Hardly had Cortés landed, however, before he requested that friars be sent to instruct and convert the Indians; and the political and economic controversies that have raged for more than a century between Church and State in Mexico should not blind us to a realization of the fact that most of what Mexico had of Western civilization prior to 1910 it owed to representatives of the Catholic Church.

The most notable educational pioneer to arrive in New Spain during the first years of occupation was Fray Pedro de

[12] Tannenbaum, *op. cit.,* p. 143.

[13] Benito Juárez, *Exposiciones.* Spanish text: "El deseo de saber y de ilustrarse es innato en el corazón del hombre. Quítensele las trabas que le miseria y el despotismo le imponen, y él se ilustrará naturalmente, aun cuando no se le dé una protección directa."

Gante, a Flemish Franciscan friar, who landed in 1523, and that same year established at the village of Texcoco, near Mexico City, the world's first true "school of action." Later, Vasco de Quiroga planned and established a communal school in which economic, social, educational, and agricultural activities were carried out in a small community as if that community were one complete family.

In 1551 the National University of Mexico was founded. The coming of the printing press to the New World in 1535, and the appearance of the first book published on this continent in 1536—almost 100 years before the landing of the Pilgrims on Plymouth Rock—gave new impetus to learning, but learning only for the children of the privileged. It was in this respect that the Colonial schools failed: the education and culture which they spread were meted out to a chosen few, never reaching the great masses of the people.

Educationally speaking, the Revolution of 1910 found the Mexicans no better off than they had been a century before. It was only through the blood and turmoil of the Revolution that the country was brought to a recognition of the rights of Mexicans, of all the Mexicans. Through it the Mexican people were awakened to the realization that "to educate is to redeem," and that through such redemption, to educate is to govern.

The Catholic Church

No portrayal of Mexico would be complete without some allusion to the part played in its history by the Catholic Church, and the struggle between Church and State.

The Spanish Conquest brought to Mexico a new race, a new economic and political system, and a new religion. It would be difficult to overestimate the debt that Mexico owes to the Catholic Church as a social institution, and it is not as such that the Church has been assailed. Rather, "the attack on the Church has been carried out in a country where the people continued to call themselves Catholics, and continued to be baptized and buried under Catholic auspices and Catholic ritual."[14]   It has not been that the Mexican people revolted against religion.   On the contrary, what they have attempted to do through the years is to divorce religion from politics and economics.

Students particularly interested in the record of the Church in Mexico have access to a wealth of material on both sides of the question, for historians, both Catholic and anti-clerical, have devoted much attention to the subject for the past 100 years or more.   No good purpose can be served herein by going into detail on this highly controversial issue.   It will suffice to state that Mexico is a Catholic country.

The essential historical facts are that, because the maintenance of its dominant position in the life of the Mexican nation depended upon the perpetuation of the feudal system, the Church bitterly opposed independence from Spain, and after 1824 the power of the Church began to wane.   Later, leaders of the Reform Movement attempted to perfect the separation of Church and State and, stinging under the loss of prestige suffered through the victory of the liberals in 1857, the Church took an active part in the negotiations which installed Maximilian as emperor of Mexico.

Under Díaz, the Church was unmolested, and when the Revolution of 1910 came, the Church aligned itself with the supporters of the Díaz regime.   As a result, its powers and activities have been greatly restricted by the revolutionary governments since that date.   But upon the spiritual life of the Mexican people this change has had little effect.   "The Church-State controversy in Mexico is a purely internal question of political and economic supremacy."[15]

The Revolution of 1910

Scarcely had the foreign diplomats and financiers taken their leave of Mexico following the centennial celebration, serene in their belief that all was well, and that the huge invest-

[14] Tannenbaum, op. cit., p. 35.

[15] George I. Sánchez, Mexico: A Revolution by Education (New York: The Viking Press, 1936), p. 171.

ments made by them in exploiting Mexican resources were safe, when the rumblings of the Revolution shook the country to its very foundations.

Unlike the French Revolution, this was not a planned, concerted movement, with a definite ideology. Rather, it was a spontaneous combustion of four centuries of disconnected, unrelated, but unceasing wrongs, grievances, and oppressions. There was not even a leader, unless Francisco Madero might be so regarded, and Madero had no program or plan of action. This was a mass social upheaval which produced many leaders, with dissimilar, often conflicting, ideals and objectives. As Anita Brenner says: "The revolution in the south was Zapata, the story of a cause, while the revolution in the north was Villa, and this was the legend of a man."[16]

Frank Tannenbaum asserts that the Mexican Revolution was anonymous, essentially the work of the common people. "No organized party presided at its birth. No great intellectuals prescribed its program, formulated its doctrine, outlined its objectives. . . . The program of the Revolution is still being written; it has been in the process of writing since 1910."[17]

Finally, long after the Revolution had begun, the peasant leader of Morelos, Emiliano Zapata, one of the greatest patriots Mexico ever produced, whose followers were said to be not an army but a people in arms, came forward with the cry of "Land and Liberty," which was then adopted as the watchword of the Revolution. Uneducated though he was, Zapata was able to express the urgent longings of his people.

Zapata and Pancho Villa were only two of the men whom the conflict brought into prominence. There were also Venustiano Carranza, Alvaro Obregón, Plutarco Elías Calles, and many others like them. These three—Carranza, Obregón, and Calles—eventually became President. The Revolution made them, gave them means and support. They were the instru-

16 Anita Brenner, *Idols Behind Altars* (New York: Harcourt, Brace and Company, 1929), p. 199.
17 Tannenbaum, *op. cit.*, p. 115.

ments of a movement; yet at the same time they each exerted a deep personal influence on its course.

It was not until the Revolution had been in progress fully four years, after the major battles had been fought, and the country was so sharply torn among warring factions that there seemed no hope of ever achieving unity again, that a statement of objectives was prepared and issued by Venustiano Carranza. Although Carranza himself failed to grasp the full significance of his own program, nearly all the reforms he advocated have since been written into law.

His proposals suggested, among other things, that agrarian laws be enacted favoring the establishment of small properties, the dissolution of the large estates, and the return to the villages of lands of which they had been unjustly deprived. Carranza further advocated laws to improve the conditions of labor and to establish a fair system of taxation. He wished a revision of laws governing the exploitation of mines, oil, water, forests, and other natural resources, so as to destroy the monopolies created during the Díaz regime. In short, he advocated all sorts of political and other reforms.[18]

In 1917, under the presidency of Venustiano Carranza, and while World War I was in progress, Mexico rewrote its constitution. The result was that Mexico emerged as the most democratic nation in the world—on paper—guaranteeing to labor and to the people in general, rights which even today are not enjoyed by the citizens of any other country. "The Constitutional Convention of 1917 was the most important single event in the history of the Revolution. It definitely marked off the past from the present and the future in Mexico."[19] Until 1917, the struggle was to formulate a program for the abolition of the feudal structure of Mexico. Since 1917, it has been to realize and consolidate the gains written into the constitution.[20]

This has been, and still is, no easy task, for the smooth opera-

18 *Ibid.,* pp. 161-162.
19 *Ibid.,* p. 166.
20 *Ibid.,* p. 171.

tion of a democratic form of government—a government for, by, and of the people—presupposes a people familiar with the forms of democracy. Such a condition does not exist in Mexico, though rapid strides are being made in that direction. The people of Mexico have never had an opportunity to learn the meaning of democracy. Peons, with their backs bent for centuries in tilling the soil and carrying heavy burdens, have had no contact with either the principles or the forms of democracy. Their evolution from slaves to citizens must begin with the fundamentals. This is the essence of the program of rural education, developed by the trial and error method—a system of socialistic instruction completely Mexican, an inspired formula for the redemption of the Mexican masses.

Rural Education

In *Mexico: A Revolution by Education,* by Dr. George I. Sánchez, there appears a foreword by Professor Rafael Ramírez, who was, for years, head of the Department of Rural Education in the Mexican Ministry of Education. Professor Ramírez writes:

> In Mexico we are anxious that our rural population modify its rudimentary manner of domestic, social and economic life rather than that it should learn to read and write. We are more interested that this population should be cultured, taking the word in its precise acceptance, than that it should be learned. Our rural education, in effect, stresses work along these cardinal lines: health and sanitation, the dignifying of the domestic life, elevation of habitual occupation, recreation and satisfactory social living. After these essentials come those subjects that American educators call "intellectual skills and tools."[21]

It was in 1921 that President Obregón established the Federal Secretariat, or Ministry, of Education, with José Vasconcelos as Secretary. With vigor and enthusiasm, Vasconcelos and his assistants immediately applied themselves to the task of formulating a program of education that would meet the needs of the Mexican people.

[21] Sánchez, *op. cit.,* p. viii. Quoted by permission of the publisher, the Viking Press, Inc.

One of their first moves was to organize a group known as missioner-teachers, whose primary responsibility was that of visiting the rural Indian centers of the Republic—by rail, automobile, horseback, canoe, and even on foot—surveying educational needs and economic conditions, selecting rural teachers, studying native industries and encouraging them, and co-operating with the Department of Agriculture in the study of soil and the cultivation of crops.

They were missionaries in the truest sense of the word, because they first had to sell the superstitious Indians and peasants on the idea of secular education, often at the risk of injury and even death. They had no funds for buildings or for materials, no precedents to guide them, and they supervised a corps of inexperienced rural teachers whose training averaged less than three years of elementary education.

Needless to say, Mexico was not transformed overnight, but by 1924 more than 1,000 federal rural schools, attended by 65,000 pupils, had been created.[22] By 1938, fourteen years later, the rural schools numbered 21,158, and in that year Mexico had 50,000 teachers, and a total school attendance, including workers and peasants in night classes, of 2,124,000. Moreover, there was constant, continual pressure from the peasants for more and better schools.[23]

The rural school is called "La Casa del Pueblo" ("The House of the People"), which tells exactly what it is. In addition to teaching children the rudiments of reading and writing, of personal cleanliness, of the native arts and industries, the teacher also instructs in sports and the regional dances, supervises the cultivation of gardens, encourages the formation of orchestras, bands, and choral groups, for all of which the school house is the center of activity.

In the afternoons, the teacher calls on the mothers, advising them on the preparation of food for undernourished babies,

---

[22] *Ibid.*, p. 67.
[23] Sylvia and Nathaniel Weyl, *The Reconquest of Mexico* (New York: The Oxford University Press, 1939), p. 319.

the use of mosquito netting, and the desirability of boiled drinking water. Then in the evenings, the adults of the community gather at the school house to be given instruction in agriculture, animal husbandry, and allied subjects, and to receive aid in filing applications to the government for the return of land.

This is a far cry from the duties of a school teacher in our own or almost any other country, but Mexican leaders recognize the fact that by no slow and leisurely system of formal education can their problems be solved, or their citizens lifted from the morass of feudalism to the plane of democratic life. To effect this imperative metamorphosis in the shortest possible time, in order to insure Mexico's place among the nations of the world, a revolutionary program of education is required, one patterned not after American or European models, but one fitted peculiarly to the needs of the Mexican people. And that is exactly the sort of plan that was devised.

As Dr. Sánchez says:

Many of the accomplishments of the new schools are still in the future, and the effectiveness of the new program must be weighed in the balance of time. There are many problems that still remain unsolved. Health conditions present a challenge to the efficacy of reform through education. Great portions of the population are still illiterate. The place of women in the social, cultural, and economic scale is yet far from satisfactory. Alcoholism still spreads its enervating tentacles over the untutored masses. The problems arising from the economic upheavals of the agrarian revolution and of labor reforms present a continuing demand upon the powers of a social education. Indeed, the work of the schools has just begun.[24]

The Public Health

Working hand in glove with the educational program, and inseparable from it, is the drive for improved public health and a decrease in the mortality rate, which is the highest in the world. In 1936, Mexico's death rate was 22.4 per thousand, or twice that of the United States.[25]

[24] Sánchez, op. cit., p. 189. Quoted by permission of the publisher, the Viking Press, Inc.
[25] Weyl, op. cit., p. 329.

With very little communication in the past, isolation of
sick people was established by natural obstacles. But today,
new roads and means of rapid transportation are reducing distances and accelerating communication. As a result, the spread
of communicable diseases among the rural population, who
are not yet instructed in their prevention, overbalances the
reduction of deaths secured through measures of control.

The chief enemy of the public health is diarrhea, which
accounts for nine times the number of deaths attributed to
tuberculosis. Second and third in importance, respectively, are
pneumonia and malaria. Since water-borne diseases are the
principal cause of death, much time and money have been
devoted to the purification of water supplies; but until the
economic level of the peasantry is raised, the Mexican will
remain subject to the hazards of hunger and cold, bad and
unbalanced diet, overcrowded dwellings, and subsequent
epidemics.

Health work is one of the most important responsibilities
of the rural teacher[26] who, in addition to his many other tasks,
must co-operate with, and strive to increase the knowledge of,
the native healers or witch doctors, who have a death grip on
the villages; for it will be decades before Mexico's eighty-odd
thousand villages have the benefits of medical service.

In 1936, peasant Mexico had only one doctor for every 6,869
inhabitants. A report of the Rockefeller Foundation in Mexico
for that year revealed that of the 4,520 doctors in Mexico, 2,000
or almost one-half were concentrated in the capital. Of the
remainder, all but 610 were located in seventy large towns.
This meant that 84,000 towns and villages had no medical
attendance whatsoever.[27]

As a result of this report, Dr. Charles A. Bailey of the Rockefeller Foundation recommended that no doctors, nurses, midwives, or dentists be issued licenses to practice until they had
served an apprenticeship in the rural areas. The National Uni-

26 *Ibid.*, p. 333.
27 *Ibid.*, p. 334.

versity endorsed this suggestion, and made five months' practice in rural areas a prerequisite of the medical degree. The student chooses his territory from a prepared list of towns with from 1,000 to 10,000 inhabitants that have no doctor, and departs equipped with a complete medical kit and quantities of health propaganda. He is required to report weekly on his work, and to prepare a monograph on health conditions for his doctor's dissertation, which material, incidentally, is of inestimable value to the Department of Health.[28]

Agrarian Reform

Although "Land and Liberty" was the battle cry of the Revolution, and despite the numerous revolutionary presidents who have held office since 1910, it was not until Lázaro Cárdenas put the Six Year Plan into operation in 1934 that any real headway was made in the matter of returning the communal lands to the peasants. In the first four years of his administration, Cárdenas carved out 39,000,000 acres of land and gave ejidos to 813,000 peasants. On New Year's Day, 1939, he could report that 1,606,000 ejidatarios were the lords and masters of 58,000,000 acres of agricultural land.

While this would seem to be a tremendous amount of acreage, actually the peasant landlords were still a minority group, owning less agricultural land than the owners of haciendas. "At the end of 1938, the land reform had benefitted slightly less than half of those in need. . . . Only 19 per cent of the plowed fields, pastures and woodlands had been turned over to the peasants after two and one-half decades of revolution and reform."[29]

With the return of the communal lands to the peasants, new problems arose. How could an illiterate peon, bred for generations in the tradition of doing exactly as he was told to do, devoid of initiative or a sense of responsibility, and knowing none but the most primitive aspects of agriculture, be expected

[28] *Ibid.*
[29] *Ibid.,* p. 177.

to transform himself overnight into an independent, self-supporting farmer? How was he to obtain modern tools, and when he did secure them, who was to instruct him in their use? Who was going to furnish the seed for his first crop, and who was to determine of what that crop should consist? How was he to live until his first crop was harvested?

In an effort to meet these and other problems arising out of the agrarian revolution, two banks were established, the National Bank of Ejidal Credit, and the National Bank of Agricultural Credit.

The first of these institutions is concerned primarily with the successful operation of the co-operatives organized in cotton, rice, sugar, sisal, and other crops. It tackled for the first time the problem of organizing the ejidatarios for communal working of the land in areas where natural conditions or other circumstances made impossible or impracticable individual cultivation of the ejidal parcel.[30]

The granting of lands to peasants in the rich and extensive Laguna Region, in the Yaqui Valley of Sonora, in that section of Lower California irrigated with the waters of the Colorado River, and in Lombardía and Nueva Italia, made necessary the organization of a different type of credit societies which permitted the use in common of animals, implements, machinery, labor, and lands for cultivation. In this manner, up to June, 1940, four hundred and seventy-one collective ejidos had been organized, working 340,647 hectares of land.[31]

The National Bank of Ejidal Credit not only performs the function of loaning money to the ejidatarios and collecting it, but also that of organizing them economically and socially to exploit the land scientifically, improve the quality of produce, and increase the quantity of crops.

The National Bank of Agricultural Credit is restricted by law to operations with farmers rather than with ejidatarios.

[30] *Seis Años de Gobierno al Servicio de México* (México, D. F.: La Nacional Impresora, S. A., 1940), p. 70.
[31] *Ibid.*

In other words, it functions on an individual-to-bank relationship, lending money and technical assistance of all types and, when required to do so, acting as purchasing agent or crop agent for individual small property owners and for farms in general, whatever their size. Its goal is to develop a prosperous agricultural system for Mexico,. modern and scientifically directed; one which "permits the creation of a new type of farmer, an authentic small operator, who, with new ideas and new attitudes, exploits the natural resources of the soil and not the poorly paid work of his peons."[32]

Both banks co-operate with the Department of Agriculture in constructing and repairing irrigation canals and building power plants; buying machinery for the peasants and farmers, and showing them how to use it; analyzing soils, experimenting with crops, fighting plant parasites, and battling stock diseases.

The co-operative farming areas are the most vital and interesting feature of the Mexican agrarian revolution. They are economic units, embracing thousands of acres of land, with processing plants, electric power systems, feeder railroads, or mechanical traction. The co-operative' involves more than the primitive communism of the early ejidos. It is organization combined with machine technique to solve the social and technical problems of agriculture.

Some of these giant experiments have succeeded, and some have failed, because of successive years of drought and other causes. However, under Avila Camacho, new and important advances have been made in agriculture, to the great benefit of the Mexican people and the war effort of the United Nations.

Brief Notes on the Cárdenas Era

All of the powerful forces of the revolution seemed to reach a dramatic climax during the administration of Lázaro Cárdenas (1934-1940). It is not yet possible properly to evaluate either the man or the influence he has exerted upon Mexican life. Like all important personalities, he had, and has, devout

[32] Ibid., p. 72.

admirers and followers, as well as virulent enemies. As his retirement from public life becomes more definite, however, his stature is increasing, even among his former opponents.

When Cárdenas came into power, he found his country, and the Revolution, in a stalemate. The bloodshed, sacrifice, and original idealism of the Revolution seemed to have come to nought through the ineffectual dilly-dallying of his predecessors in activating its guiding principles.

In breaking the deadlock, Cárdenas opened wide the door of opportunity for a new, youthful, energetic generation. He aroused and revitalized the nation with a personal touch, the like of which had never before been seen in Mexico. During his presidential campaign, and throughout his tenure of office, he visited practically every city, town, and hamlet in the Republic. Wherever his headquarters were at the moment—in the National Palace in the City of Mexico, in a railroad car, in an abandoned hut on a mountain path, even under a tree on the outskirts of a village—he received and personally greeted hundreds of thousands of peasants, workers, common men and women. He galvanized the country into action and set himself vigorously to apply in practice both the spirit and the letter of the revolutionary principles fought for during the two previous decades.

He gave lands and tools to the peasants. He established schools and hospitals. He introduced sanitary measures. He provided an opportunity for the workers to participate in government and in industry.

His chief concern was always with the common people. He steadfastly advocated higher wages, the emancipation of women, and the extension of health facilities. His zeal for the betterment of conditions among the Indians was apostolic. Having the conviction that the economic independence of Mexico—a matter close to his heart—was being retarded by the lack of trained workers, he introduced technical and scientific training and vocational programs, including arts and crafts, mechanical and manual skills, and preparation for trades, in order to offset the preponderance of professional training. He re-established freedom of religion, freedom of speech, and freedom of the press.

Under Cárdenas, the great constitutional conception of the inalienability of the national sovereignty was reborn, at considerable international risk. In hours of historic importance to the world, he supported the cause of democracy and fought against international fascism with such determination, constancy, and vigor that he succeeded in giving to Mexico a weight in international affairs far in excess of the actual military and economic might of the country.

Most noteworthy, perhaps, is the fact that Cárdenas carried out his program in a peaceful, truly liberal, tolerant, democratic manner. He proclaimed, possibly for the first time, the sacredness of human life and thought, and he had the courage of his convictions. During his entire regime, there were no political prisoners, despite the fact that controversial issues were daily debated with fury on the streets and in the press. It is said that no one can point to a single instance in which the honor or the personal safety of any man, because of his political beliefs, was ever endangered by the action or suggestion of the President. This, unfortunately, had not been true before in Mexico.

With less success, Cárdenas attempted to impose honesty in the government. He kept himself irreproachably above corruption, but the same cannot be said of all of his collaborators.

Politically, he built himself up to the point of being all-powerful. Nevertheless, at the expiration of his term of office, and in the face of tremendous pressure from the great masses of the population for whom he had done so much, he stepped out of the government, thereby setting an admirable precedent of disinterestedness, sincerity, and faith in a working democracy. Even during his tenure, and in spite of the many calumnies cast against him, he was considered the greatest president Mexico had had since the revered Benito Juárez.

In all his undertakings, Cárdenas carefully steered clear of any Communistic influence, as that term is generally employed.

Mexican collectivism is closely akin to democracy, and is a form of life that was old in Mexico when the Spanish Conquerors arrived.

Lázaro Cárdenas also made many mistakes, but they were honest mistakes, born of good faith. The harshest criticism that can be made of this man, who held the strategic post of Minister of National Defense in the cabinet of his successor, is that he was, perhaps, too eager to accomplish the complete redemption of his people. Some of his experiments, like some of those of our own government under the Roosevelt administration, were unwise, many were unsuccessful. Yet he was exactly what Mexico needed at the time he served. Of one fact there can be no doubt; that he has left a deep and lasting imprint upon the pattern of Mexican history, the real significance of which can be properly appraised only by future generations.

The opinion of Hudson Strode is as follows: "In this century only two men have made a new spirit in Mexico. Each had the apostolic soul. One was Francisco Madero. The other was Lázaro Cárdenas. Madero made a new political spirit. Cárdenas made a new social and economic spirit."[33]

And *Life* magazine's summation of the man Cárdenas, in the fifth year of his administration, was: "Cárdenas is probably the first completely fearless, honest and unselfish politician to appear since Madero (assassinated in 1913)."[34]

[33] Hudson Strode, *Timeless Mexico* (New York: Harcourt, Brace and Company, 1944), p. 306.

[34] "Mexico: Life Reports on a Social Revolution in Progress," *Life*, VI (January 23, 1939), p. 29.

Chapter 6

Social Advances Under Avila Comacho

MANUEL AVILA CAMACHO was sworn into office on December 1, 1940. Gently, but firmly, he immediately reined the nation back into a course that veered just a little to the left of middle-of-the-road.

One of his first acts was to remove the national railroads from the workers' administration, into whose hands they had been delivered by Cárdenas, and place them under governmental control. Later on, in the fall of 1942, realizing that the advice and assistance of expert railroad administrators and technicians were urgently needed if the nation's transportation system was to carry out its vital role of distributing food to all parts of the Republic and delivering to the United States the raw material necessary to our war plants for our mutual defense, Avila Camacho requested and received the services of a North American Railway Mission, headed by Oliver M. Stevens. That corps of advisers is still stationed in Mexico, collaborating closely with the national railways, to the inestimable benefit of both our countries.

Education

Perhaps the most spectacular, the most characteristically Mexican development in public education during the administration of Avila Camacho has been the national campaign against illiteracy, inaugurated by Jaime Torres Bodet, Minister of Education, and the Chief Executive on August 21, 1944. The former was named executive director of the campaign.

In announcing the revolutionary project to the Mexican people in a radio broadcast, President Avila Camacho said:

> Today the Mexican Government has made a decision of importance. I want to ask all of you to consider it with fervent patriotism as a decision expediting an emergency law by virtue of which all Mexicans over eighteen and under sixty years of age, who can read and write Spanish, and who are not incapacitated, should teach reading and writing to at least one illiterate person.

He stated that during the six-months preparatory period, ending February 28, 1945, ten million pamphlets would be printed and distributed throughout the Republic.

> We are at war, and we realize that in a total war such as the world is now undergoing, every country has two kinds of enemies: enemies from the outside—in our case the nazi-fascist forces—and enemies from the inside [the President said further]. With reference to Mexico, this last type of enemy is more than anything else a product of grave and dangerous insufficiencies.

Then, in words which indicate clearly his profound understanding of the ills that harass Mexico, Avila Camacho continued:

> These insufficiencies are our internal enemies: political—a lack which is still very much obscured in the march of our institutional life; economic —an insufficiency which proves the lack of intensive industrialization, the low production of our agriculture, the inequilibrium of conditions throughout the country and in the cities, the wealth of certain minorities and the misery and poverty of enormous human masses which form the very basis and framework of the nation; technical—a lack derived from a backward and narrow-minded tendency to scorn direct material work and to prefer, in education, instead of the concrete knowledge of indis-

pensable formulas for the better advancement of our resources, the academic forms which lead to the exercise of free professions.

All these insufficiencies spring, however, from one very grave source of insufficiency—that of instruction.

Our leaders of revolutionary extraction have done much in an attempt to carry teaching and education to all the people of Mexico; and the sums of money which we dedicate year after year toward the fulfillment of such an urgent mission are great. Nevertheless, our results from such expenditures have not even been successful enough to obtain a sufficient number of teachers and schools for the total Mexican population of school age. Hundreds of thousands of children lack the complete element of education. This is why the percentage of illiterate people has not diminished in the proportion which would be desirable in order to raise the level of culture to that point to which our country aspires.

I know very well that the education of a people is not rooted exclusively in eliminating illiteracy, but I know, with equal clarity, that the first indispensable step to that education is the teaching of reading and writing. And since half of Mexico is composed of illiterates, no other social problem which we confront could be more directly attacked with the hope of a perfect, logical solution.

It is thus that we confirm ignorance as being the most fearful of internal enemies. Consequently, in this era of conflict, one of our most urgent tasks ought to consist of fighting, by all possible means, against this enemy.

In conclusion, the President warned his people that the task would not be an easy one; that, instead, it would challenge their utmost powers of co-ordination, co-operation, and determination. However, he said: "The confidence which I have in you, my compatriots, strengthens in me the conviction that we will come out of this experience more united, more capable, and more completely Mexican citizens."

To support the anti-illiteracy program, the 1945 allottment for education in the national budget was set at 171 million pesos (approximately $35,625,000). This represented an increase of 43 per cent over the 1944 appropriation. Even at that, the sum devoted to education in Mexico is inadequate by United States standards, although Mexico is doing extraordinarily well with the resources she has. As Professor Guillermo Bonilla y

Segura, Director of the Mexican Cultural Missions, said in a lecture at the University of New Mexico in the fall of 1944, to appreciate the tremendous effort of Mexico and her accomplishments with the small financial means available, let it suffice to state that the educational budget of Mexico with which to provide for all the educational needs of a population of more than 20,000,000 is about the same we devote in the United States to care for the education of, and other social and economic assistance to, our some 300,000 Indians.

Originally scheduled to terminate on March 1, 1946, the campaign against illiteracy, "in view of its marked success," has been extended indefinitely by the Mexican Congress. An Associated Press dispatch from the Mexican capital, on February 14, 1946, quoted the Ministry of Education as reporting 1,270,000 persons in attendance at anti-illiteracy centers throughout the nation, and 800,000 others receiving private instruction. During the first year, 300,000 learned to read and write.

"To reach 3,000,000 Indians who do not speak Spanish," the AP dispatch stated, "special primers have been prepared in the languages of five tribes, [Tarahumaras, Mayas, Tarascans, Otomis and Nahoas] and books in other dialects are being edited. The Indians first learn to read their own language, then learn Spanish."

Dr. Joaquín Ortega, director of the School of Inter-American Affairs, the University of New Mexico, in an address on "Mexico, Vanguard of Latin America," said, in April, 1946:

It must be said that Mexico is educating itself. The current campaign against illiteracy is a gigantic step toward the world of letters and intelligence. Within a generation, Mexicans will be more able politically, more easily molded to progress, and more difficult to deceive. And other Latin American republics [notably Guatemala and Ecuador] are imitating the literacy program of Mexico, because when there is real leadership, as Mexico has been giving in the past few years, the others naturally follow.[1]

[1] *Diario del Norte*, Ciudad Juárez, Chihuahua, México, April 24, 1946. Address delivered to the Club Conquistadores, New Mexico A. & M. College, Las Cruces, N. M., on April 13, 1946.

Industrialization

A concerted attack on the economic and technical insufficiencies mentioned by President Avila Camacho has been made through the Mexican-American Commission for Economic Co-operation, which was created by agreement between Presidents Roosevelt and Avila Camacho in September, 1943. At its final meeting on January 29, 1945, the Commission announced that Mexico plans a $383,000,000 industrial development program within the next few years.

The developments contemplated include irrigation and power projects, and new industrial plants for the manufacture of steel and iron products, building materials, heavy chemicals, pulp and paper, and textiles. The equipment to be required in this expansion program will be purchased in the United States and has already been contracted for.

In all, the Commission approved fifty-eight development projects, and its estimate is that Mexico will require a minimum of capital equipment from abroad valued at $94,000,000 through 1947, and $43,000,000 for 1948 and immediately subsequent years "for projects of major significance to its economic development."

"It is my conviction," President Roosevelt said in his letter to President Avila Camacho which accompanied the final report, "that the basis of sound collaboration between our two countries in the economic field which has been so fruitfully begun through the work of this Commission, now terminating its task, may be widened in the years to come to the mutual benefit of both countries and peoples."

Agriculture

Progress on the agricultural front has been marked under Avila Camacho's administration. Incorporating into his declaration of war on the Axis an assertion that "our trench is in the furrow," the President has stimulated the Ministry of Agriculture and such sub-agencies as the National Irrigation Commission to unprecedented activity.

On January 1, 1944, the N.I.C. reported in operation twenty-nine "great and medium-sized irrigation works," and forty-two "small irrigation works," besides twenty projects on which work had been started. It reported, also, that during the preceding three-year period, an investment of 205 million pesos (approximately $42,700,000) had been made in dams, canals, and various works that made possible the cultivation of 111,454 hectares (approximately 278,635 acres) of land that had completely lacked water, and the improvement of another 126,700 hectares. It is estimated that by the end of the present administration, the N.I.C. will have placed at the service of the nation more than one million hectares, or 2½ million acres of land.

"All that is possible, and more, has been done," said Marte R. Gómez, Minister of Agriculture, in November, 1943; "and were it not for the fatality of restrictions on obtaining necessary machinery, much more could be done."

That the results of these efforts inspire a justifiable pride was emphasized by Gómez when he stated: "During the first half of this year (1943), we exported products of the soil, agriculture and livestock, to the value of 262 million pesos, the highest exportation in our history in a six months period. Our imports amounted to only 102 million pesos in that time, from which it can be deduced that the foreign commerce balance during the period was decidedly in our favor, as it attained the respectable sum of 160 million pesos."

The 1945 budget allowance for Mexico's sharply expanded agricultural program was 174 million pesos, an advance of 67 million pesos over the 1944 appropriation. Part of these funds were used to implement the Ministry of Agriculture's campaign to increase production through mechanization of farming methods, the national government bearing from one-third to one-half of the cost of plows, machinery, and tools purchased.

Public Health and Welfare

Into Mexico's Ministry of Public Welfare, headed by Dr. Gustavo Baz, have been incorporated the functions of the

Department of Health, and during Avila Camacho's administration tremendous strides have been made in the extension of public assistance facilities. However, the Ministry's ambitious program is still handicapped by the fact that, in 1944, Mexico had only 7,000 medical doctors when 20,000 were needed.

Because qualified practitioners are more numerous in the Federal District than elsewhere, progress there has been more rapid and satisfactory. Nevertheless, the number of hospitals of all kinds throughout the Republic increased from twenty-one in 1940 to 100 in 1943, and the Ministry's budget rose from twenty million pesos to twenty-eight million pesos over the same period of time. In many instances, hospital facilities are constructed co-operatively by Federal and State governments and private funds.

One of the most extensive projects of the Ministry is the establishment, in Mexico City, of the Great Medical Center which, when completed, will be the most important grouping of hospital units in the nation. By February, 1944, four million pesos had been spent on construction alone, apart from the cost of installing equipment, and the total cost is expected to exceed 100 million pesos. The Center will include, among other units, the Infantile Hospital, the Cardiological Institute, and the Mundet Maternity Home.

The new hospital for chronic invalids, recently constructed in Tepexpan, D. F., is the second of its kind to be built in Mexico. The first, at Villa de Guadalupe, near Mexico City, can house only 300 patients, but the new one has accommodations for 1,000. In it will be sheltered those invalids who are considered by science to be incurable, and there arrangements will be made to adapt the patients to some useful occupation, for which the institution has been equipped with gardens and workshops.

As an indication of the results obtained through improved public health services, it may be pointed out that, according to the report of the Ministry of Public Welfare for the year 1942-43, the number of maternal and child health centers established throughout the Republic increased from 115 in 1940 to 237 in 1943. Patients hospitalized increased from 14,338 in 1941 to 46,242 in 1943. In 1940, 16,123 prenatal patients were cared for, as compared to 28,724 in 1943. Maternity care was extended from the Federal District, where 6,516 cases were handled in 1940, to include service to 19,112 mothers in various parts of the Republic in 1943. Likewise, facilities for serving school lunches to the children of indigent laborers have been amplified during the past three years. In 1941, in the Federal District, 778,375 such lunches were served, whereas in 1943, 1,621,775 meals were served to children in the Federal District and elsewhere. Each child's social and economic conditions are investigated before free lunches are given, and subsequent improvement in health is noted.

In Mexico City, three large family dining halls were in service in February, 1944, with three more under construction. Families without sufficient funds to purchase food may there buy individual meal tickets each week for three pesos and obtain well-balanced meals for the entire family.

Mother's clubs and organizations to assist with children's aid have been formed under the direction of doctors and professors supervised by the Ministry. In 1943, in Mexico City alone, 2,719 mothers attended classes in cooking, nutrition, preserving, sewing, hygiene, and care of the sick.

The Ministry of Public Welfare has undertaken an extensive program to revolutionize medical techniques, eliminating antiquated customs and inadequate systems. This program includes the establishment of new techniques not only for their immediate application, but also for specific experimentation and investigation along various lines. The Ministry has made it possible for many Mexican doctors, architects, and administrators to widen their knowledge, experience, and observations in the United States and other countries in order that the new hospitals in Mexico may have the advantage of the latest scientific advancements. At the same time, through the Civil Defense Committees and other agencies, the number of youths who are being trained as nurses has been increased materially. Public health has become the people's business.

Foreign Relations

In the matter of foreign relations, and specifically relations with the United States, the Avila Camacho administration has been confronted with numerous difficulties, both tangible and intangible.

To begin with, there are the deep sentimental grievances of the Mexican people against this country, going back almost to Colonial days. Then, with the shelling of Vera Cruz in 1914 and the Pershing expedition of 1916 still vivid in their memories, many Mexicans have lived in constant fear of further armed intervention by the United States.

The widely publicized behavior of some United States financial interests in Mexico has led to a general fear of the economic potency of this country, and a common belief that, with slight provocation, the United States would swallow Mexico, depriving her of all important sources of income, her language, her culture—in short, her independence.

Mexicans in general have resented the hostile attitude and incomprehension of many individual Americans going into Mexico. They also object strenuously to the manner in which Mexico and Mexicans have been portrayed in the movies and depicted by the press in this country.

Reactionary forces in Mexico, through what might be termed "religious reluctance," have contributed to the general distrust of the United States by identifying it with Protestantism as opposed to the Catholicism of Mexico. Progressive elements, on the other hand, deeply resent the hands-off attitude that our government took when the republican elements in Spain went down before the fascistic Franco régime.

When the United States became involved in the second World War, many Mexicans experienced a feeling of satisfaction and anticipation. Weary of living at such close quarters with a powerful neighbor whom they at once feared and envied, their hope was that although they themselves were powerless to beat up the "big bully," some one else would do it for them.

Real and imaginary wrongs at the hands of the United States have been intensified by constant reports in the Mexican press of mistreatment of Latin Americans in the Southwest, and particularly in Texas.

All of these grievances were ready-made fuel for the Nazi propaganda machine, which worked tirelessly to emphasize, magnify, and capitalize upon the points of conflict, actual or potential, between our two countries. It is not surprising, therefore, that even after the attack on Pearl Harbor, many Mexicans held steadfastly to the conviction that it was not their war.

In the face of all these adverse factors, the government of Manuel Avila Camacho embarked upon a course of full co-operation with the United States. This decision was concurred in and supported by the entire Cabinet, including former President Cárdenas, the responsible leaders of the agrarian movement, trade unions, and enlightened business men. Suddenly, Mexico, too, was at war.

Since the beginning of the Avila Camacho administration, however, preparations had been under way for just such an emergency. In a quiet, unassuming, but thoroughly efficient manner, the Ministry of the Interior, under the direction of Licenciado Miguel Alemán, and in close co-operation with our own military and naval intelligence and the Federal Bureau of Investigation, had every possible troublesome spot in the Republic under control, had every person with Nazi, Fascist, or Japanese sympathies or leanings under close surveillance, and had the economy of the country co-ordinated to withstand the shock of war. Mexico was a most unhealthful place for conspirators, whether already within the country or coming into it from the United States. Besides, the army had been completely activated.

It was Alemán's responsibility to condition public opinion and the attitudes of public officials to support of the United States and the United Nations. This he accomplished, without fanfare, by enlisting the sympathy and co-operation of the governors of the twenty-nine Mexican states, the Congressmen, the press, law enforcement officers, and the courts. So successful were his efforts that when war became an actuality, Mexico's official machinery was able to go into immediate action on the side of the United Nations.

It would be difficult to overestimate the value of the service rendered to the United States by the Mexican delegation at the Río de Janeiro conference in January, 1942. The personal ability of Ezequiel Padilla, then, and until June, 1945, Foreign Minister of Mexico, was a deciding factor in winning for the United States the support and co-operation of the other American republics. Throughout his term of office, Padilla continued to interpret the friendly policies of his government, which have been clarified and reaffirmed by his very able successor, the former Ambassador of Mexico to the United States, Dr. Francisco Castillo Nájera.

After the outbreak of hostilities, and for the duration of the war, the home economy of Mexico, principally under the direction of Eduardo Suárez and Ramón Beteta, Secretary and Under-Secretary, respectively, of the Treasury, was geared to the production of strategic materials for our war production plants. Just how magnificent was their country's contribution to the war effort of the United States the members of the Permanent Commission of the Mexican Congress learned on January 17, 1946, when a complete report on the subject was submitted and read by Senator Alfonso Flores M.

Even before the United States became an active combatant, minerals were flowing across the border from the mines of Mexico. During the period 1938-1941, inclusive, the tonnage was as follows:

Lead	238,900	tons
Copper	164,800	tons
Zinc	256,900	tons
Arsenic	27,000	tons
Antimony	33,000	tons

Following the attack on Pearl Harbor, and particularly after the Río de Janeiro conference, production of strategic minerals in Mexico and their exportation to the United States were greatly accelerated. The figures which cover the two and one-half year period ending June 30, 1944, speak eloquently for themselves:

Lead	545,000	tons
Copper	265,000	tons
Mica	324,900	tons
Zinc	410,000	tons
Manganese	42,000	tons
Strontium	8,000	tons
Feldspar	32,000	tons
Antimony	8,500	tons
Arsenic	4,500	tons
Tin	355	tons
Mercury	72,000	flasks
Bismuth	326,000	kilos
Tungsten	555	tons

In vegetable and animal raw materials, also, the contribution of Mexico was considerable, as revealed by the following figures, which cover the years 1942 and 1943:

Henequén fibre	104,574	tons
Ixtle fibre	22,200	tons
Rope	3,250	tons
Fibre for Rope	11,500	tons
Cottonseed	5,066	tons
Goat Skins	393,000	skins
Animal Hair	125,000	kilos

In addition to all the above, Mexico furnished this country with 25,546 tons of raw rubber between January 1, 1941, and August 31, 1943.

With regard to the loan of manpower, the report stated that, according to data submitted by the Secretary of Labor and Social Welfare, the number of Mexican laborers who contributed their services to the United States during the war years included 167,846 agricultural workers and 135,224 railroad track workers.

In presenting this impressive report to the Permanent Commission, Senator Flores said:

Mexico has not arrived at the peace table with empty hands, but with a very considerable contribution to the war effort of our allies in their successful attempt to destroy totalitarianism and to bring about the triumph of democratic principles and the liberty of the world. . . .

It is no exaggeration to state that without the help of Mexico, the military might of the United States would have been impossible. If war production in the United States attained its indispensable rhythm and volume, it is due to the co-operation of Mexico, which has been given with absolute loyalty, with disinterest, and with generosity. The United States received from Mexico greater assistance than that which any other country could have given.

Senator Flores concluded his remarks with the statement that "Mexico, in its contribution to the war effort of the United Nations, has carefully avoided any concern for profits, in accordance with its international policy. On the contrary, our country has given to the policy of the Good Neighbor a real significance."[2]

Besides diplomatic assistance and economic co-operation both at home and in this country, Mexico undertook armed participation in the war through action of the 201st Mexican Aerial Squadron in the Pacific theater of operations. This was in addition to the thousands of Mexican citizens enrolled in the armed forces of the United States.

Through the travail of war and the mutual understanding which is born of common effort for a common end, some of the doubts and fears which existed in the minds of Mexicans at the beginning of the Avila Camacho administration have disappeared or at least greatly diminished. But there remains one notable sore spot, and that is the matter of "discrimination" against persons of Mexican descent in the United States, and especially in Texas.

[2] *Excelsior* (México, D. F.), January 18, 1946.

Part 4

*Problems of Latin Americans
in Texas*

Chapter 7

The Latin American Child and the School

THE DIFFICULTIES and inequalities suffered by our Texas people of Mexican descent are not problems that have sprung up overnight. They have been developing for the past fifty years or more. Neither can a single cause be specified for the existence of those problems.

Robert C. Eckhardt, field representative in Texas of the Office of Inter-American Affairs,[1] points out the futility of attempting to place responsibility upon only one weakness in our social structure when he says:

The problem of Spanish-speaking minorities in Texas is a complex one. To say that the bad aspects of the relation between persons of Latin American descent and persons of other descent in Texas arises from a single cause, such as "racial prejudice" or "economic" and "class" differences, is to oversimplify to the point of falsehood. Such oversimplification in analysis of the causes results in a similar error in propounding remedies. Causes of strained relations are as varied as the personalities of the thousands of persons of Latin and Anglo descent who come in contact with each other.

[1] Robert C. Eckhardt is now field representative for the division of Spanish-Speaking Peoples in the United States, Institute of Ethnic Affairs, Inc., Washington, D. C.

We may logically assume that the chief reason for the development of inequitable conditions and difficulties in the relations between these two groups of people in Texas is that the number of Latin Americans in the State has increased enormously since 1900, principally because of demands of cotton, citrus, and vegetable growers for cheap labor. This means that the majority of Mexicans who have immigrated into Texas since the turn of the century have been drawn from Mexico's peasant population, that nation's most impoverished class, economically, educationally, and politically speaking.

Carey McWilliams says that the number of persons of Mexican descent in Texas in 1900 was 71,062; in 1930, 683,681.[2] The figure in 1945 was in excess of one million. This sharp increase in the forty-five-year period was brought about, in the main, by the influx of agricultural and railroad laborers.

Viewed in this light, our problems in Texas closely parallel those which have been the chief concern of the Mexican governments since 1910, and the people involved in both instances are the children of Mexico's long-lived feudal system, released from bondage by the Revolution.

In his annual address to the Mexican Congress, on September 1, 1943. President Avila Camacho graphically described the plight of the peasant class in Mexico. On that occasion he said:

Ignorance and poverty are conditions that are intimately linked, so much so that it cannot be precisely determined whether the first is the origin or the consequence of the second. In an order in which the parents do not always have prosperous opportunities of work, and when their reduced income allows them to attend only the demands of a vegetative life, how can it be expected that their children shall enjoy that interior tranquility, a condition that is essential to the taking advantage of instruction? Drawn by the urgency of uniting their small effort to the insecure effort of their family, the adolescents and even the children must, of necessity, turn their backs on school and, with sad precocity, engage in the struggle from which it is difficult for them to emerge as victors.

[2] Carey McWilliams, *Ill Fares the Land* (Boston: Little, Brown and Company, 1944), p. 247.

Thus, during many years the chain is forged: one generation, pinched by misery, comes stumbling upon the other, submerged in ignorance. And this, in its turn, perpetuates the anguishing poverty that it has formed. To break this circle, there is only one system: that of attacking at the same time the two evils, seeking the full utilization of our resources and organizing an educational diffusion that, little by little, elevates the spirit of the masses and proportions, on a par with a complete vision of Mexico, an outlook that affirms their liberty.[3]

All we need do is substitute "Texas" for "Mexico" and we have a vivid picture of our own basic problems—that is, one side of the picture. The other side was presented by Dr. George C. Engerrand, eminent anthropologist of the University of Texas in an open forum meeting in Austin:

Americans are afraid of complete democracy. Ignorance, prejudice, and vested interests make most Americans fear giving equality to minority groups.

The problems arising from racial, linguistic and cultural minorities all over the world can be remedied only by change in our society. The world looks to us to learn how to solve minority problems, but people think we are hypocritical when we talk about democracy and allow discrimination against groups such as the Mexicans in Texas.

Any solution of the minority problem must take into consideration economic equality of opportunity, that minority members must be able to make a decent living. The only possible solution lies in different and better education based on what we have found out through science: that all races have the same potentialities.[4]

In answer to the self-posed question, "What kind of educational program will best serve the needs of the Spanish-speaking child and the democracy in which he is to participate?" Dr. H. T. Manuel, professor of Educational Psychology at the University of Texas, states:

The answer in principle is easy: the basic needs of Latin American youth are not different from those of other youth. Their desires, which education is to help satisfy, are the desires of all youth. They, like others,

    [3] Quoted verbatim from resumé (in English): "President Avila Camacho Delivers His Annual Message," *Mexico News* (published by International Press Service Bureau of the Department of State for Foreign Affairs), October 1, 1943, p. 2.
    [4] *The Austin American* (Austin, Texas), April 3, 1945.

want an opportunity to participate on equal terms in the activities in which men and women normally engage and to enjoy a fair share of the goods of life. They want action. They wish to be participants in the drama of life rather than merely spectators. They want reasonable security, but they want adventure also. They want to have a part in business, industry, government, home life, education, and recreation as full-fledged and responsible members of the group. They want opportunity, not special privilege. Democracy, on the other hand, wants Latin American youth, as other youth, to be prepared to participate effectively in the varied activities of democratic living and to share the benefits of co-operative endeavor.[5]

To determine to what extent the public schools of Texas meet accepted educational standards with regard to Latin American children, the State Department of Education and the University of Texas, in the summer of 1943, agreed to co-operate in making a study of the problems of the Spanish-speaking child of school age. Dr. George I. Sánchez set up the project, and, with funds received from the Office of the Coordinator of Inter-American Affairs and the General Education Board, Dr. Wilson Little was employed to carry it out. The study, entitled "Spanish-Speaking Children in Texas," was completed and published in June, 1944.

Dr. Little's findings are based on figures for the 1942-43 school year, taken from reports of school superintendents submitted on a voluntary basis. In view of the fact that replies were received from 75 per cent of the common school districts and 76.6 per cent of the independent school districts, in which were included 79.26 per cent of the total number of Latin American scholastics in the State, Dr. Little's study may be regarded as representative of the State as a whole. For the fiscal year ended August 31, 1944, the State Department of Education requested similar information on a "must" basis, to be included in each superintendent's annual report.

Since no separation is made on the school census of Latin and Anglo children, it was necessary for Dr. Little to resort to

[5] H. T. Manuel, "Education of the Spanish-Speaking Child," Proceedings of an Inter-American Conference, Baylor University, Waco, Texas, January, 1945, p. 30.

the not altogether accurate method of counting the Spanish names appearing on the census roll in order to determine the number of Latin American children of school age enumerated in the State for the year 1942-43; that is, those between the ages of 6 and 17, inclusive. The resultant figure was 260,759, or 20.4 per cent of the total white school population.

Contrary to popular belief, our Latin American population is not confined to South and Southwest Texas. Dr. Little's survey revealed that Latin Americans are resident in all but sixteen of Texas' 254 counties. The largest number of Latin American scholastics, 37,246, was found in Bexar County, where they constituted 53.24 per cent of the total white school population in the year 1942-43.

Obviously, however, the absolute figures on Latin American children per county do not correspond to their proportion of total children. For instance, as Dr. Little points out:

> Bexar County has the largest number of school-age children of Latin American extraction in the State; but Bexar County does not have in proportion to other white scholastics, the highest percentage of such children in the State. . . . For example, there are only 549 scholastics of Latin American descent in Hudspeth County, but this number is 68.88 per cent of the total white scholastic population of that county. On the other hand, the 7,675 Spanish-speaking scholastics in Harris County represent only 9.39 per cent of the total white scholastic population in that county.[6]

Horace Mann, the world-famous educator of a century ago, said:

> I believe in the existence of a great, immortal, immutable principle of natural law, or natural ethics—a principle antecedent to all human institutions, and incapable of being abrogated by any ordinances of man, —a principle of divine origin, clearly legible in the ways of Providence as those ways are manifested in the order of nature, and in the history of the race, which proves the *absolute right* to an education of every human being that comes into the world; and which, of course, proves the correlative duty of every government to see that the means of that education are provided for all.

[6] Wilson Little, *Spanish-Speaking Children in Texas* (Austin: The University of Texas Press, 1944), p. 18.

In regard to the application of this principle of natural law,—that is, in regard to the extent of the education to be provided for all at the public expense,—some differences of opinion may fairly exist under different political organizations; but, under our republican government, it seems clear that the minimum of this education can never be less than such as is sufficient to qualify each citizen for the civil and social duties he will be called to discharge;—such an education as teaches the individual the great laws of bodily health; as qualifies for the fulfilment of parental duties; as is indispensable for the civil functions of a witness or juror; as is necessary for the voter in municipal and in national affairs; and, finally, as is requisite for the faithful and conscientious discharge of all those duties which devolve upon the inheritor of a portion of the sovereignty of this great Republic.[7]

In support of these recognized principles, the State Constitution clearly defines the obligation to all Texas children. Article VII, Section 1 thereof reads:

A general diffusion of knowledge being essential to the preservation of the liberties and rights of the people, it shall be the duty of the Legislature of the State to establish and make suitable provision for the support and maintenance of an efficient system of public free schools.

Yet the tabulated reports of school superintendents for the fiscal year 1942-43 revealed that only 53 per cent, or approximately 138,000 Latin American children, were enrolled in the public schools of Texas during that year. Of that number, 128,123, about equally divided as between boys and girls, were enrolled in the elementary grades, first through eighth.

According to figures supplied by the Chancery Office in San Antonio, approximately 12,000 children of Mexican descent were enrolled in Catholic elementary and high schools of Texas for the school year 1944-45. If we assume the same figure for the year 1942-43, and deduct it from the 122,759 scholastics Dr. Little shows not enrolled in the public schools, we are still confronted with the appalling figure of 110,759, or 42.47 per cent of the total number of Latin American children of school

---

[7] *Life and Works of Horace Mann* (New York: Lothrop, Lee & Shepard Co., 1891), Vol. IV, pp. 115-116. Quoted by permission of the publishers.

age in the State, who are receiving no education whatever.[8]

That something is drastically wrong with the Latin American children, or with the tools and methods of instruction provided for them, or with the psychological factors and cultural attitudes involved in the situation, is shown in Dr. Little's analysis of enrollment. During the year covered by his study, 37,000 Latin American children were shown to be enrolled in the first grade, with only 19,000 in the second grade. Enrollment in the eighth grade had dropped to less than 6,000.

In the State Department of Education's follow-up study, on the year 1943-44, the statistical data are broken down by counties to show (I) total white enumeration, (II) number of Latin Americans included in the enumeration, (III) total white enrollment, (IV) number of Latin Americans included in the enrollment, (V) average daily attendance of Latin Americans, (VI) number of Latin Americans not making a grade per year.

Figures on counties selected at random from widely separated sections of the State are shown below:

County	(I)	(II)	(III)	(IV)	(V)	(VI)
Mitchell	2,444	227	2,438	77	3	66
Taylor	9,856	434	9,324	318	186	278
Tarrant	46,883	1,647	41,851	1,133	772	901
El Paso	35,386	23,206	32,110	19,639	21,754	14,370
Hudspeth	808	467	656	393	232	320
Tom Green	8,204	1,433	6,869	1,120	623	967
McLennan	19,057	1,180	17,771	883	590	712
Bexar	72,787	37,173	58,805	28,759	21,936	15,461
Zavala	2,708	2,105	1,798	1,203	99	1,058
Travis	18,391	3,894	16,257	2,763	1,778	2,160
Brazos	3,448	304	3,259	303	230	230
Bee	4,173	2,294	2,991	1,318	618	1,147
Galveston	14,812	1,655	12,868	1,137	778	830
Brooks	1,849	1,626	1,382	1,107	955	909
Hidalgo	31,344	22,787	21,800	14,526	9,896	11,498
Nueces	25,087	12,119	20,491	7,898	5,241	6,232

8 This estimate does not include denominational schools other than Catholic; but these schools have such limited enrollment that they do not invalidate the argument.

It will be noted from the above that there appears to be no uniformity whatever among the various counties, whether their Latin American scholastic population is large or small, as to percentage enrolled, percentage in average daily attendance, or percentage able to make a grade each year.

For example, Bexar County, with 37,173 Latin American scholastics for the year 1943-44, had only 28,759, or 77.4 per cent of them enrolled in public schools, of whom 76 per cent were in average daily attendance, and only 53.7 per cent doing passing work.

Hidalgo County, with 22,787 scholastics of Mexican descent, listed 14,526, or 64 per cent of them, as being enrolled in school, of whom only 68 per cent were in average daily attendance, and 79 per cent doing below average work.

Mitchell County reported 227 Latin American scholastics, yet of that small number, only 77, or 34 per cent, were enrolled in school, of whom 3.9 per cent were in average daily attendance, and 85.7 per cent failing to advance.

Nueces County closely resembles Hidalgo County, with 12,119 scholastics, and only 7,898, or 65.2 per cent, enrolled in school, of whom 66 per cent were in average daily attendance, and 78.8 per cent failing to progress satisfactorily.

With these data in mind, certain questions logically present themselves. Why are these children not in school? When they are enrolled in school, what are the factors which prevent their regular attendance and normal progress? What kind of schools are provided for their instruction?

To answer these queries satisfactorily, we must begin with the economic situation which confronts that large body of our Latin American people of the laboring class.

W. A. Shaley of Starr County, field worker for the Texas State Department of Public Welfare, in addressing a professional workshop on inter-American relations education in Austin on March 21, 1945, related:

The letter inviting me to attend this workshop was received on the fifth anniversary of a tragedy that will linger long in the minds of the people in the community where I live. On March 14, 1940, a truck carrying forty people to the vegetable fields in the Valley was hit by a train. Twenty-seven of the forty were killed, and among them were eight children of school age, eight children who should have been and would have been in school that morning, if the necessity for earning their daily bread had not forced them to join the crew of vegetable workers. I knew them all—knew their families, their living conditions, their economic circumstances.

During the first three months of 1941, representatives of the Children's Bureau, U. S. Department of Labor, made a study which was published as "The Work and Welfare of Children of Agricultural Laborers in Hidalgo County, Texas." Three hundred and forty-two families were included in the survey, of whom 329 were of Mexican stock and predominantly Spanish-speaking. To quote from the report:

In most households the father and mother and also several children were wage earners. Employment was, however, so irregular and rates of pay were so low that the combined earnings of all the workers from agricultural labor, supplemented to some extent by earnings from non-farm work, were too small to provide adequate food, clothing, and shelter for the family group. During the year preceding the date of interview, the families had a median cash income from all sources of only $350.00 to provide for their large households, averaging 6.6 persons. This was considerably less than the minimum annual income of $480.00 estimated by the Texas Social Welfare Association to be necessary to maintain relief families, averaging only 4.2 members, at a level of health and decency.[9] Yet very few of the families had received any assistance from public or private agencies during the year.[10]

To demonstrate the direct relation between the economic status of the family and the school attendance of the children, case histories are cited, of which the following are representative:

[9] Even at that, one may question the ability of a family of 4.2 members to maintain itself "at a level of health and decency" on an annual income of $480.00. Many recent socio-economic surveys have shown that the average American family of approximately 3.5 persons needs at least four to five times this amount to maintain an adequate standard of living.—P.R.K.

[10] Amber Arthun Warburton, Helen Wood and Marian M. Crane, M. D., *The Work and Welfare of Children of Agricultural Laborers in Hidalgo County, Texas* (Washington, D. C.: U. S. Department of Labor, Children's Bureau, Publication 298, 1943), pp. 4-5.

Felipe was nine years old. He had picked cotton for twenty-five weeks during the migratory period in the preceding year. His mother reported that his earnings were needed and that, consequently, he had never been to school. In addition, the family felt that it had never been in one place long enough to permit the boy to go to school.

Ramona was nine years old. For the past year she had kept house and cooked for the family. The mother was a widow and had to work. Ramona was the only member of the family available for housework, and therefore the mother did not see how she could "ever send Ramona to school."

The Servando boys were fourteen and seventeen years old. Their family had lived in the country near Robstown, Texas, when they were small, and the school was so far away that the mother said: "It was better to send the boys into the fields to work with their father than to send them to school alone." Therefore, when they were six and seven years of age they were helping their father in the fields, and by the time they were eight they were working for hire. Since that time the family had always regarded their earnings as essential.[11]

These conditions are not peculiar to Hidalgo County, nor to South Texas, nor to agricultural workers. A somewhat similar study made in 1943 of 153 Latin American families chosen at random in three Central Texas counties revealed that

the employment situation follows no particular pattern. Types of jobs vary widely. Eighteen per cent of the fathers do farm work, with only 9 per cent of the mothers working outside the home. Seventy-four of the families have children who work. The total average monthly income for the families is $88.00, the lowest being $39.00. The average number of persons living in the home is 7.5 with an average of 3.5 rooms per house. One-fourth of the people own their homes. The average rent is $9.20 per month. Inadequate toilet facilities and improper lighting are evident.[12]

Children of migratory laborers suffer, perhaps, the severest handicap. The migrants travel in family groups, the swing through the cotton-growing areas of the State begins in June or July, and by the time the season is over in December or January, the opportunity for half a year's schooling has already

---

[11] *Ibid.*, p. 41.
[12] Confidential information supplied to the author.

PLATE I   *Photo by J. A. Dodd*

SIX-YEAR-OLD BEGINNERS
learn English through story-telling activities. Stephen F. Austin School,
Kingsville, Texas

been lost. Although many of these children enroll in school for the spring term, they are, year after year, placed in the same grades, because of the time lost between enrollment periods.

Numerous other reasons for failure of Latin American children to enroll in school are engendered by the economic situation. Among these is illness, either on the part of the child or some member of the family who requires his attention. Another is the inability to dress like other children, or to take lunches that could be eaten without shame before other children. To quote again from the Children's Bureau study:

> Carmen was eight years old and had never been to school because she had acted as nurse to her blind five-year-old brother.
> Angela was seven years old. Although the family regarded schooling as important, the parents were too poor even to consider school as a possibility. Apparently no one had ever thought of sending Angela to school. Angela had no shoes or dress of her own.[13]

Even among migratory laborers, who are, generally speaking, the latest arrivals from Mexico, more than 90 per cent of the children are, by birth, citizens of the United States. They know no other country, want no other country; yet they continue to be regarded as "Mexicans" and considered as foreigners. On occasion, the word "Mexican" is even applied as a term of opprobrium,[14] and in some cases it is this attitude on the part of Anglo American children or teachers that prevents the Latin American child's enrollment in and attendance at school. He is made to feel that he is not wanted, that his presence in the class is distasteful.

In one West Texas town, where the Latin American children attend a segregated school, Girl Scout troops were organized in each of the schools and elsewhere in the city. During the past year, all the troops were to join in a celebration at the

13 Warburton, et al., op. cit., p. 41.
14 This name-calling and this bigoted attitude toward foreigners, in a nation fundamentally made up at one time or another of foreigners, together with arbitrary categories of acceptance (first, the blond peoples, then the dark ones, until the darker ones are hardly given a chance for assimilation) is the basic difficulty in the acculturation and ultimate unity of the peoples who live under our flag.—P. R. K.

high school. The Latin American group was Troop No. 10 among thirteen troops. When the time came to march into the hall, the troops were placed in line according to number— with the exception of the Latin American troop. Its members were instructed to bring up the rear. The girls were hurt and embarrassed, and said they would go home immediately unless allowed to take their rightful place in line. Their Anglo American leader, who was entirely in sympathy with the girls' feelings in the matter, delivered their ultimatum to the director. After some argument, the director of the organization, one avowedly dedicated to the development of youngsters with sound minds in sound bodies and to the high ideals of "fair play," allowed, with poor grace, Troop No. 10 to march in order.

In June, 1944, in a South Texas high school, a Latin American boy and an Anglo American girl were running a close race for the honor of being valedictorian of the graduating class. The competition was keen, and it appeared certain that the boy would win, whereupon the principal of the school was warned that if he allowed a "Mexican" to become valedictorian, he would be discharged. During the final week of school, the girl brought her grades up sufficiently to win the honor, but the principal resigned his position immediately after the close of the session.

A number of Latin Americans were members of the graduating class in another South Texas high school. On the night of the senior banquet, the Anglo American girl in charge of arrangements deliberately distributed the place cards so that the Latin Americans would be seated among Anglo students. Two or three girls, entering the dining room and finding that they were to be seated next to "Mexicans," left in a huff. But the arrangements stood, and the banquet went off in fine order.

Latin American parents are also responsible to some degree for the failure to enroll their children in school. This indifference is not surprising when we take into consideration the fact that if only 58 per cent, at the most, of our present generation of Latin American children of school age are enrolled in school, the percentage of their parents who have had any education whatever is negligible. Not having had the advantage of instruction, whether they grew up in Texas or Mexico, it is sometimes difficult for them to understand its necessity for their children.

One of the most important reasons for the failure of these children to attend school, however, is the lax enforcement of the State's compulsory school attendance law. Unfortunately, responsibility for the enforcement of this law rests upon each individual school district. Whether it employs special personnel to investigate and prevent absenteeism is strictly up to the district. Doubtless the manner in which the State school funds are apportioned to the districts has much to do with the failure to enforce the attendance law.

For the year 1944-45, each Texas school district received $29.00 per capita for all children between the ages of six and seventeen listed on its census enumeration. This money is paid by the State whether or not the children are enrolled in school. The injustice which results all too frequently is obvious.

If there are 5,000 children in the district, 2,000 of whom are Latin Americans, the school authorities will receive from the State a total of $145,000.00 for the instruction of those 5,000 children. If, however, no effort is made to enroll the Latin American children in school, the money will be forthcoming anyway, and there will be more to spend on buildings, equipment, and teachers for those who are in school. In other words, if the Latin American children are not enrolled, the State will actually be contributing $48.33 per capita, instead of $29.00, for the education of those children who are enrolled in school.

As the Children's Bureau report showed, there was a school district in Hidalgo County which was receiving the State apportionment on the basis of 2,600 children enumerated, while only 1,600 were enrolled in school.

This made possible a much smaller school appropriation by the local community than would have been necessary to provide the same level of education for all children in the district. Thus the nonenforcement of the compulsory-attendance law not only reduced the local tax levies, but made available to some of the children, especially those in comparatively fortunate economic circumstances, a better education than would have been possible if all the children had attended.[15]

It is not to be assumed, however, that diligent enforcement of the law alone would solve the attendance problem. Latin American parents can make only one choice between the entire family's being able to eat regularly, even though frugally, and regular school attendance of children who are considered old enough to work. The instinct of self-preservation is infinitely more powerful than either fear of the law or the desire for education.

Some superintendents upon being approached with regard to the failure to enroll Latin American children defend themselves with the lack of building space, saying that even now children in some of the lower grades are attending only half-day sessions because of overcrowded conditions. This argument, of course, while plausible is nevertheless beside the point. That building materials are difficult to obtain at this particular time has nothing to do with the fact that these children have not been enrolled in school and adequate facilities have not been provided, even before restrictions were placed on building materials.

Actually, a superintendent who submits a census enumeration and thereby requests State funds for the education of children who have never been enrolled in school and never will be, because insufficient building space and seating capacity precludes their attendance, is acting with intent to defraud the State and to defraud the children of school facilities. As an example, one Central West Texas school district last year reported 2,000 children of school age in the district and collected the State apportionment on that basis, whereas the total seating capacity of school buildings in the district was only 1,350. The State of Texas is not morally justified in contributing to that

[15] Warburton *et al.*, *op. cit.*, p. 32.

district on the scholastic enumeration basis, when it is obvious that 650 children could not attend school if they so desired. It so happened that the Latin American children in the district numbered 650. The working of the compulsory attendance law under such conditions is farcical.

One phase of the schooling of Latin American children which we have not yet considered at length is that of segregation. One reason is most often advanced for the separation of Latin American children for purposes of instruction, either in separate buildings or in segregated classes within the school. That one reason, regarded as pedagogically sound by some school administrators, is the language handicap from which a large number of them suffer. Many of the parents speak no English, or very little; at any rate, Spanish is the language spoken in the homes of most of the laboring class of Latin Americans.

Let us grant, then, for the sake of argument, that throughout the first three grades, Spanish-speaking children might be separated from those whose native tongue is English, to the mutual benefit of both groups, provided, that is, that special, intensive training in English is given to the Spanish-speaking children during those three years, sufficient to enable them to enter combined classes in the fourth grade.

Even under this arrangement, however, it is neither necessary nor desirable to house the Spanish-speaking children in separate buildings, for by so doing, the natural barrier of language is supplemented by the additional obstacle of physical separation. Where the children are housed in the same building, even though in separate rooms in the lower grades, but are allowed to mingle on the playground, not only will the Spanish-speaking child's knowledge and effective usage of English increase much more rapidly, but the process of assimilation will proceed apace.

The matter of segregated schools was considered in Dr. Little's study.

In answer to the question: Are children of Latin-American descent provided separate school buildings? many superintendents answered "No" and stated that such children in their school districts could attend the schools nearest their places of residence. They also pointed out that Spanish-speaking people have a tendency to gravitate into "Mexican settlements." In laying out the attendance areas within a given school district, therefore, it is not at all uncommon to find that one school is attended only by Spanish-speaking children and that another school in the same district is attended only by Anglo-American children. Children of both culture groups attend the same high school in districts of this description.[16]

While these statements are true, of course, Dr. Little goes on to point out that "separate housing for Spanish-speaking children is a fixed practice in many school systems in Texas."[17] There is no pattern for segregation. According to Dr. Little's findings, nine school districts provided separate housing facilities for the first two grades, sixteen provided them through the third grade, twenty-three through the fourth grade, thirteen through the fifth grade, twenty-seven through the sixth grade, thirteen through the seventh grade, seventeen through the eighth grade, one through the ninth, one through the tenth, and two through the twelfth.

The reasons given by school superintendents in support of this physical separation of children, as quoted by Dr. Little, while divergent and diverting, are frank:

Local prejudice and inability to speak English.

Latin-Americans favor the plan; children are much more at ease and they will naturally segregate anyway. They are not at the disadvantage of being graded in English on the same standards as Anglo-Americans who are speaking their native tongue.

Public opinion.

Children with language difficulty can be given special treatment and special methods in teaching may be employed.

So many in the first grade, and need cleaning up to be taught. Lack of English language knowledge.

School board is antagonistic toward housing in the same building.

16 Little, op. cit., p. 59.
17 Ibid.

Language handicap is the reason in the school minutes.

These children need five or six years of Americanization before being placed with American children. Their standard of living is too low—they are dirty, lousy, and need special teaching in health and cleanliness. They also need special teaching in the English language.[18]

Here we have, in a nutshell, all the reasons school administrators offer for segregation. Of course, the most fundamental ones are those vaguely stated as "local prejudice" and "public opinion." Some Anglo Americans are afflicted with prejudices and distorted opinions, growing out of ignorance and complete lack of understanding, strongly supported by the widely accepted theory that "Mexicans," aside from being congenitally inferior, are, by nature, notoriously cheap competition and tend to lower wage scales in any locality. Unfortunately, some school boards reflect these local prejudices and misconceptions.

It is altogether true that Spanish-speaking children will tend to segregate themselves in a predominantly English-speaking group unless wise and tactful teachers see to it that they are made to feel themselves a part of the group. This happens not only in the elementary schools. Spanish-speaking students from the Latin American countries attending the University of Texas, often display the same tendency to isolate themselves from the remainder of the student body by congregating in dormitories where few, if any, English-speaking students reside. Thus they defeat, in part, their original purpose in coming to the United States to study, that of mastering the English language and familiarizing themselves with our way of life and attitudes of mind.[19]

18 *Ibid.,* pp. 60-61.

19 "The solution of the difficult problems of adjustment presented by the minority of over three and one-half million people of Spanish descent and speech who live within our borders is aggravated by intolerance on the part of some members of the dominant Anglo-Saxon group, and the concomitant resistance on the part of the dominated to lose their identity to an unkind people. When a so-called 'superior' culture wants to superimpose itself upon another, it must do so persuasively, for otherwise the 'attacked' culture in a natural move of self-assertion and self-preservation (which is, by the way, the measure of its strength) instead of acceding to assimilation maintains stubbornly its own practices."—Joaquín Ortega, *New Mexico's*

It is extremely doubtful, however, that Latin American parents favor separate schools for their children. In fact, the constant agitation from such parents for the abolition of segregated schools indicates emphatically that what they want most for their children is the opportunity to become good American citizens, growing up together with other American children.

Which brings us to the subject of Americanization. Investigation was made of one so-called "Americanization" school in West Texas. Six hundred Latin American children were enumerated on the census, of whom only 357 had ever been enrolled in school. A six-room building was provided for these 600 children, which would have meant, were they all in attendance, 100 children to the room. The school term began in December instead of September, the opening date in the other schools in the district. Naturally, with the wartime shortage of teachers, all those who were really competent were employed elsewhere long before December 1, leaving only those teachers who, for various reasons, were not wanted in other schools to form the faculty of this "Americanization" school.

During the school year 1943-44, the head teacher was changed three times; some of the classes were taken over by a new teacher on an average of every three weeks; rules for such seemingly simple arrangements as going to restrooms, forming lines, and ringing the bell were changed frequently, according to the whim of the current head teacher. One classroom teacher reported that she was forced to accommodate eighty children in a room equipped with forty seats; that what sweeping and dusting took place was done by the children themselves; and that not until twelve weeks after the opening of school did she have enough textbooks to go around, although the books are provided by the State.

Out of such utter confusion and disorder, how could even a group of English-speaking children progress? What earthly

Opportunity (Albuquerque: School of Inter-American Affairs, University of New Mexico, 1942), pp. 4-5.

incentive would they have to attend school? What distorted concepts of the American way of life could they be expected to acquire?

It cannot be denied that many of our Latin American children desperately need instruction in the most elementary principles of health and personal hygiene. Neither can it be denied that their "standard of living is too low." However, it is doubtful in the extreme that segregation, in and of itself, will remedy these conditions; and it hardly seems possible that a school administrator who uses the terms "dirty and lousy" to describe the Latin American children in his district could be expected to possess the necessary sympathy and understanding, and the clear concept of what the noble profession of the educator is, to provide the specialized instruction and facilities requisite to the elevation of the standards of these children.

Furthermore, even where bathing facilities and special assistance in personal hygiene are provided, as they have been in a very few notable instances, no permanent improvement can be expected until the homes from which these children come are made sanitary. These problems will be discussed in a later chapter.

We must not lose sight of the fact that, while we reject the fundamental idea of segregation, it nevertheless appears that in some segregated schools a sincere effort is made to give the best possible instruction under the circumstances. However, United States District Judge Paul J. McCormick, of the Southern District of California, in granting an injunction in the case of Gonzalo Méndez and others vs. Westminister School District of Orange County, *et al.,* on February 18, 1946, "restraining further discriminatory practices against the pupils of Mexican descent in the public schools of defendant school districts," said:

"The equal protection of the laws" pertaining to the public school system in California is not provided by furnishing in separate schools the same technical facilities, text books and courses of instruction to children of Mexican ancestry that are available to the other public school children regardless of their ancestry. A paramount requisite in the

American system of public education is social equality. It must be open to all children by unified school association regardless of lineage.

Of the few schools in Texas in which, although segregated, the Latin American children are provided with equal facilities, one of the best examples is the Stephen F. Austin elementary school in Kingsville. The largest school in Kingsville, it had an enrollment for the year 1944-45 of 1,100 in seven grades. The principal, A. D. Harvey, has spent years in studying and teaching the most effective methods of instruction for Spanish-speaking children. During the summer, he joins the staff of Texas College of Arts and Industries at Kingsville, where many of his teacher-students are themselves Latin Americans.

His Austin school has a faculty of thirty-five carefully chosen and trained teachers, fifteen of whom are of Mexican descent. The methods of teaching are such that after six weeks of pre-first-grade instruction, children with no previous knowledge of English are able to form complete sentences in English, do number and object exercises in English, and comprehend lessons in elementary health and hygiene. By the time the children complete the first grade, they are reading aloud, going through arithmetic drills, singing songs, etc., all in English.

For the students in the upper grades, the Austin school boasts a modern home economics department, where instruction is given in homemaking, sewing, cooking, and nutrition. For the boys, a fully equipped machine shop was conducted until the instructor was drafted into the army. As soon as a qualified man is available, this department will be reopened. For all children in all grades, specialized instruction in music is provided, including choral singing, band and orchestra, and folk dancing.

The element lacking in this school—and others like it— is the opportunity to know and mingle with Anglo American children. Mr. Harvey recognizes this fault, but until such time as conditions permit the necessary change in administrative policy, he and his teachers are giving their best to the children in their charge.

With regard to segregated schools, Dr. Manuel says:

In the problem of attitude, democracy faces one of its greatest tasks. The indifference and antagonism too often found between individuals and groups is a socially disrupting force. Democracy has set a goal of co-operation which as yet we have imperfectly attained. Individuals and communities have made very different progress; some are well along toward the goal while others are backward. In some communities, though not universally, indifference and antagonism must still be listed as number-one enemies of the Spanish-speaking child. The segregation of Spanish-speaking school children in separate buildings is more often a reflection of community prejudice than it is of a regard for better teaching. In most cases inferior facilities go hand in hand with segregation. It is true that a policy of segregation is sometimes defended on the basis that it provides a better language opportunity, but if this argument is examined closely, it boils down to the amazing notion that a child will learn a new language more quickly and effectively if he is isolated from children who already know the language![20]

On this point, Judge McCormick stated:

The evidence clearly shows that Spanish-speaking children are retarded in learning English by lack of exposure to its use because of segregation, and that commingling of the entire student body instills and develops a common cultural attitude among the school children which is imperative for the perpetuation of American institutions and ideals. It is also established by the record that the methods of segregation prevalent in the defendant school districts foster antagonisms in the children and suggest inferiority among them where none exists. One of the flagrant examples of the discriminatory results of segregation in two of the schools involved in this case is shown by the record. In the district under consideration there are two schools, the Lincoln and the Roosevelt, located approximately 120 yards apart on the same school grounds; hours of opening and closing, as well as recess periods, are not uniform. No credible language test is given to the children of Mexican ancestry upon entering the first grade in Lincoln School. This school has an enrollment of 240 so-called Spanish-speaking pupils, and no so-called English-speaking pupils; while the Roosevelt (the other) school has eighty-three so-called English-speaking pupils and twenty-five so-called Spanish-speaking pupils. Standardized tests as to mental ability are given to the respective classes in the two schools and the same curricula are pursued in both schools and, of course, in the English language as

[20] Manuel, *op. cit.*, p. 33.

required by State law, Section 8251, Education Code. In the last school year the students in the seventh grade of the Lincoln were superior scholarly to the same grade in the Roosevelt School and to any group in the seventh grade in either of the schools in the past. It further appears that not only did the class as a group have such mental superiority but that certain pupils in the group were also outstanding in the class itself. Notwithstanding this showing, the pupils of such excellence were kept in the Lincoln School.[21]

We may begin to understand, then, why those Latin American children who are enrolled in school do not progress satisfactorily. In addition to all the reasons heretofore discussed—language handicap, periodic employment in agriculture or elsewhere, illness, inability to dress like other children, attitudes of some children and teachers toward them, indifference on the part of some parents—we must take into consideration the nutritutional deficiencies from which so many Latin American children of school age suffer.

Experiments conducted among Latin American children in New Mexico have revealed that not only does the absence of foods containing calcium, proteins, and vitamins from the diet cause rickets and general physical debility, but that it also prevents the child from having sufficient mental energy to carry him through a day in school. It was found that children subsisting on grossly deficient diets were mentally alert and capable of learning for not longer than the first two hours of class work. After that time, they were present in the class in body only.[22]

Above and beyond all these reasons for the Spanish-speaking child's failure to make satisfactory progress in school is another consideration of paramount importance. With frequent outstanding exceptions, our elementary teachers have been lacking entirely in a knowledge and understanding of Latin American

[21] Méndez *et al.*, vs. Westminster School District (Orange County, California).

[22] Michel Pijoan, *Certain Factors Involved in the Struggle against Malnutrition and Disease, with Special Reference to the Southwest of the United States and Latin America,* Inter-Americana, Short Papers VII (Albuquerque: University of New Mexico Press, 1943).

children; and until the very recent past, the teacher-training institutions in Texas were not actively aware of the fact that the successful instruction of Spanish-speaking children requires special teaching methods and classroom materials, in addition to a general and fairly comprehensive knowledge and understanding of their social characteristics and economic background. Add to this the fact that, in many Texas school districts, teachers in segregated schools receive from $400.00 to $600.00 a year less salary than those in the other schools and it is readily understandable why, for the most part, the inferior academic qualifications of teachers of Latin American children act as a deterrent to both attendance and progress.

Honesty demands, however, that full credit and recognition be given to those Texas teachers, principals, and superintendents who, through the years, have pioneered in giving adequate and equal educational advantages to children of Mexican descent. Their number is large, even though they do constitute a small minority among the thousands of public school teachers in Texas. Bucking administrative apathy—even antagonism at times—and confronting more frequently the opposition presented by some Anglo patrons who are prompted only by unreasoning and unfounded prejudice, these educators have stuck to their guns, winning out in the end.

Their reward is threefold: the knowledge of a sacred responsibility ably discharged; the gratification of seeing their former pupils assume their rightful places in the life of the community; and the long-delayed satisfaction of watching their untiring efforts mature into a statewide movement, on the part of both the State Department of Education and the colleges and universities of the State, to provide Latin American children with the education to which they are entitled.

Chapter 8

Revolution in Education

THERE ARE three facets of the responsibility of the public schools, colleges, and universities in Texas, with regard to inter-American relations on a local, statewide, national, and international basis. The first is to provide equal educational opportunities for all Texas children. The second is to incorporate into the curricula of all schools materials related to Latin America and inter-American relations, including the teaching of Spanish. And the third is to promote school-community relations as a means of drawing adults, both Anglo and Latin American, into the program.

Early in 1943, a movement to emphasize inter-American education in the public schools was initiated by the State Department of Education through the formulation, adoption, and publication of a two-point statement of policy. It declared, first, that the curricula of all public schools should be revised to include, in all appropriate subject-matter fields, information and activities relative to Latin American history and culture, as a means of instilling into all young Texans a knowledge and appreciation of their neighbors. The second point, dealing with the matter of segregated schools, was as follows: "Any administrative or curricular practices which isolate, or tend to isolate, the Latin American children solely on the basis of such descent, through physical separation or inequitable educational offerings, are deemed pedagogically unsound, contrary to state and national policy, and inimical to the best interests of both of those groups of children."

Almost simultaneously, the teacher-training institutions of Texas began thinking along the same lines, and in June, 1943, the State Department of Education called a conference with representatives of the colleges, public school teachers, and administrators. It was an exploratory meeting and noteworthy only as the first in a series of highly significant and productive regional and state conferences.

There followed, during the fall and winter of 1943, meetings in thirteen of the State Department of Education's twenty-four districts. These, too, were exploratory in nature, but the roots of the difficulties were gradually exposed, opening the way to the outlining of procedures for the solution of these educational problems.

Each conference was held at a college or university in the district, and at each meeting a qualified educator developed, as the keynote address, the theme of "A Sane Philosophy Underlying Inter-American Relations in Texas for Texans." It was apparent that the speakers agreed on five general principles:

1. That we acknowledge the Fatherhood of God and the brotherhood of man, and accept the truth that "God is no respecter of persons." To this extent, all men are fundamentally alike.

2. That we in Texas must recognize the fact that one-sixth of our population is of Mexican extraction; that there are differences which cannot easily be eliminated; that the two elements have a contribution to make, each to the welfare of the other and both to the general welfare; that we should minimize the differences in order to build up a greater Texas.

3. That we believe in superiority on the basis of ability, and in rewards because of merit, rather than in a superiority, or in an inferiority, of race. We accept individual worth as the doctrine of the democratic State and denounce the doctrine of superiority of race as the creed of the totalitarian nations.

4. That we believe the State and the local school districts should provide equality of educational opportunity for all children so that they

may develop to their fullest capacity the abilities with which nature has endowed them.

5. That we believe the heritage of every child in Texas should be made a matter of pride to him whether he be of Anglo American or of Latin American lineage, for through the efforts of all these peoples, the State has had a glorious past. To the civilization thus achieved, every person has a right to contribute his best efforts, thus insuring a greater Texas of the future.

During the months between June, 1943, and January, 1944, a Statewide Supervisory Committee on Inter-American Relations Education was built up, composed of approximately 250 public school teachers, administrators, and college professors. At the State Department of Education's annual conference in January, 1944, the Supervisory Committee adopted a program of work which embraced the local community, the teacher-training institutions, and the local schools.

For developing within the community a sound philosophy with regard to relationships between Anglo and Latin Americans, it was proposed that the contributions of the other Americas, particularly Mexico, to western civilization be made known through a persistent campaign of publicity by press and radio; that adult Spanish-speaking clubs among Anglo Americans and adult English-speaking clubs among Latin Americans be established wherever practicable; and that conferences and forums focusing attention upon the importance of mutual understanding and confidence as bases for a permanent Good Neighbor Policy be conducted.

It was recommended that the teacher-training institutions place special emphasis upon building up, in the minds and hearts of those who are to teach Texas children, a right attitude toward the Latin American people in Texas, together with an appreciation of their rights as citizens and the desirability of a school system which actually has the concept of democracy underlying its entire structure. Furthermore, it was urged that the colleges provide ample opportunity for interested persons to become well acquainted with Latin America, its languages, history, government, economic structure, and social life through courses designed specifically for this purpose, in order that those who desire such training will be able to take places of leadership in school and in civic groups.

For the local schools, the Supervisory Committee proposed the following objectives:

1. The adoption of a local school program which will provide equal opportunity for all children of all peoples to develop to the limit of their capacities, physically, mentally, morally, economically, and socially.

2. In-service training for teachers through reading clubs, travel clubs, and extension classes so that they may, through study, discussion, and guidance, find out how and where to place those emphases which will result in better inter-American relations.

3. A careful evaluation of the need for, and nature of, such courses as "Elementary Spanish" and "History of All the Americas," to determine whether they should become an integral part of the curriculum.

4. The organization in accredited high schools, under proper direction, of Pan American Student Forums or Inter-American Relations Clubs.

5. A series of auditorium and community programs which will bring together all agencies and people of the community into a harmonious study and knowledge of the proper relationships which should exist among the people of all the Americas.

6. The addition of suitable books, magazines, and newspapers to the school libraries at all levels so that teachers and pupils may have an opportunity to become familiar with the countries, their life and development.

7. The introduction of curriculum enrichment materials in the inter-American field at both the elementary and high school levels; not a separate course, but incorporated into existing courses in literature, history, and geography.

During 1943, three state institutions, the Texas College of Arts and Industries at Kingsville, the Southwest Texas State Teachers College at San Marcos, and the Sul Ross State Teachers College at Alpine, had conceived a co-operative plan for the furtherance of inter-American relations through better preparation of teachers and the building up of materials in the inter-American field for use in the public schools. They submitted a joint proposal to the Office of the Coordinator of Inter-American Affairs for assistance in financing such projects in each of the three colleges. The proposal met with the enthusiastic approval of the Coordinator's Office, but it was suggested that, in order to realize the greatest possible benefit from the program, more Texas colleges should be drawn into it.

Accordingly, on January 5, 1944, there met in Austin educators from ten of the State's colleges and universities, together with representatives of the Coordinator's Office, the State Department of Education, the University of Texas, and the Good Neighbor Commission of Texas. The four chief areas of work to be considered, in the beginning, were agreed to be to improve the preparation of teachers; to make available more suitable inter-American materials and teacher aids to teachers in Texas, especially in communities of Spanish speech; to project the program on a community basis by forming citizen committees which would co-operate with and advise the colleges in their program—these committees to consist of the two language groups; and to develop suitable inter-American curriculum materials on the college level.

These objectives were elaborated upon in discussion to include such specific problems as the development of more satisfactory and efficient methods of teaching non-English-speaking children, more adequately trained teachers to apply these methods, and the preparation of better materials for their use. Stress was placed upon the need for development of more practical and suitable textbooks and methods of teaching Spanish at elementary, secondary, and college levels, and the training of teachers with not only a reading but a speaking knowledge of the Spanish language.

It was agreed, further, that studied consideration must be given to the development and incorporation into the curricula of all Texas schools of materials pertaining to the history and culture of the other American republics, and the introduction into the curricula of Texas colleges and universities of courses which will prepare Texas teachers properly to interpret these new materials.

With regard to the community, the conferees urged the creation of interest on the part of Latin American parents in the school program through joint consideration, on a local level, of such matters as social welfare and community health, special attention to and guidance for Spanish-speaking Parent-Teacher Associations, an adequate program of adult education under the auspices of the colleges, the enlistment of aid from service clubs, women's organizations, and church groups in outlining remedial procedures.

It was finally agreed that the program was of such importance, and so obviously of statewide proportions, that all the colleges and universities of the State should be given an opportunity to participate. As a result, a second conference was called for February 9-10, 1944, in Austin, in which nineteen institutions joined. The seventy-four members of the conference were divided into five committees, according to their special interest, to work on (1) problems in bilingual education, (2) school-community relations, (3) objectives, organization, materials, and techniques for conducting education workshops on inter-American relations education, (4) the possibilities of enriching the curriculum at the college and university level, and (5) possibilities of curriculum enrichment in the elementary and secondary schools.

Interest and enthusiasm thus created resulted in fourteen summer workshops in inter-American relations education, which were conducted at colleges and universities throughout the State in the summer of 1944, in which public school teachers of Texas joined in studying the various problems advanced, doing research on curriculum materials, and actually compiling units and courses of study for use at different instructional levels.

In March, 1944, preceding the opening of the six-weeks summer workshops in June, a week-long professional workshop was conducted in Austin, jointly by the University of Texas and the State Department of Education, for the training of those who were to direct the individual workshops. Representatives of the Office of the Coordinator of Inter-American Affairs and the United States Office of Education participated, presenting and discussing the materials and assistance available from those two sources, and giving those in attendance the benefit of their experience in directing similar programs elsewhere.

As was to be both expected and desired, the summer workshops emphasized those problems which were of particular concern in their respective localities. Texas College of Arts and Industries, for example, being located in Kingsville and serving an area in which the population is predominantly of Mexican descent, devoted its attention to the problems faced by teachers of non-English-speaking children. Denton's Texas State College for Women, on the other hand, serving the northern part of the State, chose to emphasize materials and methods for teaching Spanish, and the building of units of work on Latin American culture, history, geography, and customs. Several of the workshops included demonstration classes composed of Spanish-speaking beginners, which served as a laboratory for experimentation in methods and materials.

In San Antonio, where Incarnate Word College, St. Mary's University, and Trinity University joined in a Tri-College Workshop, the areas of interest covered included curriculum enrichment through inter-American materials, the teaching of beginning Spanish, the teaching of English to Spanish-speaking children, the improvement of health education for Spanish-speaking children, and the construction of inter-American units of work. In addition, one hour each day was devoted to instruction in conversational Spanish for all members of the workshop.

For the purpose of bringing together and evaluating the materials developed in the summer workshops and adopting such of them as met with general approval, the State Department of Education called a conference of workshop directors and members of the statewide Curriculum Enrichment Committee to meet in Austin on October 5-7, 1944.

The combined labor and thinking of some 285 Texas teachers in the workshops had produced many significant units of work in various fields, one of the most important of which was a new high school course of study in Spanish, which has since been published and put into use. The introduction to the text states, in part:

In the production of the course of study four major needs were recognized:

1. To prepare pupils, through natural procedures, activities, and experiences, to express themselves in Spanish.

2. To meet the needs of pupils in *Texas* schools. The course, therefore, includes materials designed to foster better understanding of Spanish-speaking people and calls for the pronunciation, idioms, and vocabulary used in Mexico and other American countries.

3. To follow basic techniques of instruction: demonstration on the part of the teacher, participation on the part of the pupil.

4. To provide for different abilities. The first-year class in high school in Texas may be made up of Spanish-speaking pupils, pupils who have had Spanish from one to six years in the elementary school, and pupils who have had no Spanish at all.[1]

Many other new and valuable materials were submitted, both for curriculum enrichment and for methods of teaching non-English-speaking children. Some of them were adopted in part, but most of them have since been enlarged upon and perfected, preparatory to final adoption.

Numerous important developments were reported to the Statewide Supervisory Committee on Inter-American Relations Education, in January, 1945, by its executive secretary, Miss Myrtle L. Tanner. With regard to the provision of equal educational facilities for all Texas children, previously endorsed by the Supervisory Committee, she stated that school boards

---

[1] Joseph R. Griggs and Myrtle L. Tanner, *Suggested Course of Study in Spanish for Texas High Schools 1945* (Austin: State Department of Education, Bulletin No. 452), p. 10.

and administrators are becoming increasingly conscious of their responsibilities along this line and that the decided stand taken by the Division of Supervision in the State Department of Education with respect to elimination of segregation and discrimination is slowly but surely having the desired effect.

As a means of securing the interest and co-operation of the general public, the State Department of Education, with the financial assistance of the Office of the Coordinator of Inter-American Affairs, developed and presented a series of twenty-six weekly radio broadcasts over a statewide network, beginning with the title "Americas United," later changed to "Buenos Amigos."

According to reports of superintendents of independent school districts for the year 1943-44, one hundred and twelve of the 200 largest districts are now teaching Spanish in one or more elementary grades. However, the Spanish-teaching program in elementary schools was described as continuing to be badly handicapped by the lack of qualified teachers.

Suggested book lists on Latin American subjects and inter-American relations have been prepared by the State Department of Education for the use of the public schools, and minimum library requirements for schools of different sizes have been set up. Greatly stimulated interest on the part of both teachers and students has been evidenced by more frequent requests for materials in the inter-American field and the widespread formation of Pan American Student Forums.

In addition to the fourteen workshops participated in by sixteen colleges and universities in the summer of 1944, seven Texas institutions conducted field schools at various points in Mexico, by which more than 600 persons, the majority of them teachers, were benefited.

For several years the University of Texas has held a summer session at the University of Mexico; Texas State College for Women, at the Escuela Normal in Saltillo; and Sam Houston State Teachers College, at Puebla. In 1944, field schools were also conducted by Southwest Texas State Teachers College at

Guadalajara; by the University of Houston in Mexico City; by North Texas State Teachers College at Morelia; and by Trinity University at San Luis Potosí.

Furthermore, community conferences were held by many of the colleges during 1944, in which Latin American leaders joined in a consideration and frank discussion of local problems. The efforts of the Southwest Texas State Teachers College to promote better school-college-community relations resulted in a full-time project, to the great mutual benefit of Latin and Anglo American residents of San Marcos.

The tremendous growth in thought and action on the part of Texas educators that had been brought about in the preceding two years was indisputably demonstrated at the second professional workshop on inter-American relations education, held in Austin the week of March 19, 1945, in preparation for the 1945 summer workshops at the various colleges.

Sponsored by the State Department of Education and the University of Texas, in co-operation with the Office of Inter-American Affairs, the workshop, for the first time, placed emphasis on the health and economic conditions which contribute to the failure of Latin American children to enroll in school, or to attend regularly and progress satisfactorily when they do enroll. In addition to this all-important question, further attention was given to the problems of improving methods of teaching Spanish, methods and materials for teaching non-English-speaking children, and curriculum enrichment materials.

Considerable discussion was devoted to the advisability of pre-school training in English for non-English-speaking children, to relieve or eliminate the language handicap before the age of six. No definite conclusions were reached, but it was indicated that the matter was to receive serious study in the 1945 summer workshops.

A development that should give a real impetus to the Spanish-teaching program in Texas, particularly in the elementary grades, was described and demonstrated by Mrs. Connie

Garza Brockette, of the Division of Education and Teacher Aids, Office of Inter-American Affairs. It consists of a set of recorded exercises in Spanish, comprising fifteen ten-inch records, or thirty three-minute exercises, playable on any phonograph, and accompanied by teacher's manual and classroom guide. The series, basic materials for which were developed by Mrs. Brockette, E. E. Mireles, and Elida Wills— all Texas teachers—is entitled "Hablemos Español," and is designed to provide teachers who may lack a fluent conversational knowledge of Spanish with an effective oral technique in the teaching of functional Spanish.

These records were planned and developed by the Department of Radio and Visual Education, State Department of Education, with a grant from the Dallas and Fort Worth Junior Chambers of Commerce.

Highly significant recommendations were reported out of discussion groups formed during the workshop to consider specific problems.

With regard to improvement in the teaching of Spanish at elementary, secondary, and college levels, the recommendations were as follows:

1. Because of the shortage of qualified teachers of Spanish, especially at the elementary school level, we recommend that in all teacher-training institutions, faculty advisors insist that majors in elementary education take at least six hours in elementary Spanish; and that all Spanish majors be encouraged to take courses which would fit them for teaching in the elementary grades.

2. It is agreed that the teaching or learning of any foreign language requires certain skills making necessary the use of laboratory procedures for which purpose the following equipment should be provided as a minimum: a 16 mm. machine with sound projector; recording machine with maintenance fee for buying records needed for classes; play-back machine adapted for use of records; adequate library of records for teaching language and for cultural objectives, such as music and literature; current periodicals, newspapers, and magazines from different Spanish-speaking countries.

3. Believing that a speaking knowledge of Spanish will do much

to further cement the policy of friendship between the peoples of the Americas and realizing that a great amount of drill and actual conversation is necessary in developing the ability to use a foreign language fluently, it is recommended that Spanish classes be kept to a maximum of twenty, with adequate time provided for the use of laboratory procedures.

The group studying the possibility of increasing school attendance on the part of Latin American children through improved health and economic conditions made two recommendations. The first proposal reads as follows:

The framers of the Texas Constitution assumed for the State of Texas the duty of "general diffusion of knowledge" as "essential to the preservation of the liberties and rights of the people"; the duty of providing for the education of all its children regardless of their economic status.

Yet, a large body of our young citizenry has not been so provided for as to afford the opportunity of attaining even the most rudimentary education.

It is the conclusion of our panel that the problem of affording educational opportunities to the children of seasonal agricultural laborers in Texas presents a unique challenge to educators which is not met by present measures and cannot be answered without special attention and planning.

It is therefore the recommendation of the panel that the members of this workshop, the institutions represented here, and the State Department of Education give special attention to these questions: Under existing conditions of our farm economy, during what seasons can the children of agricultural laborers be attracted into our schools? What type of instruction should be given these children in order to make a short yearly period of schooling most beneficial to them?

It is the conviction of the members of this panel that the first of these questions can be resolved in each community by studies, such as those of the Children's Bureau in Hidalgo County and the Research Division of WPA in Crystal City, in the several counties in Texas where many seasonal agricultural laborers are enumerated.

This panel is further convinced that curricular material and methods for such a short-term school can be prepared ably by persons and groups represented in the workshop, with the co-operation of the State Department of Education.

However, there are certain safeguards that have suggested themselves

116   LATIN AMERICANS IN TEXAS

to us in the consideration of such a plan which we desire to pass on to the conference:

1. The suggested off-season school should constitute a service to those whose employment, either resident or migratory, prevents more extended school attendance, and not a deprivation of further schooling to any group or person who desires to be enrolled throughout the year.

2. The children who avail themselves of the off-season school should be given as nearly as possible a normal school environment. Such schools should be in conjunction with the established schools so that all children may play together, engage in extra-curricular activities embracing the whole student body, and utilize the same lunchroom and other such facilities.

As its second proposal, the panel suggested:

With regard to increased school attendance through improved health conditions, the panel bases its recommendations on the following findings:

1. Many bad health conditions exist in the families which can be relieved or improved if brought to the attention of proper agencies, such as State Rehabilitation, Public Welfare, Red Cross, service clubs, and other agencies.

2. Personal contact between the school and the child's family creates confidence and interest in school, thereby increasing school attendance.

The panel therefore recommends that a visitation program employing a full-time teacher, or combination visiting teacher and school nurse, be established in all the school districts of the State of Texas wherever a sizable number of children are enumerated but not enrolled.

In summarizing the discussion of the round table on "Education of Spanish-speaking Children," its chairman, Dr. George I. Sánchez, professor of Latin American Education at the University of Texas, said:

It is self-evident that the teaching of Spanish-speaking children is a problem which embraces all aspects of education. As an educational problem of broad scope, the field is open to contributions in every aspect of education. The problem does not narrow itself down to simply one of subject matter, or methodology, or administration, or English, or any one of the many educational phases which may attract attention. This being the case, the approach to the solution of problems in this field should be grounded on the recognition and acceptance that all the under-lying principles of good education are the underlying principles in the education of Spanish-speaking children.

This basic consideration is not minimized by the fact that large num-bers of Spanish-speaking children are confronted with the special prob-lems resulting from low socio-economic status, inadequate language development (in Spanish or English or both), and the like. Rather, it should be recognized that the correction of whatever maladjustments or lack of achievement arise from these conditions is the function of an educational program which, to begin with, is firmly based on those sound educational principles and standards which characterize a good school everywhere. That is to say, the first consideration in an attack upon the problems of teaching Spanish-speaking children is the establishment of a good school—a school that would be good for any and all American children. Only then will it be possible to attack special problems (i.e., the teaching of English, the adaptation of materials, etc.) most profitably.

The group appeared to be in general agreement with the above. As a consequence, it appeared clear to all that all activities which have been found successful in developing good schools for "normal" children are, without doubt, good activities in the development of good schools for Spanish-speaking children. More specifically, with reference to summer workshops, the materials and procedures used with success in workshops the country over are desirable and appropriate materials and procedures for workshops designed to improve the education of Spanish-speaking children. Among these successful procedures, the group discussed a number which appeared to have special value in this field.

It was pointed out that the teacher of Spanish-speaking children should have an understanding of their historical and cultural back-grounds. The fact that they are Hispanic and Indo-Hispanic in culture is an important factor in their educational development. The teacher should know the number and distribution of the Spanish-speaking people in the United States, something about their social and economic situation, and the various factors which characterize them as a cultural minority. In addition, the teacher should understand how, out of these backgrounds and circumstances, certain special educational problems presented by these children arise and how to meet those special problems. For instance, the teacher must understand the nature of and the reasons for the linguistic errors made by these children, and she should have training in the best methods for correcting those errors. Similarly, the current social and economic circumstances of a majority of our Spanish-speaking people call for a special enrichment of the curriculum to compensate for environ-mental deficiencies.

It was pointed out that one of the most successful ways of training teachers in this field was through the use of demonstration schools. One of the points emphasized in this connection was that demonstration schools and classes should give the teacher guidance in how to develop those vocabulary lists, plans of study, and special materials which are particularly needed by and applicable to her particular group of children. This is especially important because, since Spanish-speaking children are such a heterogeneous group, there can be no standard materials or techniques that apply without modification in each and every instance.

It was clear to the group that the teaching of English to these children constitutes one of the most pressing problems. Without question, this phase of the total question should receive special consideration in the summer workshops. In this connection, considerable discussion was devoted to the idea of encouraging the establishment of some kind of a pre-first-grade school for Spanish-speaking children in order to give them a full year of language development prior to their inauguration into the regular program in elementary education.[2]

As Dr. H. T. Manuel said upon one occasion, in discussing the "Education of the Spanish-speaking Child":

There is a certain urgency about this problem of building a democracy in the Southwest. We are now at war with powerful external enemies. We shall win that war. But what about the years after the war? Then democracy will have a great trial of another kind. We are now fighting to preserve democracy; we must continue to fight to make it strong. If we are unable to prepare people for participation in democratic processes, if we are unable to guarantee the rights of all our people, we shall be in danger of losing the democracy for which we are fighting. We can read from the pages of history a solemn warning that if democracy fails, the stage is set for revolution. But democracy must not fail. It will not fail. In it are the aspirations and dreams of a war-weary world. The only hope of humanity is in finding a practicable way to achieve the brotherhood of man taught by the Prince of Peace.[3]

That the public schools, colleges, and universities of the State not only recognize their responsibility to educate all Texas children for participation in a democracy, as well as the com-

[2] *Minutes of Professional Workshop,* State Department of Education, Austin, March 19-24, 1945.

[3] H. T. Manuel, "Education of the Spanish-Speaking Child," *Proceedings of Inter-American Conference,* Baylor University, Waco, Texas, January, 1945, p. 34.

plex problems which confront them in so doing, but have, in the brief period of three years, made notable progress in the solution of those problems, augurs well for the future of the State, for the preservation of democratic standards of life, and for the furtherance of inter-American understanding. Developments which so vitally affect the educational system of the State cannot but carry over, to some extent, into the communities of Texas.

However, as Dr. Manuel points out, "there is a certain urgency" about our problems. Until now, there has been a paucity of information available, in both the public schools and institutions of higher learning in the State, concerning Latin America and inter-American relations. Furthermore, our present adult population generally has thus been denied the opportunity of learning anything about our Latin American neighbors, whether here or in Latin America. Moreover, the adult population of Texas must become actively conscious, not only of this background information, but also of the pressing problems faced by Texas citizens of Mexican descent, and the immediate bearing upon our international dealings of relations between Anglo and Latin Americans in Texas. For all these urgent reasons an intensive statewide adult educational program is clearly indicated.[4]

[4] Beginning in April, 1943, when the Executive Committee on Inter-American Relations in Texas, of the University of Texas, administering a grant of funds from the Office of the Coordinator of Inter-American Affairs, held the "First Advisory Conference on Inter-American Relations in Texas," in Austin, and to the present writing, numerous statewide and regional conferences have been held in Texas and elsewhere in the Southwest, under various auspices. At the early meetings, attention was directed principally, in an exploratory manner, to the problems in general of Latin Americans. Later conferences have dealt, on a basis of definite planning, with specific phases of those problems, such as education.

In 1943, a conference was called at Santa Fe by the School of Inter-American Affairs of the University of New Mexico, during which Texas problems were discussed. At San Antonio, in July, 1943, and again at Denver, in October, 1944, the National Catholic Welfare Conference sponsored conferences on "The Spanish-Speaking People of the Southwest and West." In October, 1943, a press and radio conference on inter-American affairs was held in Austin, under the joint auspices of the University's Executive Committee and the Good Neighbor Commission of Texas.

One of the most important achievements of these meetings, and others which

Such a program, for the use of adults of both groups, has been outlined and published by the Good Neighbor Commission of Texas. Special groups have been set up in Austin, San Antonio, Victoria, Big Spring, and San Marcos for the purpose of adapting the program to local needs, and throughout the State religious, cultural, and civic organizations have incorporated various phases of the program into their regular activities.

The Good Neighbor Commission, with executive offices in the State Capitol, was created by Governor Coke R. Stevenson in August, 1943, and its function as a public agency of the State was confirmed by the 49th Texas Legislature through the passage of a bill signed by the Governor on April 23, 1945. As of September 4, 1945, when the bill became effective, the Commission's membership was increased from six to nine.

The purpose of the Commission is three-fold: (1) to study the problems in Texas and arrive at a definite understanding of their scope and urgency; (2) to formulate, in co-operation with other State agencies, plans for the permanent solution of the problems encountered; and (3) to put those plans into effect, with the assistance of other State agencies, local civic, cultural, religious and patriotic organizations, and interested individuals.

The Good Neighbor Commission's statewide educational program is one of "Community Organization for Inter-American Understanding," based on the practical application of Christian principles to everyday living. Inasmuch as problems vary widely from one community to another, people differ, and therefore the solution to existing problems must be approached from a different angle in each community, the Commission has predicated its program on local action. It is suggested that local good neighbor councils and committees be set up, the membership to be nonsectarian and to include both Latin and Anglo Americans. Detailed suggestions are

---

followed, was to stimulate in the mind of the general public awareness of, and active interest in, inter-American relations at home.

made covering educational programs, community action relating to school facilities, housing, health, sanitation, migratory labor, and problems in human relations.

It is stressed throughout that the acquisition of a knowledge and understanding of the complicated problems in inter-American relations in Texas, combined with co-operative action to resolve those misunderstandings and inequitable conditions, was not only a definite and vital part of the war effort but is indispensable to a just and lasting peace.

The objectives of the Commission's program, as set forth in the published outline, are as follows:

1. To promote the principles of Christ in human relations throughout the State of Texas.

2. To preserve the honor and prestige of Texas before the nation, before our allies, and before the world.

3. To educate our present adult Anglo American population on the history and culture of Mexico, on inter-American relations, and on the problems faced by Latin Americans in Texas.

4. To study the economic and educational opportunities of the Latin American residents of the community, as well as their housing and health conditions, with a view to effecting improvements.

5. To educate the Latin American adults to a realization of their privileges and responsibilities as citizens and parents, and with respect to inter-American relations.

6. To promote friendship, understanding, and respect between Anglo American and Latin American citizens of the community, thereby insuring the continuance of cordial relations between Texas and Mexico.

7. To investigate fully, in case problems in human relations arise between Anglo Americans and Latin Americans in the community, and adjust such difficulties with justice to both sides, to the end that strife may be avoided and understanding promoted.

8. To keep in mind the ultimate objective of eliminating prefixes and hyphens, in order that we may all become Americans in the truest and broadest sense.[5]

5 *Community Organization for Inter-American Understanding,* Good Neighbor Commission of Texas, Austin, 1944, p. 6.

Thus, education in all its forms—in school and out, among children and adults, for both Anglo and Latin Americans—is coming to the front as the primary force to be employed in preparing Texas to perform, with wisdom and dignity, its significant and inescapable role in the future of the American Hemisphere.

Chapter 9

Housing, Sanitation, and Health

A LLEN QUINN, writing a series of articles for the Dallas
Morning News as part of that city's slum clearance campaign, said on December 15, 1944:

No one who will take a close look at the Dallas slums can doubt they
should be cleaned out immediately. Just take a good look at that area
known as Little Mexico, which lies directly north of the business district
to the west of Cedar Springs. Thousands of persons who live in com-
fortable homes in some of Dallas' best residential districts pass by there
daily without knowing what lies behind the scenes.

Squalor is the lot of many of those who live in that area where almost
100 per cent of the houses are substandard and many in a condition
hardly fit for housing livestock on a farm. Most of them have had no
repairs for years; they are not worth the expense to the owners, but bring
a rental income far beyond their value. Many of the places that people
call home appear on the verge of collapse. Most have no plumbing.
Water is obtained from outside community hydrants, frequently close
beside a filthy, disease-breeding outside dry toilet. Unpaved streets are
quagmires when it rains, and filth abounds despite the efforts and desires
of many residents to try to put up a better front.

These conditions, of course, are not peculiar to Dallas. They
prevail in all Texas towns and cities where any sizable Latin
American population resides. The usual pattern is for Latin
Americans to live, more or less, in one section of town, partly
because they are a gregarious people and like to live close to one
another; partly because their language handicap makes it more

convenient for them to live among those who speak the same tongue; but often because they are not permitted to rent or own property anywhere except in the "Mexican colony," regardless of their social, educational, or economic status.

In smaller towns, this section is usually set apart from the other residential sections by a railroad track, a highway, or perhaps a river. As a rule, the "Mexican colony" is devoid of paved streets, sewer lines, frequently even electric power, gas mains, and garbage disposal service. One can spot such a "colony" or section in almost every case; it is "on the wrong side of the tracks."

With regard to the housing and health conditions of Latin Americans in agricultural areas, the Children's Bureau report on Hidalgo County may be considered representative.

The usual dwelling was a small wooden house, unpainted, and of makeshift construction. Generally there was one sleeping and living room, with a still more crudely constructed "kitchen house," either built separately or attached to the main structure in the rear. Occasionally there was more than one sleeping room. On the other hand, some large families cooked and slept in but one room. But many dwellings, especially in the rural settlements, were very primitive. Often the occupants had patched them together from scraps of wood, tin, palm branches, tule, or a combination of these materials. Some of these houses had no windows, and most of them had dirt floors even in the sleeping quarters.

In the rainy season the flimsy roofs and walls of the cruder dwellings were poor protection against the weather, and the houses often became flooded. Owing to the absence of any drainage system, water accumulated in the streets and roads and the people were sometimes marooned.

For the large families in this study, which averaged 6.6 members, the one- or two-room dwellings provided very little space. In nearly two-thirds of the 342 households visited there were three or more persons per room, and in almost one-tenth there were as many as seven or more persons per room. Even these figures do not fully indicate the degree of overcrowding, because one of the rooms, the kitchen, usually could not be used for sleeping purposes.[1]

[1] Amber Arthun Warburton, Helen Wood, and Marian M. Crane, M. D., *The Work and Welfare of Children of Agricultural Laborers in Hidalgo County, Texas,* Washington, D. C.: U. S. Department of Labor, Children's Bureau, Publication 298, 1943), pp. 53-54.

Another glimpse of the living conditions of Latin Americans in rural areas is furnished by a WPA study made in 1938.

The Mexican sections of Crystal City form a large semi-rural slum. More than half of the Mexicans own their houses or shacks, but most of the dwellings in the Mexican quarter are crudely built and in very bad repair. Few have electricity or plumbing. The houses are badly overcrowded; there was an average of 2.6 persons per room at the time of the survey.[2]

Confronted with these appalling conditions of substandard housing and congestion, coupled with the low level of education as established hereinbefore, and the equally low economic level of the people, to be discussed later, any conscientious person has to ask himself these questions: What standards of health and sanitation are Texas citizens of Mexican descent able to maintain? What is the incidence of disease among them? What are the birth and death rates? What is the effect, upon the community and the State as a whole, of the conditions under which these people live? We know the answers even before we ask the questions.

The report of the Department of Commerce, Bureau of the Census, on vital statistics for Texas in the year 1942, reveals that of the total of 126,424 white births registered, 10,977 were delivered by midwives, and 1,856 by means not specified. Although no separate figures are given as to Latin Americans, it is safe to assume that the majority of white babies delivered without a physician in attendance were born to low-income families of Mexican extraction.

Of these 126,424 infants, 6,543 died before reaching the age of one year, 1,765 as a result of premature birth, 936 from pneumonia and influenza, and 927 from diarrhea enteritis. Pneumonia and influenza were the principal causes of death in the age groups 1 to 4 and 5 to 14, taking a toll of 266 lives out of the total of 1,405 deaths reported for the 1-4 group, and 87 of the total of 1,010 deaths in the 5-14 group.

[2] Selden C. Menefee, *Mexican Migratory Workers of South Texas* (Washington, D. C.: Federal Works Agency, Work Projects Administration, Division of Research, U. S. Government Printing Office, 1941), p. 15.

Tuberculosis as a cause of death appeared first in the 1-4 age group, with a toll of 58, and in the 5-14 group, 70 deaths were attributed to tuberculosis. In the next two groups, however, tuberculosis was the chief cause of death, claiming as victims 549 of the 2,339 who died between the ages of 15 and 24, and 1,077 of the 5,898 who died in the age group 25-44. Tuberculosis, therefore, stands out as the principal threat to those who are in the most productive years of their lives—most productive, certainly, so far as physical exertion is concerned.[3]

That it is the Latin Americans who are most susceptible to, and most frequently become the victims of, tuberculosis is borne out all too clearly by the 1944 statistics of the Texas State Department of Health, which indicate a tuberculosis death rate among Anglo Americans of 31 per 100,000 population; among Negroes, of 95 per 100,000; *and among Latin Americans, of 209 per 100,000.* In other words, the Latin American death rate is about seven times that of the Anglo American. As a whole, Texas has a tuberculosis death rate of 10.8 per 100,000 population higher than that of the entire United States, that of the United States being 43.1, and that of Texas, 53.9 per 100,000 population.

San Antonio, with an estimated population of 107,000 Latin Americans, lists the following number of deaths from tuberculosis per 100,000 population for the year 1944: 45.6 among Anglo Americans, 88 among Negroes, and 143 among Latin Americans.[4]

Dr. David M. Gould, describing a mass X-ray survey made in San Antonio in 1942, says:

For many years San Antonio has had the questionable distinction of having the highest tuberculosis death rate of any large city in the United States. In 1941 San Antonio requested of the United States Public Health Service the loan of personnel and equipment to conduct a mass X-ray survey in that city. It was hoped that the citizens of San Antonio

[3] *Texas Summary of Vital Statistics 1942* (Washington, D. C.: Department of Commerce, Bureau of the Census, March 11, 1944), Vol. XX, No. 44, p. 541.

[4] *Like a Sore Thumb* (San Antonio: Bexar County Tuberculosis Association, 1945), no pagination.

would be stimulated to constructive action if they knew the actual number of persons suffering from tuberculosis and jeopardizing the health of the entire city. Disease, like war, cannot be quarantined in one section; eventually it spreads to neighboring areas.[5]

In describing the results of the survey, Dr. Gould states:

Tuberculosis is the second leading cause of death in San Antonio for persons of all ages. One out of every ten deaths is from this disease. Heart disease, including coronary disease, is the chief cause of death, forming 15.2 per cent of the total deaths.

It is suspected that many deaths reported as pneumonia or diarrhea actually are caused by the tubercle bacillus and would swell the total of deaths from tuberculosis considerably.

To find tuberculosis as the second leading cause of death in the country as a whole one must go back as far as the year 1910.

A chest X-ray survey of over 20,350 residents, of whom almost 19,000 were Latin Americans, revealed 993 persons, or 4.9 per cent, with reinfection tuberculosis. Similar surveys in various sections of the country reveal that an average of approximately 1 per cent of the population has reinfection tuberculosis.

An estimation is made that there are seven active cases for each death from tuberculosis among Latin Americans.

Evidence is presented that the excessively high prevalence of tuberculosis among the Latin American population exerts an unfavorable influence on tuberculosis among Anglo Americans in San Antonio.[6]

The causes of the high incidence of tuberculosis among Latin Americans in San Antonio are set out by Dr. Gould as follows:

The recital of statistics merely defines the magnitude of the problem; it does not give the answer to the question of why there is so much tuberculosis in San Antonio. Neither does it give an insight into the meaning of the disease to the individual. The misery, the broken homes, the undernourished children, the pauperization of families that stem from this chronic ailment are all implicit in the foregoing figures. It would be futile to give specific examples of what happened to individual families, because they are legion and their tragedies are so varied.

[5] *Public Health Reports* (Washington, D. C.: Federal Security Agency, United States Public Health Service, U. S. Government Printing Office, 1945). Vol. LX, No. 5 p. 117.

[6] *Ibid.,* pp. 125-126.

The most obvious reason why one Latin American out of twenty was found to have tuberculosis is poverty. These people have been exploited as a source of cheap labor; they harvest the crops, shell the pecans, wash the clothes, and dig the ditches. For this they receive barely enough to keep body and soul together. In 1939, the housing authorities estimated that 45 per cent of Latin Americans earned less than $550 a year and that 75 per cent earned less than $950 a year.

The natural corollaries of such conditions are cheap, congested, ramshackle houses, narrow, unpaved streets, few toilets, few water faucets, and a minimum of electricity.

Diets are monotonous, high in starch, low in protein, and lacking in milk, meat, fruits, and vegetables.

Under such conditions education is cursory. Many leave school before completing the grammar grades. The majority of young adults do not enter high school. These people are unable to purchase adequate medical care; community facilities and services are likewise inadequate for their enormous needs.

All these factors mean a low standard of living which undermines resistance and makes the Latin American an easy mark for the tubercle bacillus. A vicious circle is established when the tuberculous Latin American becomes poorer and sicker, spreading bacteria to his crowded family and numerous contacts, and pyramiding the poverty and disease among his people.[7]

Dr. George W. Cox, State Health Officer, reported to the United States-Mexico Border Public Health Association conference at El Paso in April, 1944, that there were 40,000 known active cases of tuberculosis in the State. For the care of these cases, there were available only 2,000 beds in State tuberculosis sanitoria. With more than 3,500 deaths in Texas annually from tuberculosis, the minimum recognized standards for hospitalization of the tuberculous require 7,000 beds, or two for each annual death.

Let us look again at the Crystal City and Hidalgo County reports for further explanation of the prevalence of disease among the Latin Americans in Texas. The WPA survey of Crystal City reports the following conditions:

[7] *Ibid.*, p. 123.

As a result of low incomes, poor housing, and bad sanitation, disease is widespread among the Mexicans. Tuberculosis and diarrhea have taken a particularly heavy toll. The local health service is unable to care for all of those who need medical assistance.

Education of the Mexicans is also on a low level, partly because family migrations make it impossible for the children to attend school regularly. In 1938 the average 18-year-old youth had not completed the third grade of school.[8]

In describing the living conditions of agricultural workers in Hidalgo County, the Children's Bureau reports as follows:

Not only were the children deprived of schooling and forced to assume economic responsibility at an early age, but also they were reared in many instances under conditions that threatened their health. Their homes generally had only one sleeping room and a separate kitchen, were too crudely constructed to be weathertight, and often had dirt floors. The younger children usually slept on blankets or canvas on the floor. In the same small room the parents and older boys and girls slept in one or two double beds, with sometimes as many as five persons to a bed. Drinking water was often taken from an irrigation ditch or other contaminated source, and food consisted chiefly of beans, rice, potatoes, and tortillas, with seldom an appreciable amount of milk or green vegetables.

Diarrhea and other illnesses were frequent among the children, owing to the use of contaminated water, the lack of sanitation, and the inadequate protection in their homes against the weather. Few children received any medical care, since their families could seldom afford the services of a private physician and very little free medical care was available in Hidalgo County. In view of the lack of health services and adverse living conditions, the health of the school-age children was surprisingly good. The rate of infant and childhood mortality in their families, however, was exceedingly high—so high as to suggest that only the sturdiest children survived to school age. . . .[9]

The toilet facilities available to these households consisted of open-pit privies, usually shared by several families. In one area, for example, six privies served twenty-six families. In another settlement in one of the larger towns, instances were reported of one privy serving as many as thirteen large families. Usually the pits were very shallow, and they often overflowed during the rainy season.[10]

8 Menefee, *op. cit.*, p. 15.   9 Warburton, *et al., op. cit.*, pp. 5-6.
10 *Ibid.*, pp. 54-55.

It is not surprising, therefore, to find that during the first six months of 1944, of a total of 657 deaths among whites in Hidalgo County, 44 were caused by dysentery, 73 by diarrhea in children under two years of age, 29 by influenza, 50 by pneumonia, 51 by tuberculosis. These figures, of course, are for the county as a whole, but considering the fact that at least 75 per cent of the residents of Hidalgo County are of Mexican descent, it is obvious that the majority of deaths from these causes occurred among the Latin American population.

Neither is it surprising to find a far higher infant mortality rate in Texas counties where Latin Americans constitute more than 50 per cent of the population. According to the State's vital statistics record for 1942, the death rate for children under one year of age, per 1,000 live births, ranged from 89.5 in Nueces County to 141.0 in Zavala County, with Duval, Kleberg, Uvalde, Webb, Reeves, Hidalgo, Cameron, Willacy, Terrell, San Patricio, Val Verde, Dimmit, and Maverick Counties falling between the two extremes, in the ascending order named.

In only three counties having a Latin American population of more than 75 per cent was the infant mortality rate for 1942 anywhere near normal. Those counties are: Brooks, 65.7 per 1,000 live births; Starr, 54.7; and Zapata, 53.2. The full significance of these figures may be demonstrated by a comparison with the infant mortality rate in some other counties, such as Dallas, 36.7; Harris, 39.6; Tarrant, 42.1.[11]

In 1940, the Texas State Health Department published a booklet entitled "The Latin-American Health Problem in Texas", the findings in which were based on statistics for the years 1936, 1937, and 1938. It was the result of a study made to determine the truth or falsity of an impression prevailing among Texas physicians and health officials that areas in which Latin American population was concentrated exhibited extremely high death rates from tuberculosis, diarrheal disorders in infants, and infant deaths in general. The study emphatically bore out this contention.

[11] *Texas Summary of Vital Statistics 1942*, pp. 545-549.

With reference to diarrhea, it was found that Texas counties with a Latin American population of more than 20 per cent showed a death rate from diarrhea in children under two years of age of 85.1 per 100,000 population, or more than eight times the death rate from that cause in the remainder of the State; the rate in counties with from 50 to 60 per cent Latin American population was 129.4. "While these rates included all children under two years of age, other studies have shown that the majority of these deaths were in infants under one year. Therefore, the excessive infant death rates are, in a large measure, due to diarrhea and enteritis," the report explained.[12]

According to statistics furnished by Dr. Lewis C. Robbins of the San Antonio Health Department, the number of live births among Latin and Anglo Americans during the five-year period 1940-1944 were about equally divided, despite the fact that the city's residents of Mexican descent comprise only $33^{1}/_{3}$ to 40 per cent of the population. But the number of infant deaths were far from being equally divided, as revealed by the following figures:

	Live Births		Infant Deaths	
	Anglo	Latin	Anglo	Latin
1940	3,104	3,415	144	525
1941	3,789	3,937	138	375
1942	4,580	4,264	160	361
1943	5,294	4,977	179	511
1944	4,789	4,843	160	523
Totals	21,556	21,436	781	2,295

There is an even greater disparity in the number of mothers who died in giving birth to these children:

	Maternal Deaths	
	Anglo	Latin
1942	5	29
1943	6	25
1944	3	23
Totals	14	77

[12] *The Latin-American Health Problem in Texas* (Austin: Texas State Department of Health, Division of Maternal and Child Health, 1940), p. 11.

Stillbirths are almost twice as frequent among Latin Americans in San Antonio as among Anglo Americans, as shown below:

	Stillbirths	
	Anglo	*Latin*
1940	77	122
1941	66	136
1942	87	152
1943	94	151
1944	105	182
Totals	429	743

In San Antonio, as elsewhere in the State, diarrhea stands out as the principal cause of death among Latin American children under two years of age. The heavy toll exacted by this disease during the five-year period is demonstrated in the following figures:

	Infant Deaths			
	Total		*From Diarrhea*	
	Anglo	*Latin*	*Anglo*	*Latin*
1940	144	525	15	220
1941	138	375	4	93
1942	160	361	12	114
1943	179	511	16	212
1944	160	523	8	226
Totals	781	2,295	55	865

The most important single cause of diarrhea is the abundant overgrowth of bacteria, especially those from open sewage, which infect the water, milk, and food of infants. The cause is as simple as it is deadly. It would seem to be easy enough, ordinarily, to keep a baby's food and water clean, and safe, and sterile; not, however, when the homes we are considering have no means of refrigeration; not when the mother is more apt than not to be ignorant of the most elementary principles of personal hygiene; not when the water used is drawn from an irrigation ditch or other source contaminated by nearby open privies, or carried long distances in an open bucket and left uncovered in an overcrowded room; not when flies, bred in open privies and covered with filth, have easy access, through screenless windows and doors, to everything the baby eats or drinks—even to the baby itself.

It is impossible to fathom the mental processes of city councilmen and other public officials which cause them to believe that sanitary plumbing is not equally important to public health on both sides of the tracks. It is almost a cliché to say that disease germs are no respecters of persons—or of railroad tracks. The common, ordinary house fly, for example, has been found, by experimentation, to fly as far as thirteen miles from its breeding place. Claude Lillingston, writing in *Hygeia* in 1935, says:

> The house fly conveys germs of disease not only on its legs but also in its digestive system through which many germs pass without being killed. The fly's habit of voiding its digestive tract while feeding is particularly conducive to the infection of human food. It has been calculated that a fly which has access to abundant food produces between fifteen and thirty "vomit spots" and fecal deposits in twenty-four hours. The diseases conveyed by the fly include dysentery, cholera, typhoid, infantile or summer diarrhea, and a certain form of ophthalmia. The fly may also carry the eggs of parasitic worms. Leprosy, smallpox, plague and tuberculosis may all be conveyed by the fly to human beings.[13]

Although manure is a favorite breeding place for flies, the open privy is the ideal spot, and far more dangerous from the standpoint of its disease-bearing possibilities.

That a threat to the health of the Latin Americans in a community is a threat to the health of the community as a whole is substantiated by the finding of the State Health Department. In its survey of tuberculosis and diarrheal disorders in infants, it was found that death rates for both Anglo and Latin Americans were uniformly high in areas where both groups were present in large proportions.[14]

Aside from their being anachronistic, the continued exist-

13 Claude Lillingston, "The House Fly," *Hygeia*, XIII (March, 1935), 242-245.
14 *The Latin-American Health Problem in Texas, op. cit.*, p. 9.

ence of hideous, disease-breeding open privies in the Latin American residential sections of even our largest cities puts Texas in the position of the proverbial ostrich with its head in the sand. To say that such indifference makes the State extremely vulnerable to criticism is an obvious understatement.

If housing and sanitation and general health conditions among Latin Americans are bad, there is also little comfort to be gleaned from a study of the diet of these people—a condition which, naturally, reflects their low economic status.

Particularly in urban areas, our people of Mexican descent have generally adopted many of the dietary habits of the Anglo American. Even there, however, the lower income group tends to cling to a basic diet of beans, cereals (including white flour, white rice, and whole corn), and quantities of lard. Small amounts of meat, milk, eggs, and cheese are used, and onions, potatoes, and tomatoes are the most popular vegetables. Coffee is used by nearly all Latin American families, and sugar is practically the only sweet that appears in the diet.

In 1931, Jet C. Winters, associate professor of home economics at the University of Texas, made a study of the diet of sixty-five families of Mexican descent, in various income groups, residing in San Antonio and Austin. In the published account of her findings, she shows that the diet of these families, based on the Hawley standards for calorie, protein, calcium, phosphorus, and iron content, measured up as follows:

	¾ Adequate	½-¾ Adequate	Less than ½ Adequate	
	Adequate	*Adequate*	*Adequate*	*Adequate*
Calories	45%	26%	22%	7%
Protein	57	16	23	4
Calcium	19	24	40	17
Phosphorus	24	39	28	9
Iron	16	36	38	10 [15]

[15] Jet C. Winters, *A Report on the Health and Nutrition of Mexicans Living in Texas* (Austin: The University of Texas, Bulletin No. 3127, July 15, 1931), pp. 17-18.

Analysis of these results demonstrated that:

10% of the diets were adequate in all 5 factors
6% of the diets were inadequate in only 1 factor
6% of the diets were inadequate in 2 factors
20% of the diets were inadequate in 3 factors
21% of the diets were inadequate in 4 factors
37% of the diets were inadequate in all 5 factors
Average number of factors inadequate, 3.4.[16]

It was also found that the principal items of diet, that is, the food purchased in the largest quantities, and most frequently, by the sixty-five families during a period of one week, were as follows:

Total No. Families—65	No. Families Using Food
Fruits:	
Apples	15
Bananas	29
Oranges	29
Vegetables:	
Cabbage	18
Onions	50
Potatoes	59
Tomatoes	59
Legumes:	
Beans (dried)	62
Cereals and Cereal Products:	
Bread (white)	45
Crackers	22
Flour (white)	50
Macaroni	22
Masa	36
Oatmeal	16
Rice	47
Sweet Bread	44
Tortillas	22
Vermicelli	28

[16] *Ibid.,* p. 18.

Meat and Meat Substitutes:

Bacon	26
Cheese	41
Eggs	59
Meat (beef)	58
Sausage	24

Milk	62

Fats:

Lard	59
Butter	58

Sweets:

Sugar	61

Miscellaneous:

Coffee	60
Chile (canned)	14
Peppers	65 [17]

Regarding the vitamin content of foods used, the Winters study found the diets analyzed to be particularly deficient in Vitamin A. Milk, butter, eggs, leafy vegetables, and glandular meats are the principal sources of this vitamin, and while these items, with the exception of leafy vegetables, appeared on almost every diet, the quantities of each used were insufficient to provide the required vitamin intake.

Milk, for example, while purchased by all but three families, was used in quantities sufficient only to supply the younger children with an average of one and one-half cups daily. Although butter appears on fifty-eight diets, the amount purchased averaged little more than one-quarter pound per family per week.

Eggs are widely used, but in greatly varying quantities. Of the fruits most frequently purchased, only bananas, and of the vegetables, only tomatoes, are rich sources of Vitamin A.

As to Vitamin B, the report states that "the increasing use of milled cereals in place of the whole-grain corn . . . may

[17] *Ibid.*, pp. 22-24.

be cutting down his Vitamin B supply to a dangerous extent.[18]
Only 10 to 12 per cent of the calories obtained from cereals came
from the whole-grain varieties. . . . The growing tendency to
substitute milled cereals for whole grains is shown by the fact
that while 45 of the 65 families studied used white bread and 50
white flour, only 22 used tortillas and 36 masa."[19]

It is interesting to note which foods were purchased in the
largest quantities. The preponderance of starchy foods is
readily apparent. The Winters report shows the following
figures, based on the number of families using each food and
not on the entire group. In other words, for the twenty-nine
families who used oranges during the week, the average purchase was 2.97 pounds. For other foods the average amount
per week per family using the food was found to be:

Onions	2.34	lbs.
Potatoes	6.16	"
Tomatoes	4.46	"
Beans (dried)	5.56	"
Bread (white)	5.91	"
Flour (white)	16.29	"
Masa	8.37	"
Sweet Bread	6.50	"
Tortillas	4.56	"
Eggs	24	eggs
Meat (beef)	4.18	lbs.
Milk	10.7	qts.
Lard	3.97	lbs.
Sugar	5.21	"
Coffee	1.68	" 20

[18] On this point Dr. Michel Pijoan, well-known authority on nutritional problems, personally made the following comment to the author: "The substitution of
wheat cereals, regardless of milling, for corn may have a salutary effect with regard
to the incidence of pellagra. It has been known that the consumption of corn increases the demand for macin; that corn contains a substance inducing pellagra when
the macin intake is minimal."

[19] Winters, *op. cit.,* p. 27.

[20] *Ibid.,* pp. 22-23.

In summarizing, Dr. Winters says:

1. Diets in which too large a percentage of calories are drawn from cereals are apt to be deficient in calcium and Vitamin A.

2. Milk has been shown to be very definitely connected with calcium adequacy, and it is also an excellent source of A.[21]

3. Diets in which too large a proportion of calories is drawn from cereals and too small a proportion from milk would almost certainly be deficient in calcium and Vitamin A.[22]

The manner in which the food budgets of the sixty-five families were apportioned is also indicative of certain grave deficiencies. The budget plan suggested by the Food Administration is:

$1/_5$ more or less, for vegetables and fruit
$1/_5$ or more for milk and cheese
$1/_5$ or less for meats, fish and eggs
$1/_5$ or more for bread and cereals
$1/_5$ or less for fats, sugar, and other groceries and food adjuncts.[23]

But the Winters report shows that the Latin American families interviewed spent "only about ⅛ of their food money for milk and cheese, nearly ¼ for meat and eggs, nearly ¼ for cereals, and about $1/_5$ for the other two classes. Both in regard to the percentage of the budget spent for milk and in the calories obtained from milk, Mexican diets are far below these standards."[24]

Other available studies of nutrition bear out the findings of the Winters report. For example, the study made of 153 Latin American families in three Central Texas counties states:

The most noticeable nutritional deficiencies lie among the foods supplying complete protein and among the green and yellow vegetables,

21 Again I quote a comment prepared for me by Dr. Pijoan: "The need for milk may be minimal if the diet is otherwise satisfactory. In fact, without proper refrigeration and care, milk affords an excellent bacterial culture medium and has been found in many areas to be one of the chief contributory causes of dysentery."

22 Winters, *op. cit.*, p. 28.

23 *Ibid.*   24 *Ibid.*

PLATE II

Photo by J. A. Dodd

CITIZENSHIP AND ENGLISH CLASS
Alazan-Apache Courts, San Antonio

PLATE III   *Photo by J. A. Dodd*

PLAYGROUND ACTIVITIES
for children in the project and adjacent community Alazan-Apache
Courts, San Antonio

PLATE IV   *Photo by J. A. Dodd*

INTERIOR OF DWELLING UNIT
Santa Rita Courts, Austin

PLATE V

Photo by J. A. Dodd

VICTORY GARDEN RALLY
Little Mexico Village, Dallas

PLATE VI   *Photo by J. A. Dodd*

NEIGHBORHOOD CANNING GROUP
Home Counseling volunteer helps her neighbors to can peaches at home
Alazan-Apache Courts, San Antonio

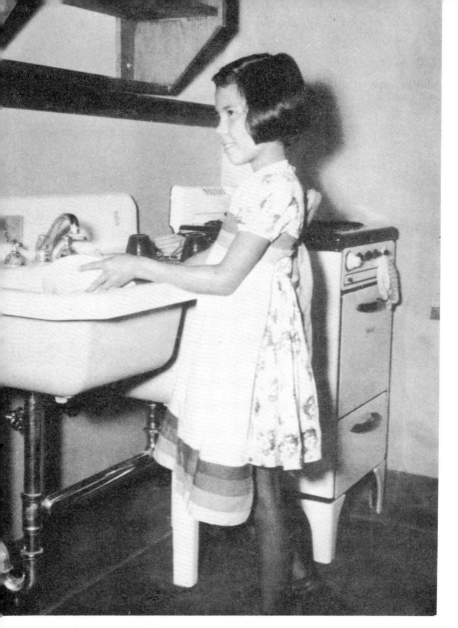

PLATE VII

Photo by J. A. Dodd

KITCHEN INTERIOR

Alamito Project, El Paso

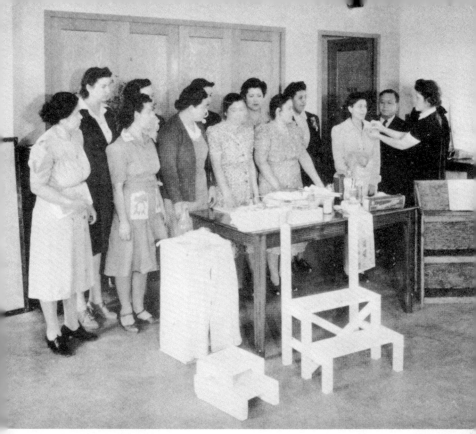

PLATE VIII   *Photo by J. A. Dodd*

RED CROSS HOME NURSING CLASS
Little Mexico Village, Dallas

PLATE IX   *Photo by J. A. Dodd*

PIÑATA PARTY
Little Mexico Village, Dallas

and fruit. Less than one-third of the families conserve any surplus foods, only two having a pressure cooker. About 29 per cent raise all the chickens and eggs needed by their families, but only 15 per cent produce what vegetables they need. Their consumption of milk per family is far below nutritional needs.[25]

As a part of the Children's Bureau study of Hidalgo County, a special health survey was made which covered all children under eighteen years of age in fifty-five families selected at random from among the 342 families that were interviewed. Included in these fifty-five families were 240 boys and girls under eighteen years of age. With regard to diet, the report states:

The diets of the children were in general a simple fare, consisting principally of pinto or navy beans, rice, potatoes, and tortillas. Vegetables and fruits were eaten infrequently by many families because they did not like them, though there was ample opportunity to obtain them from the fields or packing sheds. Of the fifty-five families interviewed, only twenty-eight, approximately one-half, reported that they used vegetables or fruits frequently. Three families did not use them at all, and the other twenty-four used them only occasionally. One family stated that the father could get vegetables easily from the packing shed, but did not because the family did not like them. He did bring oranges from the groves, but not grapefruit because, he said, grapefruit "thins the blood and causes TB."

After infancy, milk is used in only small amounts or not at all by most of the children. Of the children two years of age or older, slightly more than one-half drank no milk, and half of those who did take milk used it only in tea or coffee. Only about one-fifth used as much as a pint of milk a day, and these were usually the younger children.[26]

The lowly, but highly nutritional carrot posed an interesting and amusing challenge in one Texas community where a definite program was under way to raise the standard of living of the Latin American population and to improve school-community relations in general.

The scene was laid in San Marcos, where the normal popu-

[25] Confidential information supplied to the author.
[26] Warburton *et al.*, *op. cit.*, p. 56.

lation is about 6,000, of whom some 2,000 are of Mexican descent. There the Southwest Texas State Teachers College, in the fall of 1943, inaugurated a special school-community project in inter-American relations under the joint sponsorship of the Office of the Coordinator of Inter-American Affairs and the United States Office of Education.

Under the guidance of Willa Vaughn Tinsley, assistant professor of home economics at the College, the program was developed to interest the Latin American parents in closer co-operation 'with other local residents for several noteworthy purposes, namely, increasing school attendance, providing more adequate recreational facilities, fostering better habits of health and hygiene (including food practices), enlarging music and art activities, and improving the physical conditions of the school grounds and buildings.

It was in March, 1944, that the carrot entered the picture. But the story is best given as related by Miss Tinsley in the College's published bulletin on the subject:

At an early stage in the promotion of better school-community relations, a situation presented itself which proved instrumental as a stimulus for closer co-operation between the parents and the school and for co-ordinated effort within the school itself.

The school lunch room came into possession of a large quantity of fresh carrots which would not keep long enough to be used gradually. At a regular P.T.A. meeting the need was stressed for canning these carrots in order that this food might be available over a longer period of time.

The P.T.A. members obviously needed something tangible to do as a beginning force to bring them to the school, so that we might be more successful in getting them to return for participation in the proposed recreational program.

A government canning kitchen eight miles away at Kyle, Texas, was already operating, and those in charge agreed to do the canning if the carrots were brought to them prepared for processing. Volunteers were asked to come to the school grounds early the next morning, and to bring a clean wash tub and knife with them. A long table was placed under the trees near the lunch room kitchen so that water would be near.

Four mothers and two fathers came and worked steadily for about six hours. They were assisted by groups of older girls and boys who worked in relays. Some 1,700 pounds of carrots were carefully prepared for canning. A member of the college faculty loaned the use of his truck to haul the carrots to Kyle, with older boys going along to unload them. The parents ate noon lunch with the teachers at the lunch room. Prayers preceded the meal and speeches of appreciation followed the meal.

An ample supply of carrots was canned to furnish this food to the school lunch room all next year. However, having carrots available and getting the children to eat them is not the same problem!

The home survey showed that carrots were not a very popular food with the Latin American families. A campaign was launched in the school and in the community to popularize carrots in order to get more people into the habit of eating them. After all, a food however wholesome can nourish only if it is eaten.[27]

Miss Tinsley then proceeds to outline the steps taken to glamorize the carrot. Detailed suggestions were drawn up, mimeographed, and given to the individual classroom teachers. At all grade levels, an effort was made to introduce carrots into the daily diets of the school children by distributing clean, raw carrots at the morning recess, by appointing committees to go to the kitchen and wash the carrots before the recess period, and keeping count of the children who could be induced to eat them.

A variety of new recipes for preparing carrots was introduced into the school lunch menus, and a careful check was made to see which recipes proved to be most popular.

Children in the primary grades were provided with mimeographed outline drawings of carrots to be colored. They were taught to mold carrots out of clay. Their teachers read or made up stories in which carrots played a part, and the children were asked to make simple sentences about carrots.

Older students learned the place of carrots in the seven basic food groups and learned to show by posters the need for

27 *Building Better School-Community Relations in Latin-American Communities* (San Marcos: Southwest Texas State Teachers College, Bulletin No. III, July, 1944), p. 13.

Vitamin A in the diet. Carrots were planted in the school garden, and papers written about the use of carrots in the home. Finally, as school was dismissed in the afternoon, each child was given a sack of carrots to be taken home, together with a bilingual sheet of suggestions for using carrots. The gathering of recipes, in itself, required considerable research and experimentation.

A check-up on what happened to the carrots that were taken home to each family is most interesting: a very small percentage of families are in the habit of using carrots often, with a few never using them at all; not a single child would admit that the carrots were taken home and allowed to waste; about half the carrots were used raw, while the remainder was cooked in various ways; in every instance the children said the family "liked" the carrots. Relatively few families have carrots planted in home gardens, but the children are planting some in the school garden.[28]

Thus, one Texas community, in its desire to assist the Latin American residents in improving the quality of their diet, was plunged into an adventure of unforeseen proportions.[29]

In February, 1945, Dr. Walter Wilkins, of the United States Public Health Service, made a preliminary limited inspection of nutritional deficiencies evidenced by pupils in the Aoy Elementary School, El Paso. Aoy School is located in a slum district in which 2,500 Latin American children are to be found in an area six blocks wide by seven blocks long. One hundred and seventy-two children from the first, second, third, and fifth grades were examined for physical defects attributable to vitamin deficiencies. The signs sought were as follows:

(1) Those thought to be due to riboflavin deficiency, riboflavin being part of the B-complex vitamin found principally in milk and liver: (a) Crusty eyelids; chronic collection of mucus along the eyelashes; (b) Scarring at corners of eyes;

[28] Ibid., p. 17.
[29] Dr. Michel Pijoan's comment: "The foods to sponsor are those which are available to an area, which have high nutritional value and are not easily spoiled. The foods promoted must be carefully chosen without a set formula, but in terms of the local situation."

faint scars at the outer corner of the eye which usually follow small sores; (c) Angular stomatitis; small sores or open cracks at the corners of the mouth, usually appearing on both sides; (d) Scarring at corners of mouth; faint scars which usually follow angular stomatitis.

(2) Those thought to be due to Vitamin D deficiency, that is, rickets: (a) Bossing or a deviation in the smooth contour of the head, usually appearing on the side of the head above the ears; (b) Knock knees or bow legs; (c) Any change in the conformation of the chest such as pigeon breast, flaring ribs with protruding abdomen, beads on the ribs, etc.

(3) Those thought to be due to Vitamin C deficiency, that is, spongy, puffy, red gums that bleed easily upon pressure.

(4) Those thought to be due to Vitamin A deficiency, that is, folliculosis, or horny permanent "goose-bumps" on the skin; these may occur all over the body but are most likely to appear on upper arm, thigh, and abdomen.

(5) Those of unknown origin, but thought to be due to Vitamin A and riboflavin deficiency, that is, marked redness of the eyeball.[30]

Surprisingly enough, few evidences of riboflavin deficiency were found; not, however, because the children's diet includes abundant milk and liver, but because beans, the chief item of diet, is a rich source of all B-complex vitamins. Of the 172 children, only seventeen showed more or less slight deviations from normal where crusty eyelids were concerned; six had slight scars at the corners of the eyes; eight evidenced slight deviations, and four showed marked deviations from normal in the matter of sores or open cracks at the corners of the

[30] Dr. Pijoan also prepared the following comment on this point: "The symptoms of avitaminoses described have been recently questioned. (Dann *et al., Phys. Reviews,* 1945). Many of the symptoms are due to a multiplicity of causes, weather effects, malocclusion, etc., and nutritional deficiency contributes to the lesions with variable effect, depending on the chronicity of the deprivation" *(New England Jour. Med.,* July, 1944).

mouth; and twenty-three were found to have scars at the corners of the mouth.

Redness of eyes, which is thought also to result from riboflavin as well as Vitamin A deficiency, was found, to a greater or less degree, in 160 of the children. In the more comprehensive study that is to be made in the near future, the exact cause of this condition will be determined.

Signs of rickets, occasioned by Vitamin D deficiency, were found in almost all the children. The heads of 154 of them revealed the telltale signs; forty-six had knock knees or bow legs; and 125 were found to have deformities of the chest.

Vitamin C deficiency, as evidenced by poor gums, was discovered in 119 of the 172 children, forty-five of them showing marked deviations from normal.

An even 100 children were found to be deficient in Vitamin A, as indicated by the presence of folliculosis.

None of these 172 children ate in the school lunchroom. In order to ascertain, in a cursory fashion, whether or not one well-balanced meal a day made any apparent difference in the children's health, another 103 pupils who took advantage, at least occasionally, of the school's hot lunch program, were examined on two points: gums and folliculosis. The comparative results speak for themselves:

	Gums						Folliculosis					
	0	1	2	3	4	5	0	1	2	3	4	5°
172 children— no meals in lunchroom	53	35	39	32	12	1	72	65	28	5	1	1
103 children— 61 in regular attendance at lunchroom— 42 irregular	58	27	14	3	1	—	65	33	5	—	—	—

° Legend: Lesions were graded according to the degree of variation from normal. Thus "0" is apparently normal while "1" and "2" are slight deviations from normal, and "3," "4," and "5" are marked deviations from normal.[31]

[31] Special report supplied to the author.

In the extensive study to be undertaken at a later date, Dr. Wilkins will seek to confirm his preliminary findings through therapeutic tests, and will set up control groups for nutritional experiments.

Dr. Michel Pijoan, at the time of this writing attached to the National Naval Medical Center, Naval Medical Research Institute, Bethesda, Maryland, has conducted extensive experiments in New Mexico, Guatemala, and elsewhere, on nutrition among groups similarly situated, economically speaking, to the low-income Latin Americans in Texas. With regard to the nutritional needs of children, he says, in a letter to the author dated December 10, 1945:

The first point to make clear is that the dietary requirements of children are different from those of adults. Thus, where the dietary requirement of an adult for protein is about 1 gram per kilo, the amount required by children is about 3.2 grams per kilo.

The growing child needs more of all nutritional factors per kilo than does the adult, and it utilizes nutrients at a greater rate depending on exercise, etc., including growth. Infants should receive supplemental feeding; otherwise an anemia develops. Sufficient data exist to show that nutritional reserves in children are less easily maintained. It is, therefore, important that children are fed often and well.[32]

In this opinion, Dr. Pijoan gives support to other authorities:

The care of children during the first ten to fifteen years of life is of supreme importance. It is at this period of life that improved environment exercises its effect most promptly, and, furthermore, the improved physique built up during this period would seem to be of decisive effect at all later ages.[33]

In order to guarantee to all Texas children the opportunity to build physical strength and fitness, a school lunch program which will provide undernourished children with one good

[32] More exhaustive treatment may be found in the following: H. Parsons, *Amer. Jour. Diseases of Children*, XXXIX (1930), 1221; E. V. McCollum, E. Orent-Keiles, and H. G. Day, *The Newer Knowledge of Nutrition* (New York, 1943); Pijoan and Elkin, *Journal of Nutrition*, XXVII (1944), 67.

[33] W. O. Kermack, A. G. McKendrick, and P. L. Finlay, *The Lancet*, I (1934), 698.

meal each day is necessary. Some Texas schools have taken advantage of federal funds offered for this purpose; others have declined to initiate a program of free school lunches, or lunches sold at a very nominal cost, because, to quote one school superintendent, "We have no intention of feeding all the Mexicans in the neighborhood." Nevertheless, as Dr. Pijoan stated in connection with conditions in Taos County, New Mexico:

A school lunch is indicated for without it weight gain is impeded. The children should receive some sort of meal at mid-day. If this is done, weight gain improves and for some reason unknown to the investigators, with nutritional improvement during a period of two years, the incidence of minor infections was reduced and it is to be hoped that such a program will have a salutary effect in the reduction of tuberculosis.[34]

By a proper awareness of local conditions and some ingenuity on the part of health authorities, difficult problems can often be solved economically, as Dr. Pijoan implies:

In many areas where school lunches were out of the question, peanut butter, to which had been added dried brewers yeast and powdered milk, with crackers, was found to be helpful, although such a meal failed to make up the component of bulk.[35]

That all the conditions set forth in this chapter need not exist; that improper housing, sanitation, health, and nutrition can be remedied to a large extent by the wisdom, patience, and understanding of city planners, school officials, and other local residents; and that the results obtained by enabling and assisting low-income Latin Americans to rid themselves of the habits and environment that stunt body, mind, and soul, is demonstrated by the records of Federal Housing projects established in Latin American communities in various parts of Texas.

Most outstanding in its achievements, perhaps, is the "Little Mexico Village," which opened for occupancy in Dallas on September 15, 1942. The 102 apartments each contain living room, kitchen, a bed room for each two family members, a

[34] M. Pijoan and A. Drexler, *Comments on the Taos Report*, United States Indian Service, 1943.
[35] *Ibid.*

bath room, and ample closet and storage space. Tenants supply their own furniture, except for the electric refrigerator, kitchen range, and space heaters already installed in each apartment.

Some discouragement was caused in the beginning by the fact that the apartments were not all rented until three months after the opening date. It was found that the Latin American families were reluctant to move in because they did not understand the conditions of tenancy. They had heard that their living in the apartments would deprive them of all individual rights and family privacy. Rumors had been circulated to the effect that lights would be turned off by the management at 9:30 p. m. Some were under the impression that they would be required to buy new furniture; that their homes would be subject to constant inspection; and that they would be forced suddenly to change their manner of living. However, after the first three months, the waiting list swelled to several hundred families, of whom about seventy-five were actually eligible for tenancy.

Many activities were developed within the Village, and, with the project as a nucleus, throughout the Latin American community. During the year ended September 15, 1944, health programs successfully carried out included a city-sponsored Well Baby Clinic within the project, in connection with which a Well Baby Show was held during the summer, involving the participation of forty mothers and children. Between the weekly meetings, a city nurse called on individual families to deliver birth certificates, to create interest in the clinic, and to advise with mothers.

In the environing colony, three clinics were operated with the assistance of physicians. Free medical aid and supplies were furnished to those unable to pay; otherwise, the cost was nominal.

Two Red Cross Home Nursing Classes were completed during the year. The City Health Department exhibited films on venereal disease control clinics. Block workers distributed free material on health, and free bedside care was provided for eligible families by the Visiting Nurses Association. Through individual counseling with families, problems of diet and the home care of the sick were worked out.

A program for control of household pests and insects is supervised by the project's maintenance department. Families are quick to enlist such aid, and diligently follow the directions received. Each family is responsible for proper disposal of its garbage, and there has been excellent response to this challenge.

The Family Life Education program was initiated by the Dallas School Board, working in co-operation with the Dallas Housing Authority. Emphasis is placed on meeting the needs of the families in their new environment. In order to become acquainted with the families and to secure their interest and good will, the sponsors have promoted a varied program of activities, encouraging participation and creating a knowledge of how to utilize the community facilities to the fullest extent.

Resourcefulness and leadership among the tenants have been two of the most significant achievements of the program. Pride in the community has grown, and good relationships between project residents and the people in the community have increased.

The Family Life Education program includes organized instruction in the fields of English, home nursing, nutrition, food preparation, leadership, child care, and general home-making.

Little Mexico Village has not only benefited the Latin American families living there, but has also exerted a profound influence upon the thinking of the Anglo Americans in Dallas.

During the first months the project was in operation, the efforts made by Anglos toward co-operation and friendliness often consisted of offers of discarded clothes, toys, and furniture; calls to find domestic help; and inquiries as to families who were in need of special help, such as Christmas baskets and extra food supplies.

Through the program which has developed gradually, the Community House in the Village has become a practical demonstration center for the building of a better understanding between Anglo and Latin Americans. It is now realized that from this new environment there are emerging strong leaders who are asking to become a part of the city's life, to be recognized as leaders among the Latin Americans, and to be given civic responsibilities in keeping with their development as responsible citizens. This is a natural growth that comes from the opportunity for association in an environment where mutual understanding, confidence, and friendship—not to mention pride—can thrive. As a result, Latin Americans are being invited to serve on nutrition committees and other civic projects. During the war, some of them served in War Bond drives.

A library of 500 volumes, housed in the Community Center, represents the gifts of many clubs and individuals who have come to appreciate the project and its people. Luncheons, dinners, fiestas, and receptions are frequently held at the Village, with Anglo and Latin American groups participating. A small group of children, residents of the Village, compose "The Talent Club," and often perform for the city's leading civic and church groups. A supper club, composed of Latin and Anglo Americans, meets occasionally at the Community House for a "dutch treat" supper.

The evident success of the undertaking would certainly appear to uphold the philosophy of those who have worked so faithfully to make Little Mexico Village a success: "Better housing makes better neighbors, and better neighbors make better citizens."

Comparable worthwhile achievements have been brought about in other sections of the State, according to data available from the housing projects in San Antonio, Austin, El Paso, Corpus Christi, Dumas, Brownsville, and Laredo.

The largest of all projects in which Latin Americans are housed is the Alazan-Apache Courts in San Antonio, where 4,994 persons were living in 1,179 units on January 1, 1945.

There are three Well Baby and Maternity clinics in the area of the San Antonio project which are sponsored jointly by the

Health Department and Settlement Houses in that neighborhood. Public housing co-operates with the community agencies in carrying through an intensive educational program in positive health.

The mortality rate resulting from infant diarrhea, as we have seen, is alarmingly high in San Antonio among the Latin Americans. The City Health Department and community agencies completed a city-wide diarrhea control program about May 1, 1945, in which the Housing Authority and the residents of the projects took an active part. The response on the part of residents in Alazan-Apache was particularly gratifying. The manager wrote letters to community leaders among the residents, asking them to volunteer their services in a house-to-house canvass of the project. It was the responsibility of these volunteers to find unsanitary conditions, cases of diarrhea, and to give information on the prevention and control of the disease.

According to the San Antonio Housing Authority, this campaign proved that the project residents were capable of developing in many ways, especially in their ability and desire to organize and carry through, on their own initiative, any program which will tend to raise the standards of living of their fellow Latin Americans. The tenants have participated in similar campaigns on typhus and malaria control.

There is an active recreational program for all age groups in the project consisting of sports and athletics, arts and crafts, and parties and dances. The leadership for these programs is provided by the City Recreation Department and tenant volunteers. The youth group of approximately 300 members meets weekly for forums, discussions, and social affairs. Family nights are held from two to three times a month. In addition to these activities, there are Boy and Girl Scout troops and Junior Deputies.

Alazan-Apache residents have three self-government organizations: the Men's Club, the Women's Club, and the Teen-Age group, which take the lead in all community affairs within the project. Constitutions and by-laws have been set up for all three groups. This type of self-government is peculiar to the Latin American project, inasmuch as the other San Antonio projects have an over-all Tenants Association composed of both men and women. Perhaps this is due to the Latin American custom of separating the sexes in all their activities. However, according to the management, there are indications that the time will come soon when the two adult groups will combine as the Teen-Agers have done.

The Home and Family Life Educational Program of the San Antonio Public Schools, in co-operation with the San Antonio Housing Authority, makes definite contributions to the betterment of living conditions of Latin Americans living in the Alazan-Apache Courts and in the surrounding neighborhood.

In this educational program, activities are carried out in the fields of health, recreation, sanitation, safety, and child care. Living conditions are improved through group activities, individual and group counseling, and home visitation in the areas of nutrition, meal planning, home management, food preparation, child care, home nursing, family relationships, youth problems, maintenance and upkeep of household equipment, gardening, food conservation, consumer problems, point rationing, budgeting, and food preservation.

Programs of this nature are co-ordinated with those of other agencies and organizations operating in the immediate community as well as in the community at large. Recognizing the importance of lay leadership, home counselors working in the program have trained volunteer teachers or demonstrators in nutrition, child care, point rationing, and food preservation. A dwelling unit is provided by the Housing Authority and is used as a demonstration unit and as "Home Base" from which the counselors work.

A citizenship class, which was conducted by the Board of Education, met weekly in the community hall of Alazan-Apache Courts from the opening of the project until early in

1945. Attendance was open to all alien Latin Americans. The attendance and demand for this class diminished to such an extent that it was closed in March, 1945, but the management states that, if the need arises, it will be reopened.

The Catholic Parochial School Board sponsors a nursery school with funds provided by the government under the Lanham Act for children of working mothers. There were forty-three children enrolled as of May 1, 1945. In addition to the nursery school, there is a play school for children from three to six years of age, which meets daily from 9 a. m. to 12 noon. Leadership for the play school is provided from private funds, supplemented by a fee of twenty-five cents per week for each child.

A branch of the Public Library is located at Alazan-Apache Courts. A full-time librarian is on duty each day from 1 until 5 p. m. Story hours conducted by the librarian and tenant leaders are held weekly, and tables and chairs are provided for reference and study. Participation in the use of the library has been one of the most successful of all the activities in the project.

Tenant maintenance of units is one of the most difficult problems with which housing project management is faced. Poor tenant maintenance not only increases maintenance and replacement costs, but leads to other serious difficulties, such as infestations of roaches and bedbugs, and other health hazards. Poorly maintained projects also have a high turnover, because they provide unsatisfactory living quarters.

The San Antonio Housing Authority, in February, 1944, devised a plan to improve housekeeping and set a trial period for such operation. A score card was developed covering the items to be checked and showing the score which would be given for "excellent" on each item. These scores total a possible 100, as shown on the score card below:

HOUSING AUTHORITY OF THE
CITY OF SAN ANTONIO, TEXAS
Score Card for Good Housekeeping

PROJECT...............

UNIT NUMBER....................... NAME OF FAMILY....................

DATE OF INSPECTION.................. ADDRESS...........................

I.   KITCHEN

   1. Stove   5   _____
       a. Top, oven, and broiler free from dirt, grease and food
       b. Sides, back and bottom clean

   2. Refrigerator   5   _____
       a. Inside and outside clean
       b. Properly defrosted
       c. Free from odors
       d. Neat arrangement of contents

   3. Sink, Walls and Shelves—Clean   5   _____

   4. Garbage Disposal—Clean, covered container   5   _____
                                                                 20

II. BATH

   1. Tub and Basin   10   _____
       a. Inside and outside clean
       b. Faucets polished

   2. Toilet Area—Clean and free from odor   10   _____
                                                                 20

III. STORAGE

   1. Food   5   _____
       a. Use of covered containers
       b. Clean and orderly

   2. Clothing   5   _____
       a. Neat closet arrangement
       b. Garments hanging
       c. Adequate storage of soiled clothes

   3. Miscellaneous Articles   10   _____
       a. Adequate storage of linen
       b. Adequate storage of toilet articles
       c. Adequate storage of tools
       d. Adequate storage of toys

                                                                 20

IV. YARD

   1. Lawn   10
     a. Cut and trimmed
     b. Free from trash

   2. Shrubs   10
     a. Grass out of hedges

                 20

V. GENERAL CLEANLINESS

   1. Furnishings   10
     a. Beds—Clean and neatly made
     b. Furniture clean
     c. Floor coverings clean
     d. Curtains and draperies—Clean and hanging neatly

   2. Walls, Floors and Windows   10
     a. Clean—Free from dirt and stains
     b. Absence of cobwebs and household pests

                 20

               100

        Total Certi- Inspection
        ficate Score Score

SIGNED ....

Each unit was provided with a score card and the plan explained to the housekeeper. After a period which allowed each tenant to clean and ready her unit, she invited a representative from management to score it.

Each item was carefully judged and graded, and a copy of the score card was given to the housekeeper. Where the condition of the unit was satisfactory in its total grade, a "Certificate of Good Housekeeping" was issued to the homemaker. In addition to the certificate, the executive director wrote a personal letter to the homemaker and complimented her upon her achievement. So successful was the trial that the plan was continued.

The San Antonio Housing Authority has already announced that its post-war plans include 1,400 additional low-cost housing units for Latin Americans.

In the spring of 1945, the executive director of the El Paso Housing Authority, in a special report to which this author had access, wrote that "as a whole Latin Americans are far more appreciative of their improved living conditions than are the Anglo Americans of low income. We have Latin Americans living in both Alamito and Tays Place projects. We do not make a practice of segregating them, and we find that they get along with their neighbors in most instances."

With regard to the marked improvement in general attitudes and living standards produced by life in the El Paso housing projects, the director continued as follows:

School children are not segregated as to their Latin or Anglo heredity, but attend the school in the district in which they live. It was anticipated prior to occupancy of the projects that the school enrollment in the respective vicinities would drop when the projects were opened, due to the fact that a greater number of persons resided on the sites prior to demolition than could be housed in the new dwelling units thereon constructed. However, this was not the case. The first year after occupancy, enrollment was practically the same, and it has shown a steady increase ever since.

Teachers are high in their praise of children residing on the projects. Reports have come in to us that the morale is much better, that the children are much improved in personal appearance and cleanliness, and health conditions are much better; and that the boys and girls take more interest in their school work.

Not long ago, the following conversation was related to me by the principal of Alamo School, which is located within the limits of our project. An out-of-town teacher visited a number of our schools and expressed amazement at the demeanor of the pupils attending Alamo School. She remarked "You have a higher grade of Spanish-American students than the ones that attend some of the schools I have visited." The principal of the school replied: "No, they are of the same type, but most of them have been greatly influenced by their improved living conditions during the last year or so, and they are happier and better satisfied with their surroundings. Both their health and morale have been benefited immensely. Three or four years ago, before the advent of decent low-rent housing, my pupils were the same as the pupils at other schools."

Records of the City-County Health Department show a decided improvement in health conditions of the area in which our projects are located.

When a new tenant comes into the Project, we try to impress him with the fact that he is welcome; that we have certain rules and regulations that he must observe; that he must be considerate of his neighbors and treat them in the same manner he desires to be treated; that we expect him to be a law-abiding citizen, assist in the beautifying of his surroundings, take pride in his home and grounds; in fact, that he should give his home the same attention that he would if he were the owner. Also, we impress upon him the fact that the health of his family is a vital factor in the health of the community, and that he should use every precaution to see that a high sanitary and health standard is maintained.

It is our constant aim to impress upon the occupants of the project that it is not an institution, but a place where folks of low income can find a decent home at a rent they can afford to pay, and in order to keep it thus, they must help us to maintain the buildings and grounds in such condition that rents can continue to remain within their reach.

McAllen, Hidalgo County, is one of the Texas towns and cities which have included slum clearance in their post-war planning. Plans approved there call for a project of 300 units, which is designed to replace that many substandard homes.

To enable the housing projects of the future to contribute even more to the lives of their tenants, the Federal Public Housing Authority, as of May 1, 1945, was engaged in making a "liveability" study of projects throughout the United States, and in Texas, particularly projects housing Latin Americans.

In order to determine whether the needs of the people are being met under the present set-up, management and tenants alike were being asked: Is adequate storage space provided? Is the size of the rooms sufficient? Is separate dining room preferred to kitchenette or combination living-dining room? Is outdoor space adequate and properly apportioned? Are doors placed at most convenient points? In two-story units, are bathing facilities desired on both floors? Is size of bathroom ample? Are stairways of sufficient size to permit the passage of a piano or a stretcher?

These oases of decent and fruitful living stand out like beacon lights, emphasizing by contrast the squalid and degrading conditions under which so many of our Latin American citizens are forced to exist.

Chapter 10

Employment in Business
and Industry

B ASIC TO ALL OTHER problems of Latin Americans in Texas is the economic situation with which they are confronted. Since the beginning, the lot of the Latin American worker employed in Texas industry has been an unhappy one. His opportunities for employment have been, and are now, extremely limited. His chances for promotion in his occupation are curtailed, and his wage rates are generally established on a discriminatory basis. Some improvement was noted during the war; however, it is an indisputable fact that a majority of Texas industries still follow the practice of discriminating against Latin American workers, with regard to employment, wage scales, and opportunities of promotion.

An official statement made by Carlos E. Castañeda, special assistant on Latin American problems to the chairman of the President's Committee on Fair Employment Practice, on September 8, 1944, included the following:

Less than 5 per cent of the total number of persons of Mexican extraction in Texas are employed at the present time in war and essential industries. Such industries as have given employment to Mexican labor have restricted them to common or unskilled labor jobs largely, regardless of their ability, training, or qualifications. In the oil, aircraft

157

and mining industries, in the numerous military installations, in the munitions factories and shipyards, and in the public utility corporations, such as gas, light, and transportation companies, their employment has been limited and their opportunities for advancement restricted.[1]

Observation alone will tell us that, for the most part, Latin Americans are employed in menial occupations, such as domestic service, truckdriving, working on highways and railroad tracks, serving as hotel porters, waiters, and bus boys. This observation is substantiated by the Children's Bureau report on Hidalgo County.

Although agricultural labor predominated in the families' employment, in half (172) of the families one or more members had also had some nonfarm employment during the year. This nonagricultural work was usually limited in extent, however, as is indicated by the fact that all except eighty-three of the 1,315 workers in the study had been employed chiefly or exclusively as farm laborers.

Among the families having nonfarm employment about half (79) reported that some member had worked in a fruit or vegetable packing house or cannery. Packing-shed employment was considered, in comparison with field work, highly remunerative and desirable.

Fifty-two families, including twelve of those who had packing-shed or cannery employment, reported that a member had worked in domestic service. Thirty of the families having nonfarm work of the types already referred to, and fifty-three other families, had members who had worked at one or more of a variety of miscellaneous occupations, such as washing dishes in a hotel or restaurant, helping in a poolroom or bar, shoe-shining, road work, irrigation work, carpentry, and junk collecting. A small number of the families owned trucks, in which they sometimes peddled produce or hauled firewood, and a few families operated small grocery stores or restaurants.[2]

A Work Projects Administration publication including a study of 300 migrant families in the Crystal City, Zavala County, area in the year 1938, reports as follows:

[1] Carlos E. Castañeda, "Some Facts on Our Racial Minority," *The Pan-American* (San Antonio, Texas), I (Oct., 1944), 4-5.

[2] Amber Arthun Warburton, Helen Wood, and Marian M. Crane, M. D., *The Work and Welfare of Children of Agricultural Laborers in Hidalgo County, Texas* (Washington, D. C.: U. S. Department of Labor, Children's Bureau, Publication 298, 1943), pp. 11-12.

Most of the nonfarm employment was obtained in Crystal City during the winter. From December to April, 7 to 9 per cent of all families were employed mainly in such work, while the number dropped to 3 per cent or less from July to September, at the peak of the migratory labor season.

For the most part, only menial, unskilled types of work at wages little higher than those for agricultural labor were open to the Mexicans. The occupation reported most frequently by women in Crystal City was that of maid or general houseworker. Typical earnings in this work were $2.00 per week plus $1.00 in kind.

Among the men, wages in nonagricultural occupations were somewhat higher. Several reported having earned $10.00 to $15.00 weekly working in an ice factory or hauling ice to the loading platforms during the spinach season. Auto mechanics and helpers earned from $1.50 to $7.50 per week. A service-station attendant and a gasoline-truck driver earned about $10.00 per week each.

Several Mexicans had businesses of their own. The most prosperous of these, a store owner, reported net earnings averaging $100.00 per month through the entire year. Average earnings from miscellaneous work in Crystal City, however, were not much greater than average income from agricultural work.[3]

In April, 1945, the State's major industry—the petroleum industry—employed less than 3 per cent of Latin American workers; and in almost every instance the Latin American, regardless of education, ability, or length of service, was being refused promotion entirely, or limited in promotion to a few of the lesser paid, semi-skilled jobs.

The worker of Mexican descent in the oil industry is usually employed as a laborer and assigned to work under the direct supervision of an Anglo American foreman. He digs ditches, cleans storage tanks and oil spills, and performs any and all of the hard, menial, and back-breaking jobs. On rare occasions, Latin Americans are assigned to lend assistance to workers in skilled classifications, such as pipe-fitter, carpenter, or electrician. But, in these instances, the job classification of the Latin American is not changed, nor his rate of pay increased

[3] Selden C. Menefee, *Mexican Migratory Workers of South Texas* (Washington, D. C.: Federal Works Agency, Work Projects Administration, Division of Research, U. S. Government Printing Office, 1941), p. 36.

to the rate paid Anglo American workers performing the same task.

Occasionally, and in a limited number of oil refineries, Latin Americans are promoted to such jobs as janitors, truck helpers, truck drivers, and laboratory bottle washers. However, such promotions are so rare that they serve only to point up the infrequency of such opportunities and to emphasize the limited number and inferior quality of jobs which the industry considers "suitable" to Latin American workers.

It is interesting to note that even these limited job opportunities occur only within one branch of the petroleum industry, the refinery branch. The pipeline and production branches rarely employ workers who are not Anglo Americans. Discrimination against both Latin American and Negro workers seems to be the prevailing rule in pipeline and production operations.

Generally speaking, the conditions of Latin American workers in the few oil refineries where they are employed closely parallel the conditions of Negro workers. Both usually receive a wage several cents per hour less than the wage paid to Anglo Americans in the same job classification. The Latin American and the Negro worker are not permitted to use the drinking fountain or the toilet and bathing facilities provided for the Anglo Americans. Often, the Latin American is not permitted to punch the same time clock or to receive his pay through the same window as the Anglo American. Safety and sanitation provisions established for Anglo Americans are frequently denied both Latin American and Negro workers, and the complaints registered as a result thereof are given scant consideration.

One major oil company, during 1944, constructed a hydroflouric acid alkalization unit at one of its Gulf Coast refineries. As the process requires the use of deadly hydrofluoric acid, the company provides ample bathing facilities for the operating personnel, all of whom are Anglo Americans. Special face masks, rubber gloves, and other protective clothing are also provided for these employees, who are allowed time to bathe at the end of each shift.

A Latin American worker was assigned to care for the protective clothing of the workmen, to serve as janitor at their bath house, and to do general clean-up work in the alkalization plant. Although he had to handle acid-soaked clothing, and despite the fact that his duties required frequent contact with the alkalization plant and, as a result, frequent exposure to the danger of acid burns, he was consistently denied the protective clothing and bathing privileges granted to the Anglo American operating crew.

In the spring of 1945, the President's Committee on Fair Employment Practices ordered the Shell Oil Company to upgrade three Latin Americans, on the basis of seniority, in its Deer Park Refinery. The contract between the Shell and the union relegated Latin Americans to certain types of jobs, and their opportunities for advancement under the contract were greatly inferior to those of Anglo American employees. The FEPC not only ordered the upgrading of the three Latin Americans, but also directed the union and the company to revise their contract so as to comply with the Fair Employment Practices Act. On the last day allowed for the upgrading, the company advanced the three men, whereupon the union organization in the plant went on a wildcat strike in protest. The strike was in violation of the established policy of the oil workers' union, and the CIO International opposed it.

In March, 1946, it was reported that twenty Latin American veterans of World War II had been employed by a Gulf Coast refinery, but at a wage of fifteen cents per hour less than that paid Anglo Americans in the same job classification: Latins, 91 cents per hour; Anglos, $1.06.

The railroads of Texas afford scant opportunity for gainful employment to workers of Latin American origin or descent. Railroad operating personnel are made up of Anglo Americans, and the practice of excluding Latin Americans from such occupations as railroad engineers, firemen, brakemen, and con-

ductors has been intensified by the refusal of the Railroad
Brotherhood group of unions to extend membership to either
Latin Americans or Negroes. Railroad track repair and maintenance work performed under labor agreements with the
Railway Maintenance of Ways Union does provide many jobs
for Latin Americans, but always in the nature of low-paid,
unskilled labor supervised by Anglo American foremen.

The State's meat packing industry has, for a long time, been
the source of considerable employment for Latin Americans.
In May, 1945, approximately 10 per cent of the workers
employed by meat packers were of Mexican descent. At those
packing plants in which labor organizations have been established and collective bargaining agreements consummated, discrimination against both Latin Americans and Negroes has
been greatly reduced. The organized plants now provide for
the upgrading of all workers upon a basis of ability and seniority and for the payment of the same wage to all workers within
a classification, regardless of race, creed, color, or national
origin.

In the unorganized packing plants where labor agreements
do not exist, Latin American workers are not given the same
job opportunities, nor do they receive the same rates of pay as
do the Anglo Americans employed. One of the large packing
companies operating in Texas has the unenviable record of
using race prejudice to defeat the organizational efforts of the
workers. So far, its tactics have been successful, and the
workers, both Anglo and Latin American, are underpaid and
ill treated as a result.

In further substantiation of the statement made by Castañeda, it was reported in April, 1945, that the aircraft plants
in Texas—Consolidated at Fort Worth and North American
at Dallas—each employed a very limited number of Latin
American workers. It was estimated that approximately 3 per
cent of the total employed at the Consolidated plant, and one
per cent at the North American plant, were Latin Americans.
Although the collective bargaining agreements at both plants

provided for the upgrading of all workers upon a basis of seniority, the companies' long-held policy of employing a minimum of Latin Americans makes the new contractual rights of labor of little value to Latin American workers.

Also, in the Dallas area, a brief survey reveals that eight large branch factories, producing nationally advertised motors, tires, batteries, electrical appliances, and aircraft, have consistently barred Latin Americans from employment.

Prior to the outbreak of the war, job opportunities within the business section of Fort Worth were open to Latin Americans only in fields where the work was extremely undesirable. Girls of Mexican ancestry were employed in poultry processing plants as poultry pickers, and in one plant processing peanuts. A few months before the war, a large downtown cafeteria employed a group of young Latin American boys to serve as bus boys. After the outbreak of the war, and because of the manpower shortage, one of the leading Fort Worth hotels employed Latin American girls as elevator operators. Following the lead of the hotel, several of the downtown office buildings are now utilizing the services of Latin American girls on the elevators. Changes of a similar nature have taken place in cities throughout Texas.

While the lack of education might be advanced as one reason for the widespread employment of Latin Americans in the most difficult and least remunerative capacities, this does not explain the situation fully nor satisfactorily. There are too many instances where Latin Americans have been denied positions which they were competent to handle, or when employed, denied opportunities for advancement, simply because they happened to be of Mexican extraction.

At the beginning of the war, when the largest airplane repair shops in the world were opened at Kelly Field in San Antonio, and 35,000 civilian workers were employed, mechanics and mechanics' helpers were in great demand. Training schools were established under government supervision, and those who attended were both Anglo and Latin Americans. After identical instruction, the graduates of the schools were employed at Kelly Field, on an equal basis, as mechanics' helpers. Within a reasonable length of time, the Anglo Americans were advanced, some of them repeatedly, but the Latin Americans, despite the fact that they were in many instances more proficient in their trade than the Anglos, were retained at the lowest level of mechanics' helpers. When the matter was called to the attention of the Commanding Officer, relief was immediately forthcoming, and it was made clear that advancement would be strictly on the basis of merit.

High school and even college graduates, if they are of Mexican descent, often find it difficult to secure employment in the field of their choice. The Spanish-teaching program in Texas public schools has been retarded by lack of qualified teachers, yet young Texans with a native knowledge of Spanish, and graduates of the State's teacher-training institutions, have run up against the blank wall of prejudice in many school districts and have been forced, at length, into other employment. It is a rare occasion when a Latin American stenographer, efficient though she may be, finds herself acceptable as an employee to any but a Latin American business man or a firm engaged in foreign trade.

To cite an instance, the United States Employment Service office in Austin, one day in November, 1945, received a telephone call from a woman department-head at the University of Texas. She expressed the desire to employ a trained secretary-assistant and was told that, fortunately, the application of a young lady who possessed all the required qualifications had just been received and that she held a degree from the University of Texas. The prospective employer was delighted, and inquired as to the girl's name. When informed that it was "Martínez," she exclaimed: "Why, I wouldn't have a Mexican in my office! I want a white girl!"

As evidence of the fact that the income level for Latin American families is consistently lower than that of Anglo Americans, reference may be made to a study published by the

Bureau of Business Research of the University of Texas in April, 1943, which constitutes a progress report on surveys made in the years 1941 and 1942.

Questionnaires were distributed through the public schools, and thus a true cross section of the population was secured. Response was purely voluntary. In the year 1942, a total of 1,562 replies was received from Latin American families residing in Brownsville, El Paso, Harlingen, Laredo, McAllen, and Mercedes, communities in which they comprise a large percentage of the total population.

In no case did a Latin American family report an annual income in excess of $2,249.00. The average size of such families reporting was 6.2 persons. In comparison, the Anglo American families responding averaged only 4.6 persons and reported incomes ranging to more than $5,000.00. No indication of the occupations engaged in is given in the study.[4]

It is clear under the Federal Constitution that all persons must be afforded equal protection of the laws. This means that a law cannot be made to apply to one arbitrarily selected group, such as a race or cultural group. Therefore, in considering laws protecting the rights of minority groups, if we are to be realistic, we must limit the scope of regulation to such provisions as have a reasonable chance of adoption. And, furthermore, the regulations must apply to all persons similarly situated, and this would, of course, include Negroes, as well as persons of Mexican, English, German, Jewish, or other ancestry.

While social discriminations are onerous and insulting to persons arbitrarily discriminated against, they are not so self-perpetuating or so far-reaching in their effects as are discriminations in employment opportunities. Perhaps the major cause of discrimination of all types is difference in economic status. Unfair employment practices result in a perpetuation of this economic difference. Therefore, many persons who would

[4] *Comparison of Family Income and Expenditures for Five Principal Budget Items in Twenty Texas Cities,* The University of Texas, Bureau of Business Research, Austin, 1943.

consider legislation condemning refusal of service in restaurants and theaters impracticable or unenforceable would favor legislation to protect job opportunities for all American citizens on an equal basis.

Unfair practices on the part of either management or the unions can be eliminated, in my opinion, by the enactment of a statute along the following lines:

No corporation engaged in manufacturing, commerce, transportation, or exploring for, mining or processing of minerals or petroleum, and employing twenty-five (25) persons or more, shall refuse employment to, discharge, or discriminate against any person in compensation or in other terms or conditions of employment because of such person's national origin, language, or ancestry; nor shall any labor union deny full membership, rights, and privileges to any person, expel any person from membership, or discriminate against any member, employer, or employee because of his national origin, language, or ancestry.

This statute should be supported by proper sanctions.

Chapter 11

The Story of Cotton

COTTON WAS KING in Texas for many years, and is still a mighty factor in the economy of the State. The story of cotton is a fascinating one—fascinating, yet terrifying in its effects upon those who actually perform the labor.

The old Cotton Belt of Texas begins in the black lands that reach from the Red River between Clarksville, about eighty-five miles northeast of Dallas, and the west limit of Grayson County southwestward in a band of gradually decreasing width.

In the vicinity of San Antonio, the land becomes less black, and cotton production is spotty in Frio, Medina, and Atascosa Counties. This far south the cotton area is no longer a band of heavy production, but is a diffused, moderately productive area which embraces southeast Texas to the Gulf Coast. In San Patricio and Nueces Counties, near Corpus Christi, cotton production is high. Then up the Gulf Coast northeasterly it declines, but shows a surge of increased production in Wharton and Fort Bend Counties on the Brazos River.

Now, a little less than half of Texas' cotton is raised in the old Cotton Belt region; once it produced nearly all. However,

[1] The bulk of the material in this chapter was gathered by the author through personal attendance at, and active participation in, more than twenty county, district, and statewide meetings on farm labor all over the State of Texas, beginning with the original planning meeting held at College Station on November 28, 1944, and through personal visits to Farm Labor Supply Centers and reception centers.

the old brown loam of the Brazos bottom, the black land of the north, and the sandy loams of the coastal plain, tired with half a century or more of cotton production, still produce about 4.5 per cent of the world's supply, and about one-ninth of United States production.

The river bottoms region has seen three eras of farm economy: the Era of Slavery, *de jure;* the Era of Tenancy, which degenerated after the turn of the century into an era of slavery, *de facto;* and the Era of Tractor and Migrant. In each case, what the farm laborer gained in freedom, he lost in economic security.

At the close of the war between the states, more than 182,000 Negro slaves in Texas were freed, and these, constituting nearly a third of the population of the State, became, for the most part, sharecroppers.[2] In 1880, as Texas was becoming the leading cotton-producing region in the United States, 37.6 per cent of its farms were tenant-operated; by 1890, 41 per cent; by 1900, 49.7 per cent; by 1910, 52.6 per cent; and by 1920, 53.3 per cent.

Of this situation, Carey McWilliams says:

> The increase in land values after 1900 not only made the lot of the average tenant unendurable, but it also converted the sharecropper into a farm laborer paid in kind. Even among the tenants it was noted that three types characterized the group: a third were fairly successful; a third were on the verge of poverty; and at the bottom was a "migratory thriftless body of men not unlike the casual unskilled workers of our cities."[3]

During the past forty years, the center of cotton production in Texas has moved steadily westward, and today the area of heaviest yield is in the northwest sector of the State. Running through this country is the Cap Rock Escarpment, which extends in an irregular line from the northeast corner of the Panhandle to Martin County. Through much of its course the Cap Rock is an abrupt lift of the earth's surface of 300 to almost

[2] Carey McWilliams, *Ill Fares the Land* (Boston: Little, Brown and Company, 1944), p. 209.

[3] *Ibid.,* p. 210. Quoted by permission of the publisher, Little, Brown and Company.

1,000 feet. Below are the remnants known as buttes and rough lands, which gradually soften to the gently rolling prairies of Middle West and North Central Texas. Above the escarpment is a vast and level plain without hill or dale except where the Canadian and the tributaries of the Brazos and Red Rivers make their descent from the high plain to the lower rolling prairies.

If two parallel lines are drawn along the 99th and 103rd Meridians, and two along the 32nd and 35th Parallels, a parallelogram is circumscribed which embraces the heaviest cotton producing region of the world. (See map showing cotton production in Texas, in Chapter XIII.) It covers about one-sixth of the area of Texas, and produces about 4.5 per cent of the world's supply. This includes Lubbock, on the southerly part of the High Plains, called the South Plains, and some of the rolling prairies below the Cap Rock. Unlike the soil of the old Cotton Belt, the surface is brown earth or sandy loam. Much of the land was, until recently, in pasturage. It was then, and still is to a large extent, owned in vast tracts.

The *Texas Almanac* sums up the situation in these words:

> Until the late '80s, the crop-growing industries expanded in the eastern part of the state, while the beef cattle industry developed in the south and west. Thereafter, the rapid retreat of the cattle industry before the cotton farmer began. The last decade of the last century and the first decade of the present century witnessed the spread of the cotton farmer over Middle West Texas, and the two decades, 1910-1930, saw the development of the Great Plains area as a producer of hard wheat and cotton.[4]

As early as the eighteen-nineties, Latin Americans from both sides of the Rio Grande were following the cotton harvest afoot in East Texas, returning to their homes in four or five months. Thus, the beginning of migratory labor, combined with the rapid mechanization of farming, sounded the death knell of the tenancy system in Texas. That by 1943 sharecroppers constituted a very small minority on Texas farms is shown by the 1943-44 *Texas Almanac*:

[4] *Texas Almanac and State Industrial Guide* (Dallas: A. H. Belo Corporation, 1944), p. 138. Quoted by permission of the publisher.

Sharecroppers

1930 205,122
1935 76,468
1940 .... 39,821 [5]

As a natural consequence, the average size of Texas farms has increased, the trend being toward larger tracts, machine-cultivated and migrant-harvested:

Average Acreage

1930 ....'........ 251.7
1935 .... 274.6
1940 .... 329.4 [6]

As Carey McWilliams says:

The rapid expansion of Texas agriculture was primarily responsible for the great influx of Mexicans from 1900 to 1930. "Cotton picking suits the Mexican," was the unanimous opinion of Texas growers. . . . As early as 1911, it was not "an uncommon sight to see long trains of Mexicans in small wagons en route to the cotton fields." The use of Mexican labor was particularly striking in the newly developed cotton fields, where the plantation system was not deeply entrenched. Mr. Remsen Crawford in *Current History* for February, 1930, accurately described the situation:

"In the unirrigated plains regions of Texas and Oklahoma millions of acres formerly used as ranges for cattle and sheep and goats are being cultivated in cotton, mainly for non-resident landlords, by Mexican tenants, or hired workers, living in miserable shacks. . . . New cotton gin plants have sprung up everywhere. Old towns have greatly increased in size, and new ones have been built. The bulk of the work of making and gathering this cotton is done by Mexicans imported from over the border. As one gazes on these boundless fields one cannot help thinking of the need for agricultural relief because of the great surplus of cotton and other crops being produced. And yet the government, while expending vast sums in converting grazing areas into cotton lands, is at the same time permitting the importation of hundreds of thousands of alien Mexicans to enlarge this surplus on these same lands."[7]

[5] *Ibid.*, p. 139.
[6] *Ibid.*
[7] McWilliams, *op. cit.*, p. 248. Quoted by permission of the publisher, Little, Brown and Company.

From the beginning, it has been the big planters in Texas who encouraged the importation of labor from Mexico. The reason, of course, is obvious, and was frankly stated by one Texan in testimony before the House Committee on Immigration and Naturalization in 1926, as quoted by Carey McWilliams:

"Mr. Chairman, here is the whole situation in a nutshell. Farming is not a profitable industry in this country, and in order to make money out of it, you have to have cheap labor. In order to allow landowners now to make a profit off their farms, they want to get the cheapest labor they can find, and if they get the Mexican labor, it enables them to make a profit. That is the way it is along the border, and I imagine that is the way it is anywhere else."[8]

Other tributes to the Mexican laborer—characterized by McWilliams as "an unseemly lust for his services"—upon which the Mexican has never been able to capitalize, have been phrased thus: "The Mexican has put Texas on the map agriculturally" (*Literary Digest,* July 17, 1930). "His labors are the basis of that pyramid of economic prosperity which the southwest so proudly displays" (*Century,* January, 1926). " 'Yes, sir,' said the secretary of the San Antonio Chamber of Commerce, 'we are dependent upon Mexican farm labor, and we know it. Mexican farm labor is rapidly proving the making of this state.' "[9]

According to the Texas State Employment Service, the number of Latin American migratory workers increased in Texas until 1937, the peak year. Estimates as to the maximum number of migrants ever to follow the crops over the State vary from 250,000 to 400,000. No one actually knows, for the migrants have always been, and are now, a completely unorganized labor group. It is known, however, that the available seasonal labor supply in Texas has been greatly reduced since 1937, for which the Texas State Employment Service advances the following reasons:

(1) Inter-state migration, chiefly to the Michigan beet fields.

(2) Repatriation movement, through which 6,268 Mexican agricul-

[8] *Ibid.,* p. 249.
[9] *Ibid.,* p. 248.

tural workers returned to Mexico between January 1, 1939, and August, 1940.

(3) Tightening of immigration restrictions along the Texas-Mexico border.

(4) Inclination of cotton pickers in Brownsville area to remain at home and round out twelve months of work through diversion into local industries.

(5) Alien registration law requiring presence at legal residence.

(6) Sedentary effect of Farm Security Administration camps upon migratory labor when opportunity to enjoy semi-permanent housing under decent conditions served as an inducement to migrants to settle down and try to find local jobs.

(7) Opportunities in defense activities.

(8) Selective Service.

To these reasons may be added one more: the fact that, in the summer of 1943, the Mexican Government put a ban on the movement of Mexican agricultural labor into Texas, because of discriminatory treatment accorded some Mexican nationals, since which date there have been no Mexican national migrants to come into the State legally.

The net result was that the farm population of Texas decreased by some 260,000 to 300,000 between 1940 and 1944, principally because of Selective Service and employment in war industries; yet the farmers were called upon to produce 37.5 per cent more than in 1940; and with migratory labor more essential than ever before, the maximum number of such workers available was 100,000, of whom some 85 per cent were persons of Mexican descent already resident in Texas.

The average annual income for these families, from all sources, has increased from the $365.00 reported by the Children's Bureau in 1941,[10] to approximately $950.00 in 1944, as estimated by various federal agencies. This represents a substantial increase in three years time, but, as Joseph N. Cowen,

[10] Amber Arthun Warburton, Helen Wood, and Marian M. Crane, M. D., *The Work and Welfare of Children of Agricultural Laborers in Hidalgo County, Texas* (Washington, D. C.: U. S. Department of Labor, Children's Bureau, publication 298, 1943), p. 15.

Area Representative, War Food Administration, stated in quoting the figure: "I submit that $1,000.00 is not an adequate family income under today's cost of living by any standard you may wish to measure it. Certainly, it will not permit children whose labor contributes appreciably to the family income to attend school regularly."[11]

By a 1943 Congressional Act, re-enacted on February 14, 1944, the Farm Labor Office, Extension Service, Texas Agricultural and Mechanical College, inherited the routing and placement of migratory labor in Texas. During the 1944 crop year, Farm Labor officials became increasingly aware of the fact that the farm labor program was not operating to obtain the maximum utilization of available manpower. In an effort to analyze and correct the situation, the various problems encountered were listed. By the end of the year, it was apparent that the major obstacles to the efficient working of the program were as follows:

First, lack of understanding of the purpose of the Emergency Farm Labor Program by migrants.

Second, lack of confidence of the migrants in the personnel of the Farm Labor Office which resulted in: (a) leaving an area of work before completing the job; (b) loss of time by going to another area too soon; (c) failure to go to area suggested by field man; (d) loss of much valuable and needed manpower.

Third, poor standards of living among some Latin American and Mexican National migrants caused by economic and educational disadvantages resulted in discrimination, in some cities, against *all* migratory farm workers because of the undesirable habits of some of them.

Fourth, lack of preparation on the part of farmers and communities to provide adequate facilities with which to receive and care for migratory farm workers, such as: (a) housing and sanitary facilities in communities and on farms; (b) eating

[11] *Minutes of Professional Workshop,* State Department of Education, Austin, March 19-24, 1945.

facilities in communities; (c) lack of sufficient water and fuel supplies; (d) lack of recreational and religious facilities; (e) failure to provide suitable parking and camping space in communities.

Fifth, lack of understanding and appreciation of the migrants' position in our agricultural economy as shown by: (a) segregation and signs at public places posted so as to have the effect of discrimination; (b) lack of consideration and understanding on the part of some law enforcement officers.

Sixth, transportation and other economic problems have resulted in too large crews which cannot be placed very rapidly.[12]

The Latin American migrants live, for the most part, in South Texas, or south of a line drawn east and west through San Antonio. The usual pattern of migration begins with cotton in the Rio Grande Valley in early summer, up to the Coastal Bend area around Corpus Christi as the cotton matures there in July and August, then on to Central and North Texas for cotton, and across the State for the cotton on the Plains during October, November, and December; back from West Texas for the citrus fruit and bean harvest in the Valley, on up to Raymondville and Robstown for onions and vegetables; then the cycle with cotton begins all over again. Some 55,000 to 60,000 of the total number of migrants go into West Texas each year during the October-December season.

The migrants, naturally, are primarily intent upon making a living. Having been guided more by custom than specific direction in the past, the laborers, in many instances, failed to take the advice of County Agricultural Agents and Migratory Field Assistants of the Farm Labor Office during the 1944 migration. They depended, instead, on letters and telegrams from farmers by whom they had previously been employed. The result was that, while there was still work to be done

12 *T. E. F. L.* 20 [Texas Emergency Farm Labor Letter No. 20, addressed to all County Agricultural Agents], Farm Labor Office, Extension Service, Texas Agricultural & Mechanical College, College Station, January 5, 1945.

PLATE X

MIGRATORY FARM LABOR
RECEPTION CENTER
Brady, Texas

This shows the inside of the shed. On these concrete blocks are gas burners, and you will note the water faucets with concrete drains between each stove stand. You will also note the building is well lighted with electricity.

Above: This shows part of the grounds and a view of part of the shed.

Picture of women's rest room. It has two commodes and three showers and a concrete floor, well drained. There is one like it on the other side of the building for the men.

*Photographs Courtesy Farm Labor Office,
Extension Service, Texas A. & M. College*

in the Valley, the laborers moved on to the Corpus Christi area, arriving there a week or two weeks in advance of the time the cotton was actually ready to be picked, thus losing much valuable time and money, making themselves a burden on the community, and leaving farmers in the Valley with an unharvested crop. This process was repeated as they moved to each succeeding section of the State.

Occasionally, the County Agent in Hidalgo County, for example, was able to convince a crew leader, by a long distance call to the County Agent in Nueces County, that the cotton in Nueces County would not mature for ten days, despite urgent letters the crew leader had received from farmers in Nueces County who were concerned principally about having sufficient labor when their cotton was ready for picking. In such an event, the crew leader was induced to spend that much more time in assisting the farmers of Hidalgo County, and was still able to arrive in Nueces County in ample time to harvest the cotton there.

But in the majority of cases, the migrants failed to take the advice of County Agents, who receive weekly, and in peak seasons daily, reports on the condition of crops all over the State, the number of laborers needed, and other information.

In an effort to devise a workable solution to all the problems involved in securing the maximum utilization of available labor, and one that would be to the mutual satisfaction and profit of farmers and migrants, the directors of the Farm Labor Office, in a statewide meeting at College Station on November 28, 1944, sought the advice, suggestions, and co-operation of farmers, laborers, ginners, the Catholic Church, Latin American civic and fraternal organizations, and representatives of State and Federal agencies interested specifically in the problems either of Latin Americans or of agriculture.

Six additional planning meetings were held during the month of December in Sinton, Coleman, Haskell, Lubbock, Lamesa, and Big Spring, with representatives of the same groups and others, such as chambers of commerce. As a result of these meetings, by the first of January, 1945, the Farm Labor Office had formulated an intensive educational program for both farmers and migrants, which was vigorously promoted and which will be discussed in detail later.

First, however, let us look more closely into the problems encountered by migratory laborers, and see how certain conditions affect the utilization of labor.

Heretofore, the migrants have been accustomed to travel in family groups, in individual jalopies; but with the wartime shortage of cars, tires, and gasoline, the size of the groups or crews has increased and traveling has been done in trucks owned by a crew leader. The result is that in 1944 migrants traveled in groups as large as sixty-five, which created a difficult situation for the small farmer having no need for so many workers.

The number of Latin Americans who live in the West Texas cotton area are relatively few in comparison with the number living in the southern and southwestern portions of the State. No county in the region reflects a Latin American population of more than 25 per cent, according to Dr. Little's study.[13]

Generally speaking, the Latin American migratory worker going into West Texas is regarded as a necessary evil, nothing more nor less than an unavoidable adjunct to the harvest season. Judging by the treatment that has been accorded him in that section of the State, one might assume that he is not a human being at all, but a species of farm implement that comes mysteriously and spontaneously into being coincident with the maturing of the cotton, that requires no upkeep or special consideration during the period of its usefulness, needs no protection from the elements, and when the crop has been harvested, vanishes into the limbo of forgotten things—until the next harvest season rolls around. He has no past, no future, only a brief and anonymous present.

[13] Wilson Little, *Spanish-Speaking Children in Texas* (Austin: The University of Texas Press, 1944), p. 18.

This is an average picture of what happened in 1944. On one Saturday afternoon in October of that year, 496 migratory labor trucks were counted on the streets of Lubbock, the "capital" of the cotton-raising Plains area. Lubbock is a city of between 40,000 and 50,000 inhabitants. Each truck carried an average of fifteen migrants, of all ages, which meant an estimated total of 7,440 migrants who had come to Lubbock to spend the weekend, seek new opportunities for employment, purchase their groceries and other supplies for the following week, and find a little recreation.

Large crews have been known to spend as much as $100.00 in one day, just in the purchase of groceries, during the peak of the season. But to make a very conservative estimate, let us suppose that each of the 496 crews in Lubbock that weekend spent an average of $25.00. That is a total of $12,400.00 income to business places of all kinds in one weekend.

Yet Lubbock had made no provision whatever for taking care of this influx of people, which occurs regularly every fall, and every weekend during each fall. There was no place where they might park their trucks, take a bath, change their clothes, even go to the toilet.

Conditions in towns throughout that section of the State were, in 1944, more or less the same as in Lubbock. In some places they were even worse. In Lamesa it was stated in the meeting that toilet facilities in the City Hall, which the migrants could use most conveniently, were locked up at noon on Saturdays, and filling station facilities were used except where the owners prohibited it because of the objections of customers. As a result, the migrants were forced to disregard the lack of toilet facilities, and an epidemic of dysentery, which originated among them, spread through the entire town of Lamesa and into the schools.

As a natural consequence, the laborers came into the nearest town on Saturday, after picking cotton all week, and without having had access to bathing facilities. Their appearance and hygienic condition were as unattractive as would be those of any other group of people going through a similar experience. There being no facilities available to them in the towns, they remained in a state of uncleanliness, and were refused entrance into or service in public places of business and amusement, such as cafes, barbershops, and in some instances theaters. Some of the larger towns, however, have theaters in the "Mexican" section of town, where Spanish-dialogue films are exhibited.

A letter received by the Governor of Texas during the 1944 cotton season illustrates the reactions of migrants toward such discriminatory treatment:

Dear Mr. Governor:

At the present I am here at Wilson, Texas with 80 hands pulling cotton. The first day we went to Lubbock, Texas some of my hands were told that they did not sell or served Mexicans at certain places. . . .

I can't say that everybody is the same, because where I come from they let us go anywhere we wish. I am from Huntsville, Texas. The hands that I have are from Bryan, Texas, and they like Mexicans. . . . Let me ask you this what would the farmers of west Texas do if the Mexicans would not come to West Texas and pick their cotton? . . .

Now Mr. Coke, I tell you, do we have the rights of any Americans or are we just like nothing?

Esteban Velasco.

As an instance of how conditions in the towns affect the maximum utilization of labor, we may consider the story of a Migratory Field Man who was stationed in Hockley County during the 1944 crop season. A certain farmer in the county, who lived near the town of Ropesville, was badly in need of a large crew of pickers. The farmer got into contact with the Field Man, and late one evening the agent took a crew leader and two or three laborers out to the farm from Levelland, the county seat. They found a good crop of cotton, acceptable housing, agreed on a price, and promised to come out from Levelland to work the next day.

On the return trip, passing through Ropesville, the agent and the laborers stopped at the only cafe in town that was open. It was about eight o'clock on a cold night, and they wanted a cup of coffee. There was no one else in the cafe. The owner

came up to them and said: "What do you want?" The Field
Man responded: "I want a cup of coffee. I don't know what
the other boys want. They may want sandwiches." The owner
said: "I don't serve Mexicans." To which the agent replied:
"Well, now, these boys are out here to help the farmers harvest their crops. They have just agreed to come out tomorrow
to work for Mr. Blank. I don't see anything so elegant about
your cafe, and I don't see why you can't serve us a cup of çoffee."
The owner stated flatly: "I'll serve you, but I don't serve Mexicans." "No," the agent replied, "you can't serve me either,"
and they walked out.

The laborers were angry, of course, and the result was that
they did not return to the farm the next day, and the farmer
did not have his cotton picked until much later, when his crop,
through exposure, had greatly deteriorated in quality. Ropesville was the nearest town, the town to which they would have
to go on weekends, and since they were not welcome there,
they could easily find some other place to pick cotton.

It was necessary to station a Migratory Field Assistant in
Big Spring during the entire month of October, 1944, to
straighten out difficulties within the town. The complaint
came into the Farm Labor Office that trucks were being
molested. On the highway leading into the city, the agent
found that the local officials had stationed a constable who was
flagging down all trucks and instructing them not to stop in
the town under threat of arrest. The result was that the few
trucks that did stop there had to go through the town and
park on a garbage dump outside the city; but the majority of
them did not stop in Big Spring; they didn't even stop in
Howard County, and the farmers in that region experienced
great difficulty in harvesting their crops.

As to facilities on the farms themselves, they were practically
nonexistent in 1944. Laborers were expected to camp in fields
and ditches or under bridges. Housing that was provided consisted for the most part of unrenovated barns and chicken
sheds. In contrast with this prevailing condition—which the

farmers themselves were frank to admit—there were a very few,
like the farmer who attended the meeting at Big Spring, who
had provided adequate housing with sanitary facilities. This
particular man had built one brick and hollow tile building,
80 feet by 16 feet, complete with toilets and shower baths, for
the housing of laborers, and had a duplicate building then
under construction. But for the most part, considering the
fact that cold weather comes early on the Plains, there was no
housing on the farms.

Six years ago, under the Farm Security Administration, an
effort was made to improve the housing situation through the
construction of ten Migratory Labor Camps, or Farm Labor
Supply Centers, as they came to be called under the supervision
of the War Food Administration. These camps, built on the
order of tourist courts, are located at McAllen, Weslaco, Raymondville, Robstown, Harlingen, Sinton, Crystal City, Prince-
ton, Lamesa, and Ropesville, only the last two named being in
West Texas. During the war, the camp at Crystal City was
used as a Japanese internment camp, but the other nine were
used for housing migrants.

The Robstown Farm Labor Supply Center has a capacity
of 1,200 people. As each family registers, its members receive
a thorough physical examination, and if medical or dental
treatment is indicated, it is given, free of charge. One building
contains a well-equipped clinic and living quarters for two
nurses, with an adjoining two-room "hospital" for the care of
mothers during childbirth.

There are two types of quarters in the camp, one being
small one-room apartments for housing up to five persons.
These apartments rent for $1.25 per week, and for the use of
the occupants there are provided ample community shower
bath and toilet facilities, and a large community laundry, complete with electric irons and sewing machines. For larger
families, there are available twenty-six four-room houses, each
with private bath, which rent for $2.25 per week.

The camp is divided into districts, and each district elects a representative to the Camp Council, which governs the camp. The Council sees to it that garbage is collected and properly disposed of, lawns mowed, and the buildings and grounds maintained in good order. It also arranges for recreation and religious services in the huge community center, which is well equipped for the purpose.

A nursery school for children under six years of age is conducted in the community center. The nurse in charge inspects each child each morning for lice, sores, sore eyes and throat, etc., and administers treatment whenever necessary. The nursery is equipped with small beds, tables, and chairs. The children play games, receive instruction in English, take naps, and are properly fed during the day while other members of the family are busy in the fields.

According to the camp manager, life in the camp is excellent training for the migrants, many of whom come in contact there for the first time with facilities such as flush toilets. As an indication of how their living standards are affected by the experience, a number of the families, after living temporarily in the camp, have settled permanently in Robstown, building small homes of perhaps two or three rooms, but in each house there is to be found at least a shower bath and a flush toilet, the first the family has ever owned. The self-government which the migrants enjoy in the camp is also a new and beneficial experience.

These migratory camps have obviated the necessity for individual housing facilities on the farms in the regions where they are located. The laborers go out from the camp each morning to the various farms and return to the camp at night. More camps of this type would go far toward relieving the housing situation in West Texas, where they would also contribute to the improvement of conditions in general.

The lack of religious facilities in West Texas constitutes a serious problem. The great majority of the Latin American migrants are of the Catholic faith. West Texas is largely Protestant, and there are many towns without Catholic churches and without the regular services of a priest. The normal events of birth, death, illness, and marriage take place among the migrants just the same while they are in West Texas as they do when they are in South Texas. The fact that it is many times impossible to attend church services, have babies baptized, or receive the last rites in the case of a dying person, contributes in no small way to the dissatisfaction of the laborers.

Practically without exception, the farmers and townspeople who attended each of the meetings in West Texas admitted existing conditions and agreed that improvements must be made, and immediately, if the 1945 cotton crop was to be harvested efficiently. The citizens of that region realized that the time had come when the position of the migrant in the agricultural economy of the State must be recognized with tangible improvements.

The program of the Farm Labor Office, as developed in the planning meetings described, and as later put into effect, heralded a new era in Texas agriculture. Through it, the hit-or-miss, catch-as-catch-can relation that had theretofore existed between farmer and migrant began to be superseded by a system of referral and placement, with the Farm Labor Office as the middleman operating to the economic advantage of both employer and employee.

In January, 1945, there was inaugurated, by County Agricultural Agents, a series of educational meetings, on a county and community basis, in all cotton-growing areas, for the purpose of acquainting farmers, local public officials, and citizens generally, with the seriousness of the farm labor problem and the imperative necessity for (a) improving housing on the farms; (b) providing reception facilities for migratory labor in community centers; (c) correcting mistreatment of labor by business and law enforcement interests; and (d) providing religious and recreational facilities for migrants.

Housing on the farms must, of necessity, be left up to individual farmers, but in connection with reception centers in the towns, the Farm Labor Office was able to offer material assistance to county and municipal authorities. Requirements to be met by local sponsors of such reception centers included (a) adequate sanitation facilities, including toilets and showers; (b) an adequate sanitary water supply; (c) buildings to provide a minimum amount of shelter; (d) adequate parking space; (e) the prohibition that the center should be used only by migratory labor during seasonal peaks of labor requirements, as a place where migrants could gather in awaiting placement by the County Agent, and as headquarters for the migrants while in the community on shopping and holidays; and (f) adequate fuel to be provided by local sponsors.[14]

As for its share, the Farm Labor Office offered to contribute to each community $300.00 to be spent for lease, alterations, and repair of properties, if needed; and, through the local County Agent's office, to provide for personnel to look after the property during peak periods, act as camp manager, guard, and placement officer. Title to the property was to rest with the community sponsors establishing the facilities.

Inasmuch as County Agents' offices are frequently located in court houses—and court houses, to the wary migrant, represent the "law"—this fact alone contributed to the incomplete success of the Farm Labor program in 1944. Migrants simply did not contact the County Agent, who could have assisted them in finding employment without delay. The presence of a placement officer, under the County Agent's supervision, in each local reception center proved to be most beneficial to the program in 1945.

In addition to assisting in the construction and operation of reception centers, the Farm Labor Office also agreed to pay fees for medical care for a migratory worker under these conditions: (a) the migratory worker must be at a reception center, traveling en route to a specific county under a County Agent's referral, or working on a placement made by the County Agent; (b) all cases paid for must be of an emergency nature; or when not of an emergency nature, it must be established that

14 *T. E. F. L.* 20, *op. cit.*

the migratory worker cannot receive necessary and proper treatment because of inability to pay for the services; (c) the County Agent must approve cases for which the Farm Labor Office is to pay before treatment is given; (d) the fees paid for the services rendered by doctors and hospitals should be in line with those regularly charged; (e) bills must be submitted to the County Agent, on approved cases, by the doctor or hospital, in duplicate, for his approval and transmittal to the Farm Labor Office for payment.[15]

Climaxing the program outline is the statement of the Farm Labor Office:

Plans for the construction of reception centers in communities should be submitted by the County Agent to the Extension State Farm Labor Office for approval by April 1, 1945. Construction should be completed at the earliest possible date. We expect to publicize in Spanish all the facilities established through the use of pictures and booklets, by the time migratory labor begins its movement early in the summer. It is important that this be given immediate attention. Pictures of reception centers must be available to the State Office by May 1, 1945.[16]

This was a beautiful program to contemplate, an unheard-of program for Texas. In action, it was even better. By March 15, 1945, ninety-seven communities had made definite commitments for the construction of reception centers. All of these did not materialize, for drought in the South Plains area reduced the cotton crop from the normal 700,000 acres to less than 300,000 acres. But by June 15, reception centers in forty-one towns had been completed. Unsuspected resources were tapped, unanticipated interest and activity were stimulated, and unprecedented ingenuity manifested itself. As a result, migratory laborers found working and living conditions in the cotton-growing areas vastly improved in 1945.

New construction was not possible in most instances, because of the exigencies of war, but new construction was not found to be necessary. Big Spring and Post erected new hollow tile

[15] Ibid.
[16] Ibid.

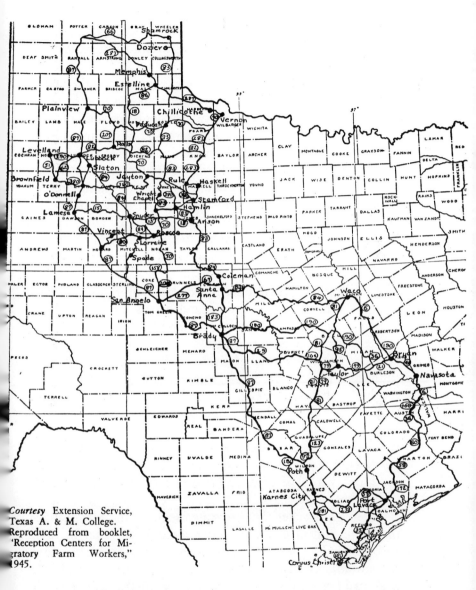

Courtesy Extension Service, Texas A. & M. College. Reproduced from booklet, 'Reception Centers for Migratory Farm Workers," 1945.

MAP SHOWING LOCATION OF RECEPTION CENTERS FOR MIGRATORY FARM WORKERS AND THE HIGHWAYS LEADING TO THESE CENTERS

Large dots indicate reception centers. The name of the town or city is given. Encircled numbers are the numbers of highways leading to the centers.

reception centers; but, for the most part, buildings already in existence and standing idle were converted into centers, the cost ranging from $600.00 to $10,000.00.

Granaries and fair buildings, through repairs and the installation of partitions and sanitary facilities, took a new lease on life. School buildings, long since abandoned because of consolidation of districts and the transportation of children to the towns for schooling, were refurnished and properly equipped. A tabernacle that once echoed with the sound of voices raised in praise and worship was reconditioned to play another role— a role upon which God undoubtedly looked with equal favor. In one community, the concrete foundations of an erstwhile C.C.C. camp remained, complete with sanitary connections. Low-cost housing units were constructed thereon and fixtures installed.

Something of the same sort took place with regard to housing on the farms. Where ways and means—and priorities— could not be found to build new structures, those already in existence were made serviceable and sanitary. In some instances, farmers with a relatively small amount of acreage in cultivation planned on a co-operative basis. For example, on the highway between Lorraine and Colorado City stands a school house that had been unoccupied for five years. The four or five farmers who live in the immediate vicinity converted its four classrooms and auditorium into four small apartments and recreation hall. Thus they were able to house comfortably a large crew of laborers for employment on all their farms.

These great material improvements are not the only changes that were evident to the migrants throughout Texas in 1945. A corresponding development was revealed in the thinking and the attitudes of many Texans; for farmers and townspeople alike had been awakened to the realization that migrants are people and that, being people, they merited more consideration than had been shown them in the past. Treatment accorded the cotton pickers improved tremendously in some counties,

such as Haskell, McClellan, Refugio, Wharton, and Calhoun,
In many others, a changing attitude was apparent. Unfortunately in some sections of the State, attitudes had not changed;
the people were not yet convinced.

But the educational process is essentially a two-sided affair,
and simultaneously with the meetings held with farmers and
other interested persons in the cotton-growing areas, Spanish-
speaking migratory field assistants were carrying the new
gospel to the workers while they were concentrated in South
Texas. Individually, and in groups, in barbershops, grocery
stores, and beer parlors, at fiestas and in their homes, at meetings in the Farm Labor Supply Centers and in churches, they
were informed as to their part in the farm labor program.

They were impressed with their importance to the harvesting of crops with which to feed and equip the nation, the men
in the armed forces, and our allies. They were acquainted with
the function of the Farm Labor Office and the manner in which
the County Agents and Migratory Field Assistants were prepared to enable them to earn more money. The necessity for
their working a full day at least five days a week was stressed.
The migrants were advised of the improved living conditions
they might expect to find prepared for them in 1945, and of
their responsibility in utilizing and profiting by those improvements. After reception centers were established, the migrants
were provided with copies of a booklet, "Centros de Recepción
para Obreros Ambulantes," describing each center and giving
specific directions for reaching it.

In a bilingual leaflet entitled "The Task of the Agricultural
Worker in the War," the migrants were told:

Last year there weren't nearly enough workers to get crops harvested
quickly, and the government says there will be many thousands less
agricultural laborers this year. That means all men, women, boys and
girls should go when and where they are needed most. Sometimes,
though, that may mean staying at home. Your own neighborhood or
county has first claim on you when crops are in the field to be gathered.
That's one of your duties as a citizen.

All of us must keep our agreements and whenever possible stay with a job until we have finished it. The farmer should keep his promise about pay and work to be done; and the worker must carry out his part of the bargain, too. Becoming tired of a contract or finding a better job doesn't justify breaking an agreement when work has been started. Living up to a contract is not only honorable; it's good business, and will help all workers get better opportunities and more advantages as time goes on.

Better working conditions, better treatment and more consideration for workers on farms are our aims. The farm labor program of the A. & M. College Extension Service is working every day to be of greater help to laborers on the road. Its main purpose is the more efficient use and placement of farm labor to help win the war and feed the starving people of Europe. This Service congratulates you on your fine job in harvesting last year's crops, and on your spirit of co-operation in your job. That job, though, still remains to be done this year; and your responsibility increases until Victory is finally won.

That the response received from the migrants equaled in sincerity and enthusiasm the reaction of farmers was demonstrated at the statewide conference held on January 11, 1946, at College Station, during which Dr. Ide P. Trotter, director of the Extension Service, Caesar Hohn, State Farm Labor Supervisor, and Migratory Field Assistants reported on the operation of the program during the 1945 crop year to representatives of the same groups and organizations who had participated in the planning meeting on November 28, 1944. Despite the unpredictable difficulties presented by the drought in West Texas and the hurricane in the Coastal Bend area, labor responded to direction and local citizens co-operated, to their mutual benefit.

The end of the war has not put an end to the activities of the Farm Labor Office, for in December, 1945, Congress extended its powers for another year. During the meeting on January 11, plans were laid for consolidating the gains realized in 1945 and intensifying efforts in counties which, for various reasons, failed to respond satisfactorily in that year. The tactics to be pursued are the same as those employed in 1945.

Special attention was devoted, in the January conference, to the matter of education for migratory workers, and particularly for their children. To enable the group to reach a concrete agreement, Dr. Trotter appointed a committee from the members of the conference, with Arnulfo Zamora, President General of the League of United Latin American Citizens, as chairman, to formulate recommendations for the consideration of the group.

The report of the committee embraced five suggestions, which were unanimously approved by the conference. The first was in the nature of a request that the Farm Labor Office, at an early date, secure from crew leaders as accurate information as possible regarding the age, sex, and grade in school of each migratory child; whether or not he or she can read English or Spanish, or both; place of residence; and how many months of each year the child is away from home following the crops.

The second recommendation was to the effect that as soon as such a census is compiled, and a logical "off season" ascertained when most of the children will be available for purposes of instruction, the proper authorities be petitioned to establish "off season" schools in order that children in agriculture may receive at least the rudiments of an education, as provided in the State's constitution.

A third recommendation requested the Farm Labor Office to consider the possibility of providing educational facilities within the reception centers. It was suggested that films, dealing with health and other subjects, with Spanish dialogue, could be exhibited; that phonograph records and Spanish-language radio programs could be utilized for educational purposes; and that intensive courses of instruction in the three "R's," citizenship, good manners, etc., patterned after the texts prepared and used by the Army, and similar to those employed in Mexico's anti-illiteracy campaign, could be introduced.

The other two recommendations called for the appointment of members of the conference to discuss with State educational authorities all the problems involved in providing instruction for migrants; and the request that the three State agencies who have already evidenced an active interest in the matter—the State Department of Education, A. & M. College, and the Good Neighbor Commission—join in calling a conference to discuss the problems and devise workable solutions.

For reasons "beyond its control," the Farm Labor Office was not 100 per cent successful in its program in 1945. But valuable groundwork has been laid, experience has highlighted both strong and weak points, and another year should see widespread improvement along all lines.

Chapter 12

Other Migratory Labor

ALTHOUGH COTTON represents the most important source of income for the majority of Latin American migratory workers, other seasonal agricultural labor rounds out the year's employment. During the winter and spring months, many of them engage in harvesting fruits and vegetables in the Lower Rio Grande Valley and Winter Garden Area. Some 20,000 migrants left Texas in 1944, and again in 1945, for the sugar beet fields of Michigan, Minnesota, Iowa, Wisconsin, Ohio, Illinois, Nebraska, Montana, Colorado, Wyoming, and North Dakota. Still others find their chief employment in sheep shearing, migrating to the cotton fields between shearing seasons.

Citrus fruits and vegetables, such as tomatoes, carrots, radishes, cabbage, beets, spinach, and broccoli, abound in the lush, irrigated Lower Rio Grande Valley, comprised of Hidalgo, Cameron, and Willacy Counties. It is to this section of the State that thousands of Latin Americans return when the cotton season is over. Despite the great productivity of the region, agricultural laborers find it difficult, even through the combined efforts of the entire family group, to make a living.

The Children's Bureau report on *The Work and Welfare of Children of Agricultural Laborers in Hidalgo County, Texas* states:

191

The inability of the families to earn a satisfactory living from agricultural work even in periods of peak harvest activity is illustrated by their low earnings in the winter-vegetable harvest. Since the study was made at the time of this harvest (January 15 to March 28, 1941), it was possible to obtain particularly detailed information on the families' work and wages in gathering winter vegetables. . . . Most of them worked in the vegetable fields, gathering, bunching, tying, or crating carrots, beets, or other vegetables, although some were employed in the citrus groves or in other farm and non-farm work.

The median earnings of the families from all types of employment came to only $6.90 for the week, and one-third of the families earned less than $5.00. For the 262 families who worked exclusively in farm labor during the sample week, median earnings were only $5.95. In contrast, the eighty families with some members employed at non-agricultural jobs had median earnings of $9.95.

Low rates of pay for field work, together with irregular employment, account for the families' small weekly earnings. Even at the height of the vegetable harvest, most workers probably averaged about three days' work per week. On days when they had employment, they often were away from home from early morning until late at night, but much of this time was unremunerated. Often workers spent several hours waiting at the packing house while the contractor received his orders for the day. Additional time was spent by them in riding to the fields, moving from field to field, and waiting at the end of the day to be taken home.

Even when several members of the family had fairly steady work, their combined labor did not offset the low piece rates. In the Gómez family, for example, which included six boys and their mother and grandmother, the 19-year-old boy, who was considered the chief wage earner, and two of his brothers, aged 17 and 14, worked six days during the representative workweek, pulling and tying carrots and beets at 12 cents for 72 bunches. The total working time of the three boys, excluding time off for meals and time spent in transportation, was, therefore, approximately 138 hours. Their combined weekly earnings, paid to the eldest boy, totaled $9.08, considerably more than most families were able to make in one week. Their average hourly earnings came to less than 7 cents.[1]

[1] Amber Arthun Warburton, Helen Wood, and Marian M. Crane, M. D., *The Work and Welfare of Children of Agricultural Laborers in Hidalgo County, Texas* (Washington, D. C.; U. S. Department of Labor, Children's Bureau, Publication 298, 1943), pp. 14-15.

Of the 342 families interviewed for the study, 202 had migrated during the cotton season just past, and 140 had remained in Hidalgo County. The nonmigratory families had earned a median cash income of $305.00 during the preceding twelve months, as compared with $365.00 earned by migratory families. The highest annual income reported by migratory families was $800.00. Fifteen families were in this bracket, but the majority of them fell far below that munificent figure, fourteen of the 202 earning less than $200.00, forty-nine earning less than $300.00, fifty-one earning less than $400.00. Earnings of the 140 nonmigratory families were consistently lower.

Two-thirds of the families of agricultural laborers in this study earned less than $400.00 during the year preceding the interview. These earnings represent the total cash earnings received from all types of private employment. The median earnings for the year were only $340.00, in spite of the comparatively large number of workers per family (3.8). One out of every eight families made less than $200.00.[2]

In other words, the weekly family income for two-thirds of the 342 families was $7.69; the median earnings per week were only $6.54; and one out of every eight families earned less than $3.85 per week in 1940.

The great Winter Garden Area, the most important spinach-growing district in the United States, centers around Crystal City, and embraces Maverick, Zavala, Dimmit, Webb, LaSalle, and Frio Counties. The rapid development of this area since 1924, like the mushroom growth of citrus groves and vegetable fields in the Valley since 1920, was made possible only by the wholesale importation of Mexican labor. In 1938, a study of 300 families of Latin American agricultural workers who considered Crystal City their permanent residence was made by the Division of Research, Work Projects Administration. In the resultant publication, *Mexican Migratory Workers of South Texas,* it is stated:

Most of the 1938 work histories of the 300 Mexican families studied had one element in common: more than nine-tenths of the families

[2] *Ibid.,* p. 15.

worked in spinach at some time during the winter harvest season, which
normally lasts from late November to the end of March. When all the
spinach was cut and shipped, 19 out of 20 families migrated north or
east to work in other crops. Almost a third got in a few weeks' work
in the Texas onion harvest before going on to beets or cotton. Over 60
per cent of the families worked in the sugar-beet fields throughout an
area extending from Michigan to Montana. A third of all the family
groups worked at picking cotton from July until late autumn. Almost
half of this latter group also found work in chopping cotton before the
picking season started.

These four crops dovetailed with one another so neatly that in only
one month of the year, April, did total family unemployment rise above
4 per cent. In spite of this regularity of employment, however, wages
were so low that many of the Crystal City families were in need at the
time of the survey.[3]

A consideration of the work patterns of the Crystal City
agricultural families is interesting because they differ somewhat
from the work patterns of families that regard other sections of
Texas as their permanent residence. The four principal crops
engaged in are spinach, sugar beets, cotton, and onions.

Work in the spinach crop is highly seasonal. Prior to harvest time
little hand labor is needed in the spinach fields because tractors and field
machinery are widely used. In the summer, when the weather is too hot
for many vegetable crops, the land is cultivated to prevent the growth of
weeds. Late in August or early in September the first plantings are
made. The seed, although sown with a grain drill, is in effect broadcast by means of an attachment to the drill. The borders, or ridges which
separate the beds, are usually built up by the use of a disc cultivator.
From planting until harvest—60 to 90 days, depending on the weather—
little labor is required except for controlling the flow of water through
the fields. No weeding is done, as a rule. Planting continues periodically
until the end of the year, so that the harvest is almost continuous during
the winter season. The industry depends heavily upon the large and
mobile supply of labor furnished by the Mexicans during this period. . . .
At least nine-tenths of the spinach laborers are "cutters" who work on
their knees in the fields, clipping the mature spinach plants and sorting

[3] Selden C. Menefee, *Mexican Migratory Workers of South Texas* (Washington,
D. C.: Federal Works Agency, Work Projects Administration, Division of Research,
U. S. Government Printing Office, 1941), pp. 12-13.

out defective leaves and weeds. The cutters, although they do the most
fatiguing type of work, are the lowest paid of the spinach workers.[4]

Under favorable conditions, an adult cutter can average
fifteen to twenty bushels of spinach a day. However, because
of decreasing yield per acre, irregularity of employment, and
the setting of higher standards of quality by the growers, it had
become almost impossible by 1938, for the cutters, who are paid
at the rate of five cents per bushel, to earn more than an average
of fifty cents per day.

During the calendar year 1938 the average weekly earnings of Crystal
City workers in the spinach harvest amounted to $3.13 per person in cash
and kind. One spinach job in six paid $5.00 or more per week, and one
in twenty-two paid $10.00 or more. A quarter of the jobs paid less than
$2.50 per week to each worker.[5]

Jobs in connection with the spinach harvest, to which the
figures quoted above apply, include, in addition to the cutting
operation, other types of labor, such as loading spinach onto
trucks, hauling it to loading platforms, unloading it, icing it,
loading it into freight cars, and icing and sealing the cars. "In
one family five members worked in the local spinach cannery
and each earned an average of about $3.60 per week."[6]

Here again it is the large growers, those who plant from
500 to 4,500 acres each, who demand and perpetuate this great
pool of cheap labor. During cool weather, a field of spinach
ready for harvesting may stand for as long as two weeks without damage; but in warm weather it must be harvested
immediately.

Sugar-beet work, which was found to be the most important
single source of income for more than half of the 300 families
studied in Crystal City, is likewise highly seasonal, three operations being involved. Families begin to leave the Winter
Garden area in early April, and from that time until late in
May, a continual stream flows northward to the beet fields.

[4] Ibid., p. 16.
[5] Ibid.
[6] Ibid.. p. 17.

The first operation consists of blocking and thinning, and takes place during May and June, requiring long hours of work. Blocking involves chopping out overcrowded plants so as to leave a tuft of beets at intervals of ten to twelve inches. Thinning is done by hand, and leaves only the strongest, healthiest plant in each tuft.

During the summer, one or two hoeings are required to keep the soil loose and free from weeds, and the pressure of time is not so great in this phase of the work.

The final operation consists of pulling and topping, which is the harvesting process. After the beets have been loosened by a horse-drawn lifter, they are pulled, then topped with a long knife. The harvest season occurs in October and early November.

During the slack seasons between operations, the migrants generally try to find other employment in either agricultural or nonagricultural work.

Almost half of the beet workers traveled in their own cars (in 1938), a quarter paid for their passage on other workers' trucks, a fifth traveled with labor contractors, and the rest rode with friends and relatives. The fare charged by truck drivers and contractors ranged from $10.00 upward per family, according to the beet workers; the usual rate was $10.00 per adult and $5.00 per child. One family of twelve paid $87.50 for a one-way passage to Iowa. Under this type of arrangement from 20 to 45 persons or more were sometimes crowded into a single truck, and the trip north was made in 40 to 50 hours without stopping except for gasoline and oil. At the end of the season several families who had gone north in trucks bought used cars in which to return to Texas.[7]

The fable that migrants "get rich" in the beet fields is effectively exploded by the earnings reported by the Crystal City laborers. Of the total of 188 families who engaged in beet work, 13 per cent earned less than $200.00 per family; 23 per cent earned less than $300.00; 14 per cent earned less than $400.00; 16 per cent earned less than $500.00; while only 9 per cent earned $1,000.00 or more. For individual workers, weekly

7 *Ibid.*, p. 21.

earnings during the seven-months period averaged $6.33 for forty-nine hours of work per week.[8]

The average cash earnings of Crystal City Mexicans from work in beets amounted to $400.00 per family, or $135.00 for each individual worker in 1938. One family in eight earned less than $200.00 from beet work. Income in kind (covering such items as rent, wood, and water) received while doing beet work brought the average earnings from this source up to a total of $439.00 per family. The average size of family among the beet workers was 5.6 persons.[9]

Inasmuch as detailed consideration has already been given to the conditions surrounding employment in the cotton fields of Texas, it will suffice, at this point, to note that cotton was second in importance only to beets as a source of summer employment among the 300 agricultural families studied in Crystal City. An even 100 of the families spent some time in chopping or picking cotton, and for eighty-seven of them, cotton was the chief source of income for the year 1938.

Of the 100 families who migrated to the cotton fields, twenty-nine earned less than $200.00; twenty-four earned less than $300.00; ten earned less than $400.00; fifteen earned less than $500.00; and only three families earned $1,000.00 or more.[10]

The average cash income of Crystal City families from cotton work amounted to $278.00 in 1938. Almost a third of the cotton-picking families earned less than $200.00 from this work. This was much lower than average income from sugar beets, in spite of the fact that there were 3.7 workers in the average cotton-picking family as compared with less than 3 workers in the typical family employed in beets. Annual earnings per worker in cotton averaged $75.00, or a little more than half as much as the average earnings per worker among Mexicans employed in sugar beets.[11]

Third in line as a source of income for migratory laborers included in the Crystal City study was the onion crop.

The onion harvest begins in south Texas at the beginning of April and reaches its peak in May. In north Texas it lasts into July. The

8 *Ibid.*, p. 22.   9 *Ibid.*
10 *Ibid.*, p. 30   11 *Ibid.*, p. 29.

average duration of onion jobs was less than two months, however, in 1938. Most of the workers who harvested onions before leaving for the sugar-beet fields worked only in April, while most cotton workers did not leave the onion fields until late in May.[12]

Eighty-nine of the 300 Crystal City families interviewed worked in onions, only two of them giving onions as their principal source of income for the year 1938. For 29 per cent of the eighty-nine families engaged in the onion harvest, their total income from that source was less than $25.00; for 27 per cent it was less than $50.00; for 21 per cent, less than $100.00; for 15 per cent, less than $200.00; and only 8 per cent earned more than $200.00.[13]

Upon combining the income to the 300 families from spinach, cotton, sugar beets, and onions, and including miscellaneous types of other farm and nonfarm work engaged in during the year, it was found that the average cash income per family in Crystal City totaled $506.00 in 1938. For those who received income in both cash and kind, including housing, wood, and water, the average income was raised to $561.00. "Since the families averaged 5.5 persons, the average yearly income among the Mexican migrants was approximately $100.00 per person in 1938."[14]

Broken down to weekly income, therefore, the 300 families earned an average of $9.73 per week in cash, or $10.78 in cash and kind, during the year 1938.

Employment of migratory labor in the sugar beet areas of the United States has been the subject of exhaustive studies by the Children's Bureau of the United States Department of Labor and other agencies from time to time. Twenty thousand Latin Americans resident in Texas left the State in 1944, and again in 1945, to engage in that type of labor. It is not surprising to find that conditions surrounding their employment in the northern states faithfully reflect the conditions under which they live and work in Texas.

[12] *Ibid.*, p. 35.   [13] *Ibid.*
[14] *Ibid.*, p. 37.

In discussing the conditions prevailing in Michigan beet fields, Edgar G. Johnston says:

Housing is frequently substandard, especially where accommodations are those furnished by the local farmer. Shacks, trailers, tents, abandoned farm houses and even stables have served as "home" for migrant beet workers in Michigan. In recent years there has been a tendency for the sugar companies to furnish houses for a nominal rent, usually paid by the beet grower, and in one area, during the past year a housing project was completed with the construction of a series of neat bungalows, financed by the federal government.

The health problem was dramatized in 1941 by the simultaneous outbreak of diphtheria epidemics in Saginaw County and in the Blissfield area, and an epidemic of bacillary dysentery in Van Buren County. Investigations by the Michigan Department of Health revealed serious lack of sanitation and, in some instances, deplorable living conditions. The incidence of tuberculosis and venereal disease has been markedly reduced in recent years through the co-operation of the Department in providing medical examinations of prospective beet workers in Texas before their annual migration to Michigan. The low economic status of beet workers' families and their unfamiliarity with their Michigan environment tend to make the employment of a "family physician" a rarity, and attention to health problems is likely to be given only in emergencies and—sometimes grudgingly—on a charity basis.[15]

Michigan's decision to examine all prospective beet workers for tuberculosis and venereal diseases before transporting them out of Texas was brought about, not out of compassion for the ailing, but because that State's institutions are required, by law, to hospitalize all persons suffering from those diseases. This, of course, constituted an unwelcome responsibility for Michigan's hospitals and sanitoria. As a result, until 1945, beet workers were employed only after going through a clinic set up in San Antonio by Michigan doctors. This meant that the efficiency of the labor supply left in Texas was further decreased by a preponderance of the physically unfit, brought about by the siphoning off of those who were free of disease. However, in 1945, because of the shortage of doctors in Michigan, as well

[15] Edgar G. Johnston, "Michigan's Step-Children," *School of Education Bulletin* (Ann Arbor: The University of Michigan, October, 1943), Vol. XV, No. 1, pp. 1-6.

as a general labor shortage, the examinations were discontinued until after the war.

Perhaps even more glaring is the fact that the workers who were found, through examination, to be suffering from either tuberculosis or venereal disease were not hospitalized, or even treated, in Texas. No follow-up was made on the findings of physicians conducting the examinations for Michigan beet growers.

With regard to income from the Michigan beet harvest, Dr. Johnston says:

> The beet work for which the "Mexican" migrants are brought to Michigan has a slack period in August and September and must be supplemented by work in onion fields, beans, and pickles if the family is not to dip too heavily into its season's earnings to tide through idle periods. The total income from all sources for the average family is meagre in terms of accepted minimum living standards. Earnings differ among the various beet growing sections and from year to year. The median Spanish-speaking migrant family included 6.3 persons of whom 3.5 persons were under 16 years of age. The yearly income from sources other than beet work and relief for 67.2 per cent of 943 families interviewed for this study was less than $100.00. The median yearly income from all sources except relief was $430.00 from the close of the harvest in 1934 to the close of the 1935 harvest season.
>
> A somewhat more favorable picture for Michigan in 1941 is shown in Thaden's study. Total earnings from beet work for four migrant families from Texas—one low income family, two average income families, and one family earning more than the average—were $487.64, $572.46, $610.84 and $787.70. The average annual earning per beet-worker for about five months' work in beet fields ranged from $95.41 to $162.55. . . . Higher minimum wage rates for 1942 and 1943 and the assistance of representatives of the U. S. Department of Agriculture in more systematic distribution of workers to other jobs during the slack season in beet work have probably improved the economic status of beet working families during the current season, but not to a sufficient degree to provide economic stability.[16]

Because of the provisions of the Sugar Act of 1937, the employment of children under fourteen years of age in the beet

[16] *Ibid.*

fields is illegal. This has created a problem in the public schools of sugar beet states; but judging from the tactics employed by some recruiting agents working in South Texas in the spring of 1945, Illinois, at least, was due to be relieved of the responsibility of providing educational facilities for the children of migrant workers.

The expedient is a simple one. The recruiters refused to transport children under fourteen years of age, the reason being that they were paid by the beet growers at the rate of $35.00 a head for laborers transported. Children who are prohibited by law from engaging in beet work, and whose presence in northern states serves only to complicate matters for the public schools, are just so much excess baggage.

Another form of migratory labor, and one which hearkens back to the romantic period of Texas history, is that of sheep and goat shearing. The machine has taken away much of the picturesqueness of sheep shearing, but there are customs that linger, giving color to the State's oldest industry.

The migratory shearer enjoys one distinct advantage over those engaged in other migratory pursuits, for his pay is much higher for his day's work, and his annual net income greater than that realized from any other type of seasonal employment.

In 1940, there were sixty-four counties in Texas that sheared 15,000 sheep or more each, Val Verde County topping the list with more than half a million. The sheep-raising area has its center in the Edwards Plateau and spreads into the adjoining counties, particularly to the east, where it extends as far over as Travis and Williamson Counties, and up to Bosque County.

In the eastern half of the sheep-producing region farm flocks predominate, and these sheep are shorn, as a rule, by small local crews of either Anglo or Latin American laborers. Often this amounts to nothing more than that the owner of one of the flocks shears his own and his neighbors' sheep, so that there is no migration to speak of east of the Edwards Plateau proper.

The migration of labor involved in sheep shearing is confined almost entirely to the western part of the sheep-raising area, where extensive ranches and large flocks of sheep are to be found. Most of these crews are made up entirely of Latin Americans. The owner of the equipment is the *capitán* of the crew, which is usually composed of his relatives or close friends. In rare instances, the shearing machine will be owned and possibly managed by an Anglo American ranchman, but the crew members will be Latin Americans.

The majority of the sheep shearers live in Uvalde, Del Rio, and San Angelo, although the crew leaders, or *capitánes,* frequently reside elsewhere. In a letter to the author, dated January 13, 1945, J. B. Kidd, Farm Labor Field Assistant, says that a survey made in 1943 revealed that the members of more than sixty shearing crews, ranging from five- to sixteen-drop machines called Uvalde their home. Del Rio reported a like number of crews living there, migrating each year through the Edwards Plateau, into the northern part of the State, and some of them following the shearing on into the northwestern states. San Angelo is believed to be headquarters for at least another sixty crews of varying size, and still others are found throughout the sheep-raising area.

There are four shearing seasons in each year, taking into consideration the fact that goats are shorn twice each year by these same crews, beginning approximately on March 1 and September 1. In the area extending from Sanderson to Ozona, across south of Sonora and Rocksprings, and around toward Hondo, sheep also are shorn twice a year.

The reason for two shearings of sheep in the area described is that browse forms a large percentage of the sheep feed there. Acacia shrubs which prevail in this brush have a cat-claw type of thorn which pulls out much of the wool if the sheep are permitted to grow a full twelve-months fleece. The added factor of milder climate below the Edwards Plateau Cap proper greatly encourages the semiannual shearing of sheep in that area.

Goat shearing far south, where the brush country impinges

PLATE XI

A truck load of migratory laborers parked in Sinton, San Patricio County, Texas

on the Edwards Plateau and is laced by the streams that flow from the highlands, begins in March, before winter has broken in half of Texas. By April 10 or 15, the crews start the spring shearing of sheep, traveling north and west, with some variations, depending upon climate, altitude, and natural protection for the sheep after being shorn. Normally, sheep shearing is completed between the latter part of May and the first of June in Texas, with the high open country around Eldorado, some parts of the Panhandle, and portions of the northwestern trans-Pecos area the last to be served, mainly because of climatic conditions.

In September the process is repeated for goats, and the fall clip of sheep lasts until Christmas. Therefore, the diligent shearer who works for an enterprising *capitán* puts in from eight to nine months each year at a task in which he is highly skilled. Sheep are shorn on a contract basis at so much a head, paid by the rancher to the contractor-*capitán*. For the last two years, 1944 and 1945, the price has been pretty uniformly twenty-five cents a head. The *capitán* retains from ten to twelve and one-half cents of the payment, and the shearer receives from twelve and one-half to fifteen cents. It is possible for an expert shearer to clip an animal in three minutes, and many an individual will shear 150 sheep a day to earn $22.50. Seldom does a shearer try to do more than that in a single day.

Migration of sheep shearers is unlike that of cotton pickers, in that only men take part in it. Sheep shearing is, traditionally, a man's job, and women and children are taboo. If, as it does happen infrequently, a shearer is accompanied by his family, he establishes his camp some distance from the main camp, which is thrown up as near the shearing pens and as close to water as possible.

A crew consists of the *capitán*, whose duty it is to make contacts and contracts, set shearing dates, and carry on all business transactions both with the ranchmen and with the members of his crew. He has his shearers, one or two wool pickers, two boys to pick up the wool, one or two wool tiers, depending on the size of the crew, one or two wool sackers, and his cook, for the crew camps out at each shearing location.

Many counties that produce large numbers of sheep and goats, such as Glasscock and Upton, do not have shearing crews that live within the county and are entirely dependent upon migratory crews to shear their flocks. Upon completion of shearing in Texas, some individual shearers, as well as some full crews, migrate into northwestern states, where shearing normally takes place later than it does in Texas.

There is nothing new about the system of shearing sheep in Texas except the pay scale. In all other particulars the system is as old as the industry itself. It was the same in the old hand-shearing days, now obsolete in the State for a quarter of a century.

Before sheep shears, fashioned like a barber's clippers and powered with gasoline motors, were introduced about the time of the beginning of World War I, the price paid for shearing sheep averaged five cents a head, divided between shearer and *capitán.* Today sheep shearing is a business requiring extraordinary skill and dexterity. In the hand-shearing days, it required these qualities, plus great strength of wrist, arm, and fingers to force the sharp blades, whose cutting power came from heavy steel springs, through dense wool. In those days, a highly skilled worker could shear as many as fifty sheep, and perhaps a few more, in a sun-to-sun working day, with a brief pause for the noon meal and a siesta. The $1.50-a-day wages received by the best shearers was net, and was ample to meet the economic needs of the day.

Transportation in those earlier, more leisurely days was by buggy, hack, and wagon, drawn by burros, mules, or horses, and sometimes a combination of all. Then, as now, the *capitán* furnished food and all equipment except the shears. Nowadays the *capitán* may supply a "chuck wagon" in the form of a truck that goes along with the shearing machine. It is still common practice for the ranchman to furnish a mutton to the crew for every thousand sheep shorn. All other food is provided by the *capitán* and in generous amounts, to sustain men whose labor is so arduous.

The shearing machine, which is mounted on a chassis drawn by a truck, has a shaft down the center ridge with drops for the power cables to the individual shears off each side, so that the shearers work along straight lines under canvas at opposite sides of the machine, and at opposite sides of the catch pen which encloses perhaps a hundred unshorn sheep at a time.

The grace of a skilled shearer, stripped to the waist, with his torso satin-shiny from lanolin (the oil that oozes from a fleece), is a sight to behold. Catch a view of him at the moment he releases a freshly shorn sheep with a quick pull on the string that has bound the animal's four legs. The shearer gently nudges with a lifting motion the rump of the abashedly naked sheep, its remaining nip of fleece the color of buttercups against skin as pink and soft as an infant's. With quick appraisal, the shearer's eyes already are scanning the dirty gray unshorn sheep that remain, looking for the smoother body that will facilitate the speed of the clipper head.

With a quick pounce, and the seizure of one hind leg, the sheep is dragged to the canvas-covered ground from which a youth has gathered and bunched the shorn fleece and carried it off to the wool tiers' table. Firmly grasping the animal's hind leg, the shearer employs his free hand to run the shears rapidly along the legs and the belly, removing the scant wool from those parts preparatory to tying the legs and cutting the more luxuriant wool from the rest of the body.

Rain is the one element that puts a sudden stop to the business of shearing, and when it rains, which it does on the most untoward occasions, shearing is halted until the wool of the sheep has been dried by several hours of sunshine. Shears will not readily cut through wet wool, and wet wool cannot be tamped into sacks, because it will spoil. The work is shut down. On those occasions, the guitars and mandolins that are cached somewhere in every outfit are brought out, and there is a festival of song. Indeed, balladry frequently accompanies the whirr of the clippers, too, but the effect is not as musical or pleasing to the ear as when the chorus rose to the click of the old hand shears.

The financing of the crews is an interesting procedure. As a rule, crews shear for the same ranchmen year after year, and the ranchman expects the same crew back next year unless other arrangements are made. Soon after January the first of each year, the *capitán* contacts the ranchmen, arranges the shearing dates, and collects some money in advance. This may be $50.00 or $500.00, but usually about 20 per cent of the total shearing fee. The *capitán* then uses the money to put his machine in shape, to take care of incidental expenses, and to advance funds to his shearers, who often rely entirely upon the *capitán* to see that they have money during the full year. It is not uncommon, says J. B. Kidd, for the *capitán* to have from $50.00 to $100.00 loaned to each of his shearers before the shearing season starts.

At the end of the season, the organization of the crew is ordinarily not abandoned. Instead, the *capitán* will contract for fence-building, prickly-pear grubbing, cedar cutting, or some other type of ranch work, in which all members of the crew may be employed. Some of the shearers, with their families, join the cotton migration in the fall.

If the life of the sheep shearer seems almost Arcadian by comparison with that of other migrants, the reason is perhaps that this occupation was from the beginning a skilled one and retains to this day many characteristics of a skilled trade. Furthermore, the sheep shearer won a place for himself in the economy of the ranching counties before the great waves of importation and immigration of laborers from Mexico set in. His higher wages, his having enjoyed for a longer time a certain degree of acceptance in his community, and perhaps even the tinge of the romantic connected with his occupation—all give him a comparatively enviable position among migratory workers.

The lot of the majority of all other migratory workers, although conditions are improving, could by no stretch of the imagination be called "rosy."

Chapter 13

Social and Civil Inequalities

TIME MAGAZINE, in February, 1944, reprinted a cartoon by García Cabral in which Cantinflas, famed Mexican comic of stage and screen, was the character portrayed. In the first panel, Cantinflas was meditating upon a sign displayed by a Texas cafe which read: "No Mexicans Served." The second panel showed Cantinflas putting the finishing touches on a sign over a Mexican restaurant which said: "Here We Serve Anyone— Even Texans."

The cartoon, which appeared originally in *Novedades,* Mexico City newspaper, was amusing—much more amusing than *Time's* comments which accompanied the reprint. There was just enough truth in *Time's* article to defy its being denied categorically; yet the interpretation given was completely misleading as to the true state of affairs in Texas.

It has been remarked that the Bible can be used to prove any contention or point of view—by merely lifting one verse out of its context. In like manner, by ignoring all of the conditions in Texas that we have been considering, and by emphasizing only certain phases of all the problems existing in relations between Latin and Anglo Americans in the State—by taking things out of context, so to speak—one could easily lead the uninformed to believe that all Texans are barbarians, that all persons of Mexican descent are shamefully treated in Texas, and that no one is making any effort to correct the situation; in short, that an atmosphere of open hostility prevails.

The one-syllable answer to the question "Are Latin Americans refused service in public places of business and amusement in Texas?" would have to be "Yes." But in order to be truthful, and speaking for the State as a whole, that reply must be modified by the addition of the phrases "some Latin Americans" are refused service in "some places of business" in "some Texas towns." At the same time it is admitted that in some rural and semi-rural communities, Anglo American operators of cafes, beer parlors, barbershops, and theaters are adamant in refusing service to any and all Latin Americans.

During the first four months of its existence, ending December 31, 1943, the Good Neighbor Commission of Texas received from Mexican Consuls, Latin American organizations, and individuals 117 complaints of "discrimination." Some of the reports related to segregated schools, and other alleged conditions of inequality, but at least 110 of them involved refusal of admission to or service in public places of business and amusement. The reports covered the year 1943, and some of the incidents were alleged to have taken place in 1942.

Personal investigation was made of a number of the complaints, but not all, in accordance with the Good Neighbor Commission's statement of policy, which declares that "due to economic and administrative limitations, the Commission cannot properly constitute itself into a judicial and executive body to investigate every incident and impose remedies. Rather, the complaints received will be regarded in the light that they represent symptoms of basic maladjustments which the Commission will seek to overcome by soliciting the co-operation of the various departments of the State Government, as well as of those agencies and institutions which can render services in an attack upon the basic causes of these fundamental maladjustments."

Instead, the reports were analyzed as to the character of the complaint, the section of the State in which the incident was alleged to have occurred, and the name and population of the town. Each incident was then spotted on a map of Texas. The following facts were thus revealed: of the total of 117 incidents, sixty-seven occurred in West Texas, four in East Texas, and forty-four in South Texas. A very negligible number were noted along the Border, where there is the heaviest concentration of Latin American population, and the greatest number were reported from that Plains section of West Texas which has already been described as the most important cotton-growing area of the State.

By superimposing upon the map the migratory labor routes, as determined by the United States Employment Service, it was further demonstrated that there existed a very close relationship between cotton, migratory labor, and refusal of service; for the greatest number of reported incidents in South Texas, also, was from the cotton-producing counties of the Coastal Bend area. This is not to imply that all incidents reported from those areas involved migrants, for such is not the case; but rather that attitudes of Anglo Americans in those sections of the State have been influenced, apparently, by their contacts with migrants.

With this as a starting point, and in the light of additional information secured, it became increasingly obvious that the matter of refusal of service in public places of business and amusement was not actually, in and of itself, the chief problem, even though it was, and is, the one which receives the most publicity here and in Mexico. Rather, the Commission became more firmly convinced that such incidents, in the main, represent "symptoms of basic maladjustments" instead of outright antagonism toward Latin Americans as such. These basic maladjustments, of course, are the conditions which we have already discussed in detail: low wages and intermittent unemployment; lack of adequate educational facilities; absence of Latin American children from school even where facilities are provided; substandard housing, lack of sanitation, and poor health.

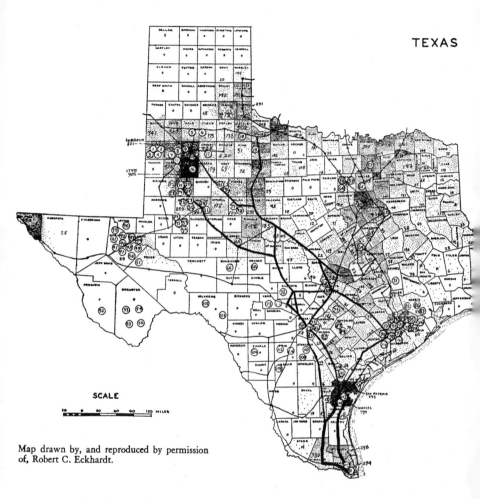

TEXAS

Map drawn by, and reproduced by permission
of, Robert C. Eckhardt.

Dots indicate density of cotton production. Each dot represents 100 bales of cotton ginned in the
county in 1943 (based on 1943-1944 Texas Almanac).

Figures in each county represent cotton ginnings in hundreds of bales; e. g., Lubbock County 801—
80,100 bales.

Heavy lines indicate major migratory labor routes; lighter lines indicate minor migratory labor routes.

Each numbered circle indicates one incident of discrimination reported during 4-months period Sept.-
Dec. 1943, incl. (Figures for reference.)

PLATE XII   (*U. S. Army Signal Corps photo*)

SGT. JOSE M. LOPEZ
of Brownsville, Texas, receives the congratulations of Major General
James A. Van Fleet upon being awarded the Congressional Medal of
Honor, somewhere in Germany

This line of reasoning admittedly does not hold true in approximately 15 per cent of the reported cases, where service or equal accommodations are refused to Latin Americans or Mexican nationals in uniform, or to those who are patently of the upper social and economic strata. Refusal of service to such persons is indicative of yet another basic maladjustment: that of prejudice on the part of some Anglo Americans in Texas, growing out of ignorance and the deplorable human tendency to generalize on insufficient evidence. We will consider this aspect more closely in a moment, but first let us continue with the results of the Commission's study of the 117 cases reported up to December 31, 1943.

It was notable that refusal of service took place, almost without exception, in fourth- or fifth-class cafes, beer parlors, barbershops, etc. In those few cases where a higher type of establishment was involved, it was found that the employee responsible was indulging his or her personal prejudices and not interpreting the policy of the management.

It must be noted, too, that not all of the complaints registered were *bona fide*. In some cases, the facts had been distorted by the complainant, either through misunderstanding arising out of the language difficulty, or because he was "carrying a chip on his shoulder," or by reason of an apparently premeditated attempt to cause trouble. There are also cases where "incidents" have been precipitated, deliberately, by prominent Latin Americans and Mexican citizens, for their publicity value as a means of stimulating anti-Texas and anti-United States sentiment in Mexico, or for other political reasons. While such action on the part of prominent persons might be explained as a natural social phenomenon—a part of the mechanism of self-defense of ostracized minorities—it is, nevertheless, an extremely poor technique, which frequently results in creating more, instead of less, antagonism toward Latin Americans in the locality where the "incident" occurs.

The analysis likewise revealed that the 117 cases of alleged discrimination took place in sixty-nine different towns. The size of the towns complained of is indicative of one of the most important causes of misunderstanding and conflict:

19 were towns of less than	....	1,500 population
26 were towns of between	....	1,500- 5,000 population
11 were towns of between	....	5,000-10,000 population
5 were towns of between	....	10,000-25,000 population
3 were towns of between	....	25,000-75,000 population
5 were cities of more than	....	75,000 population

In other words, forty-five of the sixty-nine towns against which complaints were registered, or practically two-thirds of the total, were small towns of less than 5,000 population.

The complaints received by the Commission since January 1, 1944, follow the same pattern, indicating graphically that in Texas the traditional provincialism of small towns and rural areas has exerted a strong influence on the treatment accorded persons of Mexican descent.

It is extremely difficult—in fact, impossible—to compose a satisfactory reply to the writer of the following letter, which was received by Governor Stevenson in February, 1945, or to others like him:

Dear Sir:

I was born in Texas 23 years ago. I have been in the Service for 3 years. I was on furlough and on my way home I stopped at a Highway Cafe to eat supper. I was very hungry. So the manager says "You are Mexican." I said yes. He said for me to get out. Well, I was very embaressed of my uniform as well as of my self and as a soilder of the United States army. *I can assure thats not what I am fighting for.*

I am sure that is very wrong. I am sure that you can, and will help me, and I will fight harder, so that this war may end sooner. In the front lines we do not ask the next man what race he is. Nor does my Commanding Officer.

Yours truly,
Sgt. Ramón Espinosa.

The classic case of this type came to the public's attention in March, 1944, and concerned a young Sergeant from Mission, who had been a turret gunner in a B-17 bomber crew stationed in England, and whose squadron had engaged in the first aerial raids on Germany.

After completing his twenty-five missions, on one of which he was wounded, the Sergeant returned home on furlough during the summer of 1943, bringing with him the Air Medal with three oak leaf clusters, the Distinguished Flying Cross, and the Purple Heart. At that time, he was honored by the citizens of Mission at an open air meeting, and presented with a fine watch as a token of their esteem.

His next assignment was to Sioux City, Iowa, where he served as a gunnery instructor until March, 1944, when he returned to Mission to be married.

A few evenings after the wedding, and in celebration of that event, the Sergeant and his wife, together with two other young couples, went to the Blue Moon night club, between Pharr and San Juan, to dance. But they were refused admission to the resort because, as the doorman explained, "We do not permit Mexicans in here."

One of the couples in the Sergeant's party was Anglo American, but of course the entire group left the club in protest. When the manager was questioned later with regard to his policy, he stated that he did not discriminate against men in uniform, and that the Sergeant would have been admitted had he been by himself; however, in order "to avoid trouble," he could not be permitted to bring his wife into the club.

The editorial in the Valley newspaper which recounted the incident ended with this question: "While we are engaged in fighting to the death against similar hostile influences abroad, how can we tolerate them right under our noses here at home?"[1]

Subsequently, the young Sergeant was assigned to combat duty in the Pacific, where, a few months later, he was killed in action.

Shameful as this incident is, by no stretch of the imagination may it be regarded as typical of the treatment accorded Latin

1 *The Valley Evening Monitor* (McAllen, Texas), March 30, 1944.

Americans by the operators of public places of business in Texas. Had it been typical, it would not have attracted so much attention. The story, which happens to be true in every detail, has all the elements of a sure-fire newspaper story. Here was a soldier in the uniform of his country; more than that, a wounded veteran who had been decorated for valor in the defense of his country—in defense, even, of the operator of the Blue Moon. The manager's admission that he respected the uniform but not the man wearing it, and that he had no respect whatever for the man's wife, would be merely pathetic were it not so tragic.

On the other hand, without excusing or condoning in the slightest degree the attitude and actions of the club management, there are at least two facts revealed which prove that the incident was atypical of treatment accorded Latin Americans in Texas. In the first place, the returning hero had been honored by his townspeople, Latin and Anglo American alike. In the second place, two members of his party were Anglo Americans.

What actually occurred was that this young man was made to suffer for the many ills which beset the majority of Latin Americans in the Valley, as well as for the ignorance of the manager of the Blue Moon.

"Ignorant" is not a word that we like to apply to ourselves, yet call it by whatever name we may, it adds up to the same thing; and as Mexico's Avila Camacho has said, ignorance is the "most fearful of internal enemies." "Provincial," "uninformed," "unaware" may be more palatable. All of them describe the mental state of most Anglo Americans in Texas with regard to Latin Americans in this country or in Latin America. This total unawareness is due to a diversity of causes.

To begin with, our educational system, from the elementary grades through college, has been at fault. Except for those who have done special research in the field, the present out-of-school population of Texas has had no instruction in the history, the geography, the literature, the peoples, the culture, the politics, or the social and economic structure of Latin America. Until the very recent past, the history of Texas was taught with a bias that could not fail to generate prejudices against Mexico and Mexicans. Because of the thousands of illiterate Mexican laborers that have flowed into the State during the last fifty years, as we have seen, furnishing, through no fault of their own, a vast reservoir of cheap labor and thereby enabling a "colonial economy" to persist in Texas, unreasoning prejudices have been intensified.

Ignorance and lack of understanding have given birth to many false generalizations about Latin Americans—generalizations that are bandied about as solemn truths and which have been accepted and passed on without examination or any attempt at analysis.

Our citizens of Mexican descent are people, individuals, just like the members of any other group. As individuals, they have their virtues and their vices, just like the members of any other group. Yet because we Texans—the great majority of us—have never made any effort to know Latin Americans as people, to understand their problems or their characteristics, we accept and repeat generalizations concerning them which we are totally unable to substantiate with facts.

Anyone can tell you that "Mexicans can afford to work for less, because they don't require as much to live on"; that "Mexicans migrate because they like to travel around; it's a lark for them, and you couldn't make them stay in one place"; that "Mexicans are tricky and can't be trusted"; that "Mexicans like to live in a segregated district or send their children to a segregated school because they prefer to be together"; that "the building of modern housing for Mexicans is a waste of money, because in no time at all they will have all the window panes knocked out and will chop up the floors for firewood."

Nor is this virus confined to the untutored members of our society. Unfortunately, even a college degree furnishes no immunity to its insidiousness. Some of our worst offenders are among those who have had the advantage of a good formal education, and who might, therefore, be expected to be logical and objective in their thinking. The catch seems to be that they don't think; they merely accept without question theories and attitudes that originated no one knows where.

This point may best be illustrated by a near-catastrophic incident which occurred at a meeting of the United States-Mexico Border Public Health Association in El Paso in 1944. Present were some 150 persons prominent in medicine, sanitary engineering, and public health work in both countries. About sixty of the conferees were from Mexico.

One of the principal speakers on the opening day of the conference was a doctor from the Texas State Department of Health. His subject, as listed on the program, was "Tuberculosis in Texas." Upon rising to speak, he announced that he had changed his subject to "Tuberculosis Among Latin Americans in Texas."

After his opening remarks, he stated that tuberculosis was much more prevalent among Latin Americans in Texas than among any other racial or national group; that it was due to their Mexican extraction; that Mexicans were simply a diseased race, and therefore more susceptible not only to tuberculosis but to any other disease. He proceeded to develop this theme for a period of twenty minutes or more.

Fortunately for the success of the conference and for the maintenance of amicable relations between the two countries, there were Anglo American Texans present who could, and did, emphatically refute his statements before the Mexican doctors could get the floor. Statistics such as those recorded by the Children's Bureau in the Hidalgo County study were cited in rebuttal, as conclusive evidence that the economic status and living conditions under which so large a part of our Latin American population is forced to exist constituted a much more logical explanation of the high tuberculosis death rate among them than the mere fact of their Mexican ancestry. The day was saved, but it was a near miss.

Here was an educated man, a doctor of medicine, a specialist in tuberculosis; yet he was totally devoid of any knowledge or understanding of Latin Americans and their problems, about which he had elected to speak as an authority.

The erroneous impressions that many Anglo Americans, through ignorance, have acquired about Latin Americans as a group prevent them from making any individual distinctions. It has been demonstrated that most instances of refusal of service occur in towns and villages of less than 5,000 population, and that the Latin Americans most frequently refused service are those in the lower income brackets. We have seen, also, that this discrimination may often be described accurately as a "social dictinction" rather than as discrimination against Latin Americans. However, the two tend to become confused in the minds of entirely too many people who, as a result, discriminate against *all* persons of Mexican descent, regardless of social, economic, or cultural status. If this were not, unfortunately, true, there would never be a case of discrimination against a Latin American of higher social status—and there have been such cases.

We may consider, for example, the case of a prominent business man from the State of Chihuahua, who reported as follows:

As a Mexican citizen, I come before you respectfully to bring to your attention something which, in my judgment, ought not to exist. I had to make a trip to Temple, Texas, by automobile, to take my wife to the Scott & White Clinic.

Since my wife was quite tired from the trip, we decided to spend the night at a place called Legion, Texas, near San Antonio. We went to a tourist court and pressed the button. The owner came out, and I asked him if he had a vacancy. He said he had one with two beds. I expressed my desire to see it, and he and I walked about a half block to the court.

In the meantime, my wife drove the car up in front of the court, and, without getting out, inquired of me, in Spanish, "How is the apartment?" This startled the owner, and he asked, "What nationality are you?" I replied, "Mexican."

Then he told me, "I am sorry, but we have an agreement with the neighbors not to rent to Mexicans." I told him I was sorry to have bothered him, and we left.

A similar instance is that of the Mexican official who, after touring the United States by automobile on a mission for his government, was returning to Mexico by way of El Paso. In passing through West Texas, he allegedly was refused service in cafes in Sonora, Junction, and Fort Stockton. The cafe owners were requested to furnish an explanation and apology. One failed to reply, one denied any knowledge of the incident but asserted that he followed no such policy, and the other responded as follows:

In reply to your letter of October 2nd, stating that Mr. García was refused our service, I wish to state that such act was done without my knowledge and without authority.

I hereby express my deepest regret for such act by my employee, and I assure you that any employee committing such act in the future shall be discharged from our staff and shall not be re-employed.

I want to thank you for the information, as it is not my intention to refuse service to any one, regardless of nationality, so long as such person is orderly in conduct and clean in personality.

Please convey my apologies to Mr. García. Ask him to please accept, and if the opportunity presents itself, I would like very much to meet him in person.

A Mexican citizen residing in Houston reported that he and his wife, after a movie one night, stepped into a small cafe outside the business district and ordered a cup of coffee, only to be told that Mexicans weren't served there. His affidavit concluded with the statement that "I have lived in Houston for 18 years, and this is the first unpleasant thing that has ever happened to me."

At first glance it would appear that anyone living in a metropolitan area, where the Latin American population constitutes a relatively small minority, who can balance one unpleasant experience against eighteen years of admittedly cordial relations with Anglo Americans, is not deserving of too much sympathy. While there is no denying, of course, that the act itself was unjust, we might reason that the complainant obviously failed to take into account the fact that, among half a million people, there are bound to be a few with prejudices, groundless though they are.

There are two standpoints from which to view this complaint—the quantitative and the qualitative. From the quantitative aspect, the fact that the complainant had encountered only one such prejudiced person in eighteen long years is indicative of a very significant point which is consistently overlooked by those uninformed or deliberately malicious individuals who would brand the entire State of Texas as being hostile to persons of Mexican descent.

More than one million Latin Americans reside in Texas. The total number of reports of discriminatory treatment received by the Good Neighbor Commission up to May 1, 1945, did not exceed 300. Even granting that the majority of actual refusals of service and other instances of unfair treatment are never made known to the Commission, the ratio of overt incidents to the number of Latin Americans living in the State is weighted in favor of those who never suffer such humiliations, again emphasizing the symptomatic nature of open acts of discrimination. It stands to reason that every unpleasant contact a Latin American has with Anglo Americans in Texas is offset by dozens of pleasant experiences. Yet, human nature (and justice!) being what they are, the good results of a preponderance of pleasant associations and equitable treatment are often completely canceled out by personal pique over one instance of unjust treatment. Here, again, generalization is dangerous.

From the qualitative standpoint, however, the complaint is fully justified. For eighteen years this man had lived in peace and harmony with the numerous Anglos with whom he came in daily contact. Then, suddenly, he was confronted with the senseless prejudice of one individual. He was shocked and angered, and rightly so. In this case, it is not the fact that he had been insulted only once in eighteen years that is important, but rather the fact that it was possible for the incident to happen at all.

It is a shameful state of affairs when Latin Americans in Texas—whether citizens of this country or visitors from Mexico, and regardless of social and economic status—must be ever conscious of the *possibility* of being humiliated and on guard against it. Without doubt, the chief reason more cases of refusal of service are not reported to the Commission is that Latin Americans, being forewarned that their presence in certain places of business is not welcomed, studiously avoid entering such establishments and exposing themselves to insult.

We must bear in mind, too, that there are some twenty-five or thirty far west, central west, central and southeast Texas counties in which, generally speaking, Latin Americans have no rights of any kind. Reports of mistreatment are seldom received from these counties for the simple reason that their Latin American residents, who were brought in originally as cheap labor, have been kept so consistently submerged by the Anglo Americans living there that they have more or less accepted their servile position. There is no Latin American leadership in these counties, for leadership among minority groups seems often to be unable to arise until the minority has achieved a modicum of self-respect and some respect from others. Even a blanket policy of refusal of service in Anglo American business establishments in such counties is of minor importance in comparison with the denial of the fundamental rights of education, equality before the law, a living wage, full citizenship privileges, and decent living conditions.

An excellent example of deliberate distortion of the facts in alleging discrimination may be found in the case of a girl whom we shall call Angela López. Angela was a citizen of the United States by birth. She decided upon a nursing career, and after the expenditure of much time and effort on the part of her priest, as well as financial sacrifice on the part of her family, her application for training was accepted by a Catholic nursing school some six hundred miles distant.

Her sworn affidavit stated that she had arrived at the institution on the appointed day, had been kept waiting two hours, and then had been informed by the Sister in charge that she was sorry, but this was a school for "white" girls, and since Angela was a "Mexican," she had best go somewhere else.

Upon investigation, the facts in the case were found to be that, when she arrived at the institution, Angela had been received, assigned to a room, and furnished with a copy of the regulations governing students, one of which was the request to speak English at all times, inasmuch as the girls were being trained for nursing careers in the United States. Also, being a newcomer and having an unusually dark complexion, Angela, on her first appearance in the dining room, had occasioned a certain amount of whispering and head turning. The first that was known of Angela's dissatisfaction was on the evening of the first day, when she telephoned from the railroad station to tell the superintendent that she was not happy there and had decided to go home.

The Sister's letter concluded with the observation that "inasmuch as we now have sixteen Mexican girls in training here, it can hardly be said that we discriminate against Mexicans."

In this case, since Angela "couldn't take it," she was confronted with the necessity of doing something to "save face" with her parents and her priest. The obvious device was to cry "discrimination."

Psychologists might argue that Angela's actions were normal and logical as an escape from a deep sense of personal frustration. Even so, the pertinent fact in this discussion is that Angela *did* perjure herself to build up a case of "discrimination."

One very real brand of discrimination which is particularly onerous springs not from active antagonism toward Latin Americans, nor yet from blind prejudice. It is an expression, rather, of a smug and mistaken paternalistic attitude which is encountered particularly in the isolated communities of West Texas. It is an attitude which seems to imply that the Latin American residents in the locality are amiable but simple-minded children, and must, for their own good, be kept in their "place"—an attitude which, naturally, puzzles or infuriates the Latin Americans.

To illustrate, there is the case of the owner of a small but flourishing grocery store in a West Texas town of some 5,000 population. We shall say that his name is Feliciano Mendoza.

During the early summer of 1945, Mendoza called on the town's leading dealer in ladies' apparel and asked him to order a fur coat for Mrs. Mendoza. The dealer's response was:

"Well, now, Feliciano, those things come pretty high, you know. I doubt that you could afford one."

"How much are they?" Mendoza inquired.

"Oh, they run from $150.00 on up."

Mendoza brought out his wallet, extracted bills in the amount of $300.00, and spread them on the counter.

"Will that buy two coats?" he asked.

The dealer smiled indulgently, slowly pushed the bills back across the counter, and said:

"Now, Feliciano, I don't want to see you waste your money. I tell you what you do. Schwartz, next door here, has some second-hand fur coats. You go in there and buy your wife a coat cheap and save your money."

The assertion has been made frequently of late that discrimination is on the increase in Texas. This, of course, in the face of the facts and the great improvement made in the situation in the course of recent years, is not true. Such an assertion springs from ignorance, misinformation, or deliberate misrepresentation.

What has happened is that the world upheaval since 1941 has rocked our society to its very foundations, pointing up the injustice of many conditions which we have allowed to prevail without ever being consciously aware of their existence. Latin Americans who, for years, have accepted or tolerated in silence the conditions we have been discussing, have acquired a new courage, have become more vocal in protesting against the restrictions and inequalities with which they are confronted.

Without doubt, the paramount factor in the generation of

this new consciousness among Latin Americans in Texas has been the entrance of so many of their sons into the Armed Forces. In the administration of the Selective Service Act, at least, it can never be alleged that discrimination against Latin Americans has been practiced. Neither do bullets show any partiality in choosing their targets.

On the contrary, during the war, one needed only to scan the daily casualty lists in any newspaper from San Antonio south to be convinced that so far as military service, devotion to duty, heroic performance under fire, and making the supreme sacrifice for the preservation of the democratic way of life were concerned, our Latin American youth contributed its full share. The Spanish names appearing in the casualty lists of any South or Southwest Texas paper consistently numbered from one-third to as much as three-fourths of the total.

Proportionately, Latin American families in Texas have contributed more to the Armed Forces than have Anglo American families, for they have more sons to give. This abundant gift of their own flesh and blood and bone could not but stimulate their pride and interest in their rights as citizens of the United States, could not but intensify their resentment of existing conditions and inspire them to unprecedented efforts to remedy these conditions.

(See Appendix for some typical citations to Latin Americans of Texas.)

Clarence Laroche, in an article which appeared in the Brownsville *Herald* on January 21, 1945, paid high tribute to those Latin American sons of Texas who distinguished themselves in the war. Said he:

The Mexico-Texan, like a famous Brownsville poem says, is "one fonny man." But when it comes to this business of fighting for his country, our enemies can't see anything so funny about him. . . .

Today on the battlegrounds of the world, where free men are fighting for their dignity and honor and the cause of freedom, the names of Mexico-Texans stand out . . . García . . . Longoria . . . Hidalgo . . . López . . . Villarreal . . . Vásquez . . . Segura . . . Rubio. . . .

Brownsville and the Valley stand out along with such cities and areas as San Antonio, Laredo, El Paso and other border towns, for the fighting Mexico-Texas breed. Our boys have proved themselves.

There's "persistent" José López of Brownsville, who was assigned to protect a flank of his group in the Second Division battling Von Rundstedt's breakthrough. López continued fighting by himself despite overwhelming odds, and did not stop until he was sure his division was safe. He fired 500 rounds of ammunition from his machine gun and is credited with killing 100 Nazis.[2]

Pvt. Pedro Rubio of Austin probably saved the life of a buddy somewhere in France when, under German machine gun fire, he operated on a soldier to remove a bullet lodged in a thigh. It was a pocketknife operation. Later, this Mexico-Texan and an Anglo-Texan, Pvt. Lloyd Cockrell of Lampasas, got the wounded man out of range of fire.

Then there was Pfc. Vicente Gonzales of Rio Hondo, who got the Silver Star for crawling under a sheet of machine gun fire to give first aid to two buddies and drag them to safety during the bitter Normandy campaign. Later he sustained a broken arm when a German 88 shell exploded near him.

Sgt. Roberto T. Gonzales, of Mission, was killed in action. He was a waist gunner on a Flying Fortress and had completed twenty missions when he was killed. Later, at formal military ceremonies at Moore Field, near Mission, his widow was presented with the five medals awarded to him—Distinguished Flying Cross, Air Medal, and three Oak Leaf Clusters.

They're plenty clever, too, these Mexico-Texans. On Saipan, Pfc. Ariel Hernández of a U. S. Marine engineering unit on front-line duty, used his knowledge of the Japanese language to persuade thirty-one forlorn looking sons of Nippon to surrender.

"They were scared," Hernández told reporters who sought to laud him for the unprecedented number of captives.

There were hundreds of Mexico-Texans with the great Thirty-sixth "Texas" Division at Salerno, and border country boys in particular gave great account of themselves. At Cassino, Pfc. Arturo Rivera of Mission captured six Nazis.

"A shell blast lifted my helmet right off my head," Rivera told interviewers afterward, "and I saw that Germans were manning a cap-

[2] On May 26, 1945, Sgt. López was awarded the Congressional Medal of Honor. He holds, in addition, the Purple Heart, the Bronze Star and five battle stars. Other Latin Americans from Texas who have received the nation's highest award include Marcario García of Sugarland, Cleto L. Rodríguez of San Antonio, Lucian Adams of Port Arthur, Silvestre Herrera of El Paso, and Alejandro R. Ruiz of Barstow. (See Appendix for full text of citations to these men.)

tured tank's guns. They had captured the vehicle and turned its guns on us. They knew that we had prisoners, but they didn't care how many of their own men they killed, apparently, as long as they could kill us, too.

"I was hit in the shoulder and neck by machine gun bullets from the tank. Two of the Jerry prisoners were killed and one was wounded."

Despite the wounds, Associated Press reported, Pfc. Rivera herded the remaining prisoners out of range of the tank and delivered them to his Infantry battalion command post.

From El Paso, Ernesto Alonso was promoted to a Captaincy for his ability, courage, and initiative while in battle in the Italian campaign.

Also from El Paso, Master-Sgt. Roque O. Segura was posthumously awarded the Silver Star for bravery in the Italian campaign. According to the citation accompanying the award, Sgt. Segura carried out his orders, and led his men to the assigned objective in the face of murderous enemy fire. . . .

That lists a few of them . . . so don't sell the Mexico-Texan short, for

" . . . there is neither East nor West,
　　Border, nor Breed, nor Birth,
　　When two strong men stand face to face,
　　Though they come from the ends of the earth."

These lines from Kipling express a thought that is especially significant when applied to the Latin American Texans who fought side by side with Anglo Americans the world over. They must have wondered sometimes, some of them, how it happened that their first experience with democracy was in fighting for it. They must have wondered, since the Army considered them of sufficient importance to teach them—many of them—how to read and write in order to fight and die, why they had never had the opportunity to go to school as other children did in order that they might work and live. They must have wondered, too, about the man-made rules and customs that made them privileged to occupy the same trench or ship or plane with Anglo Americans when, perhaps, they were not allowed to attend the same schools, patronize the same theaters and restaurants, or hold the same jobs as Anglo Americans in their home town.

We may profitably reminisce with W. A. Shaley, of the Texas State Department of Public Welfare:

One evening in 1939, I was calling on a Latin American family in Donna. Just before I left the house, the 15-year-old son came in from a long day's work in the vegetable fields. He was the sole support of his mother and three younger brothers and sisters. He had brought home his day's earnings—53 cents. . . . I wonder what that boy was thinking when he died on Guadalcanal?[3]

Pfc. Henry Castillo of San Antonio, writing from "somewhere in Luxembourg," voiced his thoughts in the following words:

The squad consisted of a German, a Frenchman, a Spaniard, a Mexican, an Italian, a Jew, and guys with names like Joe.

They helped to take a little town called Konzen, part of the Siegfried Line . . . but it never made the news. They started off one morning in waist-deep snow. Slipped, staggered, fought up the hill. Poured in their M1 and BAR fire. Chucked grenades wherever they did the most good. Cleaned out the snipers. Moved the line another millimeter forward on the map.

Then they blasted foxholes and took turns standing guard. Through the cold grey day. Through the bitter night. Went far off on patrols. Sought out the enemy. Came back wet with snow and sweat. Bone-weary and spent.

They shucked straw from a nearby loft. Cleaned out the cellar of a wrecked barn. Built a small stove. Made a home for the squad for the night. Volunteered for a dozen details. For wire. For chow. For bedrolls. For ammo. Ran errands. Made reports. Stood by for signals. And slept fitfully together in odd moments in between.

They were infantrymen. A mongrel crew. Dirty, tired, hemmed in by death and danger. Kids. Old and grim and taught [sic].

But the squad had something to teach the world. A sense of belonging to a unit . . . and a family. What man can do when teamed with others. An understanding of life. The meaning of misery and sacrifice. The desire to help the other guy to live, so that thereby he himself might stay alive.

Too bad everyone can't belong to one small squad in one small battle. To learn how men of different breeds and creeds can live and work

<hr/>

[3] *Minutes of Professional Workshop,* State Department of Education, Austin, March 19-24, 1945.

together when they must. How unreal are the luxuries, privileges, prejudices and politics that separate men.[4]

We will do well to consider what these boys have been thinking—and are still thinking. They have been made literate, many of them. They have learned what it means to eat well-balanced meals. They have been trained as mechanics, as radio operators, as aviators, as technicians of all sorts—training that they would never have received otherwise. They have been doing the same job, at the same pay, as Anglo American soldiers, and have acquitted themselves with equal credit.

It would be sheer, blind idiocy to think they have not resolved that this brighter and better world for which they fought shall be a brighter, better world for their children as well as for the children of John Jones.

And John Jones has changed his ideas, too. He has learned that José is a "right guy"; that he is a good man to have around when the going gets tough. Although he may have been unaware of, or indifferent to José's problems before he knew José, he will not be indifferent to them in the future.

One of the most odious and indefensible injustices suffered by Latin Americans in some parts of Texas is the denial of civil rights of one kind or another. For example, in four Texas counties, qualified voters of Mexican extraction are not allowed to participate in the Democratic primaries, by virtue of a so-called "White Man's Union," which prohibits both Negroes and Latin Americans from entering the polls.

Considering their potential voting strength, Latin Americans are singularly ineffectual in Texas politics. Except in the city of Laredo, and in certain South Texas counties, where many elective city, county, and school officials are of Mexican descent, Latin Americans are without due representation on school boards, city councils, and other governmental or quasi-governmental units. Even in San Antonio, where the Latin American population numbers 107,000, and where more than 50 per cent of school-age children are of Mexican descent, none

4 *The Pan-American* (San Antonio, Texas), I (April, 1945), 16.

but Anglos have ever been elected to membership on the school board.

Only a part of the blame for this state of affairs can justifiably be put upon the majority group. There are at least two other important factors involved. One has its roots in the nature of the Latin Americans themselves. The other is the poll tax.

Anglo politicians in most cities having a sizable Latin American population appear to have promulgated an effective, but unwritten, law which, while consenting to the appointment or election of Latin Americans to minor political posts, forbids and prevents their securing a top-ranking post. Thus, when an ambitious and capable Latin American announces for office in opposition to an Anglo incumbent or candidate (who is in all probability the candidate of the local machine), Anglo politicians follow the tried-and-true formula of "divide and conquer." They immediately sponsor the candidacy of another Latin American, preferably a personal enemy of the man who has previously announced, and thereby split the Latin American vote and assure the election of the Anglo candidate.

The important point is that this practice could not prevail were it not rooted in the shortcomings of the Latin Americans: their exaggerated individualism and consequent lack of interest in co-operation toward a given goal; the personal, and frequently petty, jealousies and animosities which separate them and prevent their working together for the common good; even the desire and willingness on the part of some to curry favor with the political "powers that be" at the expense of the best interests of their own group.

Unity of purpose and a determination to subjugate personal considerations to loftier ends must be developed by Latin American leaders and political aspirants before the group as a whole can hope to secure adequate representation in city, county, state, and school government.

The fact that thousands of Latin Americans, because of their low economic status, are disfranchised is another factor of no small significance. The abolition of the poll tax in Texas is requisite to the achievement of a truly democratic, representative government at all levels, for all the people.

In an estimated fifty counties, wherein the Latin American population ranges from fifteen to forty per cent, persons of Mexican descent have never been known to be called for jury service, even in the trial of civil suits.

In one Central Texas county, a Latin American was charged with killing an Anglo. He was indicted for murder by a grand jury composed entirely of Anglo Americans, although more than 30 per cent of the county's population was of Mexican extraction. Upon the date set for the trial, 100 men were summoned as prospective jurors, all of them being Anglo Americans. The defendant's attorney filed a motion to quash the indictment on the grounds that never in the history of that county had a citizen of Mexican descent been summoned for jury service. Rather than establish the precedent of allowing a Latin American to serve on either a grand jury or a trial jury, the authorities released the accused, and he has never been brought to trial, although the alleged murder took place three years ago.

In some Texas cities, persons of Mexican extraction are denied the right to own or rent real estate, except in designated sections of town, regardless of their economic status or social acceptability. These restrictions are imposed, not by city ordinance, but by clauses in real estate contracts, which ordinarily prohibit the transfer of property to, or occupation thereof by, "Negroes, Mexicans or Chinese."

In counties where the fee system is in use, false arrests of Latin Americans frequently occur. Where the constable or other law enforcement officer is paid on the basis of the number of arrests he makes, instead of a monthly salary, he naturally "picks on" those residents of the community who are least able to protect their rights.

Thus it happens that in one town of 7,500 population, of whom some 3,000 are Latin Americans, the record of arrests for disturbing the peace and similar misdemeanors during a two-months period in 1945 revealed that of the total of seventy-seven arrests, forty-eight were of Latin Americans, and only twenty-nine of Anglo Americans. In other words, Latin Americans in that community are subjected to arrest about four times as frequently as Anglos.

The argument might be advanced—as has been done—that this proportion of arrests among Latin Americans is only normal and natural "since they are the more lawless element in the population." Comparative statistics, however, prove conclusively that such is not the case,' but that the abnormal number of arrests among Latin Americans in this particular Central Texas town is due, rather, to the evil influence of the fee system.

Corpus Christi, for example, is a city of more than 100,000 population, 50 per cent of which is of Mexican descent. In addition to the Latin Americans who permanently reside there, some 24,000 migrant laborers pass through Corpus Christi each year in their trek through the cotton areas of Texas. Yet statistics show that in only 33.7 per cent of the arrests made in that city are Latin Americans the culprits. It would appear, therefore, that the fee system of remunerating law enforcement officers must be abolished.

The term "coyote"[5] has been used to describe a certain breed of small-time racketeers who operate, generally, on the court house steps of county seats throughout Texas. These individuals, many of whom are themselves Latin Americans, act as procurers for lawyers of questionable integrity. Lounging at the entrance of the court house, they intercept humble, unsuspecting Latin Americans—most often those who do not speak English—and succeed in extracting from them exorbitant fees for simple services which, if the victim had been allowed to proceed unhindered into the court house, would have been rendered free of charge. One such "coyote" extorted $30.00

[5] It is an interesting fact that in the State of New Mexico the term "coyote" connotes a person of mixed Anglo and Hispano blood who is loyal to neither group. It is almost always used deprecatingly.

from an elderly laborer for a Notary Public's certificate that under the law could not have cost more than fifty cents. This and similar abuses, which could not flourish without the connivance of dishonest politicians, clearly indicate the need for more free legal aid bureaus or clinics, widely publicized, and operated as genuine public service institutions.

The celebrated case at Levelland eloquently demonstrated two points: the inequality of Latin Americans under the law as it is administered in many parts of Texas, and that a law of any kind is effective only if the persons charged with its enforcement are convinced of the necessity for making it effective.

Levelland is a town of about 3,000 population, situated in Hockley County, near the New Mexico line, and is the headquarters for migratory laborers in that county during the cotton season. On one Saturday afternoon in October, 1943, some 3,000 cotton pickers had congregated in the town. One of them, a seventeen-year-old boy, entered a cafe to purchase a package of cigarettes.

Without saying a word, the owner threw a full soft drink bottle at him, hitting him in the head. The boy turned to the door, holding his head in his hands. Other laborers, conversing in groups on the streets and in the plaza, gathered around to see what had happened. When some one took the boy to the Sheriff's office, the crowd remained where it was, quietly awaiting developments.

The Sheriff was greatly disturbed, not only because of the act itself, but also because he could visualize mob action resulting, and he hurried to the cafe with his deputy. In the meantime, the cafe owner, in a spirit of bravado, had thrown another bottle into the assembly, which was caught by an Anglo American farmer in the group and returned to him through the plate glass window of the cafe; whereupon, the owner emerged from the building, brandishing a revolver in each hand, and threatened the crowd.

At that moment, the Sheriff arrived. Posting his deputy

to keep order inside the cafe, he prevailed upon a Latin American whom he knew to ask the crowd, in Spanish, to move back across the street into the plaza, as they were blocking traffic, and to assure them that the matter would be straightened out. With no display of violence whatever, the crowd gradually dispersed.

In this case, the facts were readily apparent, fully verified by numerous witnesses. The cafe owner was arrested and charged with the minimum offenses which his actions would support: "rude display of firearms" and "simple assault." Actually, he could have been charged with "assault with intent to murder," a felony. Despite the mildness of the charges brought against him, however, the cafe owner was acquitted by the jury.

Here there was no question in anyone's mind regarding the defendant's guilt. The failure of the jury to sustain the law can be interpreted only as signifying that the jurors had not yet been educated to the point where they were willing to concede that laws for the protection of the general public apply with equal effectiveness to the protection of Latin Americans. Although a law has a power and a majesty of its own, its full benefits may be enjoyed only when there is forceful public opinion behind it. This is our task: to educate public opinion —in this instance, police officers, sheriffs, judges, and jurors— to the point that justice will be meted out on the merits of a case, rather than upon local prejudices or the ignorance of those charged with the law's enforcement.

During the 1945 session of the Texas Legislature, a bill was introduced which was directed toward the eradication of discrimination in Texas. This measure, however, proposed to cover only one phase of the problem: that of the refusal to serve Latin Americans, whether citizens of this or that American republic, in public places of business or amusement. It advocated that refusal of service be declared a criminal offense, punishable by fines or imprisonment, or both.

During the time the proposal was pending in the Legislature, bitter public debate was aroused. Quite naturally, there were two schools of thought on the efficacy of a law of this type, its chances of being passed, and the possibility of enforcing it if passed. The issue was beclouded by extremists on both sides and tainted with personalities. It will suffice to say that the bill was not enacted into law.

There is nothing to be gained at this time by reviewing all the various arguments advanced for and against the proposal. Experience has proved, nevertheless, that a powerful and operative instrument, fundamental in character, must be intelligently devised to attack discrimination at its very roots; and for this reason alone does it serve a constructive purpose to mention one point that carried considerable weight in the minds of thoughtful persons.

In all justice it must be stated that these individuals, in opposing the measure, were acting in good faith. They acknowledged the evil of discrimination as practiced in public places, and earnestly desired that an end be put to it. But at the same time, they feared that a law of the type proposed, imposing sanctions, would create widespread antagonism on the part of uninformed or prejudiced persons, and would subject many innocent and defenseless Latin Americans to humiliation and make them the victims of retaliation. Furthermore, in enforcing a statutory law, it is necessary to depend upon the will of local enforcement officers and agents, as illustrated by the Levelland case, and it was feared that attempts to secure justice under the proposed law would lead to constant bickering in the courts and to an aggravation of inter-group animosity.

On the other hand, there were many who believed that in order to correct flagrant cases of social injustice, the only effective way was to provide legal sanctions against recalcitrant offenders.

Refusal of service in public places of business and amusement is only one phase of the problems in Texas. In all, there are six major issues at stake, all of which involve the civil rights of American citizens of Mexican descent. They are as follows:

(1) Refusal of admission to or service in public places of business and amusement.

(2) Arbitrary segregation of children in the public schools.

(3) Refusal to sell or rent real estate to persons of Mexican extraction, regardless of social, economic, or cultural status.

(4) Discrimination in employment, including inferior wage scales, curtailment of promotional opportunities, and denial of union membership.

(5) Refusal to permit citizens of Mexican extraction to vote in the Democratic primaries.

(6) Refusal to permit qualified citizens of Mexican descent to participate in the administration of justice through jury service.

In Chapter 10 of this book a statute was suggested, supported by sanctions, which would prohibit discrimination on the part of either employers or labor unions. Sanctions are deemed appropriate in this particular case, because affecting, as they would, only impersonal entities—corporations and trade unions —they would not tend to create widespread and uncontrollable personal animosities, would not place man against man, or group against group. At any rate, the risk of arousing personal feelings would be limited, if not altogether negligible, in comparison with the salutary effects of fulfilled justice. It is easier to enforce fair practices when dealing with responsible, well-disciplined institutions, than when dealing with the complexity of individual passions.

In the final chapter, there is outlined in full a proposal to change the method of apportioning State school funds in order to assure equal educational facilities and opportunities for all Texas children.

But in order to provide, at the root, a principle declaring unlawful the segregation of Latin Americans, or of any other group not specifically mentioned by the Constitution or the laws of the State, in any realm of community, state, or national life, a statement of policy should be incorporated into the Constitution.

It is expensive in time, money, and effort to attempt to attack the basic problems piecemeal. Individuals, vested interests, and pressure groups who would resist any and all efforts to enact legislation dealing with one phase of the problems, and imposing petty sanctions, would find it more difficult to oppose the enunciation of a principle on which all right-minded, straight-thinking people are in agreement.

Furthermore, a statement of policy in the Constitution is mandatory. It does not involve the imposition of minor sanctions, which in due course provoke retaliations. Many people who would disregard a subsidiary regulation or a particular statute would not defy a constitutional provision which is clear-cut, emphatic, imperative.

There is currently much discussion of the need for calling a constitutional convention for the purpose of redrafting the State's Constitution. The present document was adopted in 1876, since which time it has been amended repeatedly until it is now cumbersome and unwieldy, and burdened with many provisions that are statutory in nature. In all probability, the contemplated redrafting will be undertaken in the reasonably near future, at which time certain principles should be proposed for inclusion in the new instrument. However, failing a constitutional convention, an amendment should be offered to the present Constitution.

For example, Article 1, Section 19, now reads: "No citizen of this State shall be deprived of life, liberty, property, privileges or immunities, or in any manner disfranchised, except by the due course of the law of the land."

This point may well be elaborated upon by the addition of the following provisions:

Section 20. Every citizen of this State shall be entitled equally with every other citizen of this State to participate in the full measure of rights, privileges and immunities guaranteed under this Constitution and under the laws of this State, and no citizen of this State, or subject thereof, shall be arbitrarily segregated from other citizens or subjects of this State in the exercise of these rights, privileges and immunities, except where such segregation shall be provided for by laws in which provision is made that equal facilities shall be afforded to each of the segregated groups.

Section 21.   Any segregation of citizens or subjects of this State in its public school system, either by law or by administrative act, which is not specifically provided for in this Constitution shall be deemed arbitrary and in violation of this Constitution if the same shall not be done by written provision setting out clear criteria for division and based solely on individual qualifications.

Section 22.   The term "citizens of this State" shall mean all citizens of the United States residing in the State of Texas; and the term "subjects of this State" shall mean all persons, whether citizens or aliens, who are domiciled within the State.

Upon the adoption of the foregoing principles, it will be necessary to launch an intensive educational campaign, in order to make known the policy of the State and assure its effectiveness in every town and village.

The public and official recognition of these principles, their incorporation into the Constitution of Texas, and their activation throughout the State are requisite to general progress, prosperity, and security; for as Archibald MacLeish says:

Unless we are now prepared to accept, not for ourselves alone but for the world, and not for belief alone but for action, the literal and universal truth of the principles that all men are born equal; that they are endowed by their Creator with certain unalienable rights; that among them are life, liberty, and the pursuit of happiness—unless we are prepared to accept these truths, we will lose not only the hope of peace which now is darkened, but ourselves as well. To stand on one side or the other of that choice is the hard and inescapable lot of every one of us.

To stand on the people's side, which was in the beginning and has always been and always must be the American side, is the right of those who have the courage and the will to choose.[6]

" . . . the courage and the will to choose"!   That is Texas' problem.

[6] Archibald MacLeish, "Victory Without Peace", *The Saturday Review of Literature*, XXIX (Feb. 9, 1946), 5. Quoted by permission.

Part 5

Looking Ahead

Chapter 14

The Task Before Us

S O NOW WE KNOW what's the matter with Texas. We know, too, that the prospects for the future are by no means hopeless. On the contrary, they are bright indeed. In the brief span of three years, notable progress has been made, as we have seen; yet the work accomplished to date is, in reality, only the prelude to the task. Now we are ready for the main performance. Many things remain to be done, and in looking ahead, those are the things we must consider.

The principles and procedures agreed upon at the Inter-American Conference on Problems of War and Peace early in 1945, as the means of preserving and perfecting unity among the American republics, may well serve as a blueprint for the guidance of Texas in solving the problems of its Latin American people and in promoting harmony between Latin and Anglo American citizens.

Industrialization

In view of the fact that equality of opportunity for economic advancement is a fundamental prerequisite for the correction of all the other ills from which Latin Americans in Texas suffer, let us study the far-reaching implications of one provision of the Economic Charter of the Americas which was adopted at the Mexico City meeting. It is stated in this Charter that the

American republics declare their firm purpose to collaborate in a program for the attainment of

. . . a constructive basis for the sound economic develop of the Americas through the development of natural resources, industrialization, improvement of transportation, modernization of agriculture, development of power facilities and public works, the encouragement of investment of private capital, managerial capacity and technical skill, and the improvement of labor standards and working conditions, including collective bargaining, all leading to a rising level of living and increased consumption.

As Luis Quintanilla has succinctly phrased it, "The larger the number of actual beneficiaries of democracy, the stronger democracy will stand."[1] We have seen, in the preceding chapters, that a large number of Texas' citizens could not accurately be described as "actual beneficiaries of democracy." One of the primary causes of this state of affairs is that Texas is, and has always been, largely an agricultural state. Until the outbreak of the war in 1941, according to United States Census data, we had 38 per cent of our gainfully employed population in agriculture, or 16 per cent more than the average for the United States as a whole. In contrast, only 12 per cent of our gainfully employed were engaged in manufacturing.

Inasmuch as a large proportion of the agricultural labor in our State has been and is performed by people of Mexican descent, and since this kind of work, migratory or otherwise, is the most poorly paid of all labor, the economic standards of Latin Americans in Texas have been kept at a minimum level. Furthermore, with the cessation of hostilities with Japan in 1945, strategic materials began to be released for the manufacture of farm machinery. The rapid mechanization of agriculture, which will inevitably take place in the next few years, will permanently displace thousands of Latin Americans now essential to the cultivation and harvesting of crops throughout the State.

[1] Luis Quintanilla, *A Latin American Speaks* (New York: The Macmillan Company, 1943), p. 221.

Increased industrialization is obviously the answer, not only for the benefit of Latin American agricultural workers, but to provide ample employment opportunities for returning servicemen and to assure the progress of the State as a whole. And what are the prospects for industrialization in Texas?

The establishment of war plants in various parts of the State gave Texas industry an impetus that would not have been forthcoming in many years of slow, peacetime expansion. With the end of the war, these wartime industries pose certain urgent problems that must be solved immediately if the State's industrialization is not to suffer a serious setback.

In the first place, how can the industries that were established in the State during the war be held here and kept going, or, through reconversion, turned into production in new or related lines? And second, how can Texas most effectively capitalize upon the army of trained machinists and industrial workers, the technical skills, the managerial abilities which were developed in or acquired by the State during the war years?

The second consideration is, perhaps, the most immediate, for upon being released from war industries, trained management personnel, technicians, and workers—an asset that Texas has long needed and has heretofore been unable to develop—will move out of the State, unless domestic industry expands rapidly enough to absorb them. Many of them, in fact, are already gone. Should Texas industry fail to develop, the State's raw materials will again move to the North and East; war plants will be dismantled completely, or greatly reduced in size; their new machine tools will be used to retool northern plants; buildings now in use will disintegrate; and Texas industry will be right back where it was in 1941.

Excessive freight rates have always acted as an impediment to the development of industry in Texas, but this clouded condition is tending to clear, and there is good reason to hope for complete rate equalization. The Interstate Commerce Commission ruled in May, 1945, that freight rates in the East should be increased by 10 per cent and those in the South and Southwest decreased by the same percentage. In addition, the I.C.C. instructed the railroads to make plans for equal classrates east of the Rockies. These actions provide an excellent stimulus to capital investment in industry in Texas—by Texans and by outside capitalists.

It is the earnest hope of the State's Postwar Planning Commission that Texas capital will seize upon the opportunity that is now before it and establish, in towns large and small throughout the State, industries to utilize the great wealth and vast assortment of raw materials that are at hand. Huge industrial plants controlled by out-of-state interests, such as the Sheffield Steel Company at Houston and the Dow Chemical Company's magnesium plant at Freeport, have made, and will continue to make, a great contribution to the State. Certainly, investments in Texas by individuals and corporations from other sections of the United States are not to be discouraged. Nevertheless, Texas has unlimited capital of her own, and it is on Texas capital that the Postwar Planning Commission is pinning its faith for the immediate and widespread expansion of industry.

The scope and variety of possibilities are practically limitless, both for the diversification of present industries and the establishment of new ones. The so-called oil industry of Texas, during the war years, made marked progress in the field of chemistry as well. Oil and gas are both carbohydrates, the same as coal, and are sources of synthetics. There is every indication that, within a five-to-ten-year period, Texas will develop an important plastic industry.

Also, it is very likely that the synthetic rubber industry will continue for several years, during which time, under the stimulus of private capital, we may see some drastic reductions in manufacturing costs, thus bringing the synthetic product down to the competitive price of natural rubber, in which case its continuation in reasonable volume is assured. In any event, there should be a good portion of present synthetic rubber manufacture continued as a permanent Texas industry, for the synthetic substance has definite advantages over the natural rubber in some products.

There is considerable room for expansion in the steel industry. Regardless of freight rates, Texas manufacturers can produce heavy iron and steel products and ship them within her own boundaries more cheaply than they can be brought in from the north.

The possibilities of plants for processing agricultural products are legion, and may consist of milling in the cotton and grain areas, or of plants for freezing, canning, or drying Valley fruits and vegetables. Texas has both the climate and the soil for agricultural development, and since products are most economically processed as close to the point of growth and as soon after picking as possible, the establishment of such plants in the Lower Rio Grande Valley and Winter Garden Area, as well as elsewhere, would provide employment for thousands of workers. The sooner this is done the better.

Texas possesses extensive deposits of high-grade clay, feldspar, and other minerals used in the manufacture of porcelain and glassware, but so far, the deposits are practically untouched. In the past, some feldspar has been shipped to Mexico, and some clay to eastern factories; but with the exception of small plants manufacturing container glass, art pottery, novelties, and building tile, no factory has yet been established in the State for the exploitation of these raw materials. The unconcern of Texas capital is, to date, the chief obstacle to large-scale development along this line.

In an effort to stimulate activity in the porcelain and glassware industry, and for the purpose of developing trained artisans for the benefit of such plants, the 49th Legislature appropriated funds for the establishment of a ceramics development program at the University of Texas. Through the operation of a semi-industrial laboratory and plant, the industrial uses of Texas' raw materials will be demonstrated, particularly for the manufacture of porcelain products. Latin Americans possess a natural aptitude for work in ceramics, and for that reason their enrollment in the new program is especially to be desired.

Another field for development which is practically unexplored is that of seafood and allied industries. Texas boasts of a coastline 624 miles in length, yet in all that rich expanse there are no important marine industries. Enterprising promoters could, through colorful advertising, make Texans seafood-conscious. Shippers of fresh fish, shrimp, lobsters, and oysters would prosper. Oyster beds could be profitably cultivated and exploited. Canneries could be established. Related industries, such as the manufacture of cans, fish nets, boats, and fishing gear would flourish, as would plants for processing fertilizer and shell. All that is required is Texas capital, initiative, and imagination.

It seems incredible that Texas' raw cotton and wool should be shipped to northern and eastern mills for processing, only to be repurchased later, as finished goods, by Texans at many times the original sales price. The entire State would profit enormously through the establishment of cotton and woolen mills within the immediate production areas, and year-round employment opportunities for thousands of Texans would thereby be assured.

These are only a few of the possibilities for the expansion of industry in Texas, and in the process of industrialization we shall necessarily and incidentally comply with various other provisions of the Economic Charter of the Americas: development of natural resources, improvement of transportation, development of power facilities and public works, and the encouragement of investment of private capital, managerial capacity, and technical skill.

But there is one further important point in the Charter, namely, "the improvement of labor standards and working conditions, including collective bargaining, all leading to a rising level of living and increased consumption."

Capital cannot be attracted to Texas, nor interested within the State, unless labor costs are reasonable. On the other hand, low wages will not develop the State, nor make possible the solution of the problems of its present large low-income group. Capital, therefore, must be liberal and progressive. Labor must be co-operative, interested in the betterment of all its members, as well as in the public welfare.

It should be emphasized that by no means all the present discrimination in employment in Texas is practiced by management. On the contrary, the great majority of labor unions refuse to admit Latin Americans and Negroes to membership, thereby making impossible their employment by management, even if management should be so disposed.

If labor has the right to organize—which it definitely does have—then every man or woman who can meet the requirements of physical fitness and skill has an equal right to membership in such an organization and the benefits to be derived therefrom, regardless of race, creed, or national origin. The organization of labor on any other basis is contrary to the precepts of democracy, a threat to the realization of the Atlantic Charter and the Economic Charter of the Americas, and inimical to the best interests of Texas. Furthermore, discrimination by the unions belies the very principles upon which they first came into existence.

In the wake of industrialization, full employment, and the payment of decent wages will come a rising standard of living for all our people, which will, in turn, increase the demand for consumer goods and expand the service institutions of the State, thereby creating more business and more employment. Dealers in furniture, electrical appliances, and building materials, grocery, drug, and clothing stores, hotels, restaurants, and theaters, railroads, bus and air lines, laundries, and dry cleaning establishments—all these and many more will profit immeasurably. There is not a business man in the State who will not benefit from the payment of a decent living wage to every employable Texas citizen.

Legislation

Those who advocate legislation as the preferred medium for solving Texas' problems must be discriminating in the type of laws they propose. No one can dispute the fact that the world's advance from savagery to civilization has been brought about, to a great extent, through enlightened legislation. Such legislation has consisted of measures fixing hours and wages; laws promoting general education; prohibitions of child labor and industrial hazards; laws safeguarding the public health and welfare; and guarantees to labor, including that of equal pay for equal work.

Each succeeding session of the Texas Legislature sees new laws added and old ones revised, indicating, usually, a continuing progress. Two notable contributions to the general welfare of the State—actions facilitating the solution of the problems of the State's large low-income population—were made by the 49th Legislature. Most revolutionary, perhaps, was the Sanitary Code, introduced as Senate Bill No. 81, which became effective on September 4, 1945. It represents the most determined attack Texas has ever made on menaces to the public health and places our State far in advance of many others.

Among the conditions declared to be nuisances dangerous to the public health are breeding places for flies; all sewage, human excreta, waste water, garbage, or other organic wastes deposited or exposed in such a way as to be a potential instrument or medium in the transmission of disease; conditions harboring rats in populous areas; the maintenance of open surface privies or overflowing septic tanks, the contents of either of which may be accessible to flies.

The law provides that, in order to eliminate such menaces to the public health, every owner of property in or on which there is a nuisance shall, as soon as he learns of its presence, "proceed at once and continue to abate the said nuisance."

At the same time, every local health officer, upon receiving information and proof of the existence of a nuisance within his jurisdiction, shall issue a written notice to the person responsible for the nuisance, ordering its abatement. Copy of that notice will be sent, at the same time, to the local city, county, or district attorney. If, after a reasonable time, specified in the notice, the order for abatement has not been complied with, the local prosecuting attorney, upon advice of the local health officer, will institute proceedings against the offending property owner.

Regulations governing the construction and maintenance of outdoor privies are clearly defined, as are those for the collection and disposal of garbage and refuse, and sanitary standards for school houses and grounds.

One of the most vital points in the entire Code is the inclusion under its provisions of unincorporated villages, which have heretofore been affected neither by the general law nor by the laws governing incorporated towns and cities. In the future, unincorporated communities will be under the direct jurisdiction of the County Court. When it is understood that the most disastrous epidemics of polio, typhus, diarrhea, and other diseases during recent years have originated in rural communities and "boom towns" which have mushroomed outside the city limits of industrial areas, the full import of this provision can be appreciated.

For violation of any section or subdivision of the Sanitary Code, any person, firm, or corporation so offending "shall be fined not less than $10.00 and not more than $200.00, and each day of such violation shall constitute a separate offense."

A second highly significant legislative act, signed by Governor Stevenson on June 22, 1945, is Senate Bill No. 167, providing State Aid to Rural Schools in the amount of $14,000,000 annually.

In order to be eligible for State Aid under this Act, school districts must have not fewer than 20 nor more than 1,250 enumerated scholastics, or, in the case of rural high school districts, an average of not more than 200 scholastics. No school district shall be eligible to receive any type of aid authorized under the provisions of this law unless it shall have provided for the annual support of its schools by voting, levying and collecting, for the current school year, a local maintenance school tax of not less than 50 cents on the $100.00 of property valuation in the entire district.

No school shall be granted salary aid whose average daily attendance is less than 65 per cent of the scholastic census enrollment.

The amount of aid to be applied for is to be determined by the excess of operating expenses over all revenues of the district, if such expenses are greater.

Three types of State Aid are available. The first provides for the allotment of funds to assist the State's small, rural districts in defraying salary costs. This provision of the Act specifies "one teacher for any number of scholastics from twenty (20) to thirty-five (35), and one additional teacher for each additional thirty (30) scholastics or fractional part thereof, residing in the district."

It also sets the salary scale for teachers in districts applying for and receiving aid under the Act as follows:

Classroom teacher in unaccredited school[2] ....$135.00 mo. for 8 mos.
Classroom teacher in accredited school ...... 135.00 mo. for 9 mos.
Home Economics teacher .... 135.00 mo. for 10 mos.
Vocational Agriculture or Trades and
    Industries teacher .... 117.50 mo. for 12 mos.

In addition, each teacher shall receive $3.00 per month for each year of college credit over one year, not to exceed $15.00; and $1.50 per month for each year of teaching experience, not to exceed $15.00 per month.

Other types of aid available under the Act are for defraying a portion of the tuition required in rural areas and to assist in furnishing transportation.

[2] One must be grateful for improvement, but the salaries paid Texas teachers are nothing for Texans to become "chesty" about. In our neighboring state of New Mexico, for instance, where the per capita wealth is far below that of Texas, the minimum teachers' salary is hundreds of dollars a year more than that in our State. —P.R.K.

The funds appropriated for all purposes under the provisions of this law are allocated as follows:

For Salary Aid	$ 8,001,129
High School and Elementary Tuition	900,000
Transportation Aid	5,000,000
Administrative and Legislative Expense, including Salary of Legislative Accountant	98,871
Total Annual Appropriation $14,000,000	

Inasmuch as so many Latin American children reside in rural areas—and it is in the rural areas that their attendance records are so poor and their rate of progress slowest—the law providing State Aid for Rural Schools should prove beneficial. Not only will the rural districts be able to employ a higher type of teachers, but the assistance to which they will be entitled on tuition and transportation should bring about a marked improvement in school attendance.

However, further legislative changes are required if Texas, in conformity with its Constitution, is to furnish equal educational facilities and opportunities for all its children. This brings us again to a consideration of the method of apportioning State school funds.

The total sum spent for the public school program in Texas each year is approximately $85,000,000, of which $37,000,000 comes from the State Available School Fund and $14,000,000 from the Rural Aid Fund. The balance of some $34,000,000 is borne by the counties.

Under the present law, the State Available School Fund is apportioned to school districts on the basis of census enumeration. Thus a district may enumerate all its children of scholastic age and receive from the State in the neighborhood of $30.00 for each child enumerated—whether or not that child is ever enrolled in school. This system enables counties with low school attendance to receive from the State far more per capita for the education of children enrolled than counties with a high percentage of school attendance.

School attendance in Texas has a regional aspect, and is intimately linked with the economic status of the population and the real wealth or poverty of the counties. To illustrate the comparative wealth of Texas counties, Robert C. Eckhardt[3] has found that twenty-five counties have more than $5,000.00 of income per scholastic enumerated, while seventeen counties have less than $1,500.00 of income per scholastic. If one draws a line from Corpus Christi westward, most of the seventeen counties will be south of this line and between the Gulf of Mexico on the east and the Rio Grande on the west. The twenty-five wealthiest counties are the counties containing the large cities or large oil developments.

Eckhardt's study shows that the South Texas region is the most backward in school attendance, and therefore school districts in South Texas receive more money from the State, on the enumeration per capita basis; yet, at the same time, the South Texas region is lowest in per capita wealth. This situation is exactly comparable to that in the United States as a whole: the South, the Number One economic problem of the nation, is also the Number One educational problem.

When we remember that the South Texas region is heavily populated by Latin Americans, we can readily see that it is Texas children of Mexican descent who suffer the greatest lack of educational facilities.

Successive sessions of the Texas Legislature have considered proposals to amend the State Constitution so as to change the method of apportioning State school funds on the basis of enrollment rather than census enumeration. This amendment, however, has never been accepted; doubtless because it would only work a further hardship on those counties least able to finance a school program. Such a method might prove successful if each Texas county were as rich as every other county in natural resources, and if the population were about equally distributed. But this is not the case.

[3] Robert C. Eckhardt, *State Aid and School Attendance in Texas,* Report to the Office of Inter-American Affairs, October, 1945.

Any change in the constitutional method of apportioning school funds must, in Eckhardt's opinion, take four points into consideration:

(1) *The law must afford an incentive to the counties to get their children into school.* In order to do this, it will be necessary to put a premium on enrollment. A base allotment from the available school fund, perhaps one-half of the $37,000,000, should be distributed on an enrollment basis to encourage an increase in attendance.

(2) *The law must provide a means of solving specific problems caused by peculiar economic conditions.* A specific fund should be appropriated, in addition to the available school fund, to provide special classes or courses within regular school buildings and to more nearly meet the educational needs of children engaged in seasonal agricultural labor. Furthermore, as technology develops the cotton-picking machine, we must prepare the children of migratory laborers for other and better occupations. Such special training should be carried on at State expense, for these children are "flotorial" Texans, so to speak, and not really permanent residents of any county or school district. The transient worker in Texas is the very foundation of one of the State's greatest industries, and there is no banker in a Texas rural community, no depositor in such a bank, whose prosperity and security is not based on the labor of these migratory workers. Therefore, the education of the children of migrants, who may live in LaSalle County and pick cotton in Lubbock County, is the responsibility of the State as a whole. They must be given at least a rudimentary education so that they may be good citizens now, and in order that they may be prepared for a job outside agriculture when they are displaced by machines.

(3) *The law must assure an equitable division of State expenditures without regard to racial, national, or economic background.* After apportioning half of the $37,000,000 available school fund on the basis of enrollment, there would remain

$18,500,000, plus the rural aid fund of $14,000,000. A portion of these funds should be used to give an additional incentive to increasing attendance, and to offset initial cost of providing adequate facilities for children who are brought into school during the current school year. The largest increase in school attendance might be expected in South Texas, where attendance is now low. Increasing school attendance will result in added financial burdens. The initial cost of affording adequate facilities for an increased enrollment will be higher per student than current operating costs. Therefore, counties which have increased attendance should receive an additional sum of money for each child enrolled above last year's enrollment. This added fund should be distributed to the counties only where it is shown that all children enrolled are being provided for equally. This provision will tend to discourage use of State funds to educate only a select few within the county while many other children receive a mere semblance of education, and sometimes none at all.

(4) *The law must take into account the real wealth or poverty of the counties.* At present, the State has a rural aid fund of $14,000,000. This affords a rough sort of equalization between school districts, but it is only about 17 per cent of the total money spent on the school program in Texas. The discrepancy in per capita income between, let us say, Webb County in southwest Texas and Midland County in the Permian Basin of West Texas is far greater than 17 per cent. The per capita income of Midland County is almost twice that of Webb County. Texas, therefore, needs an adequate equalization fund. Instead of 17 per cent of total educational expenditures, this fund should be approximately 25 or 30 per cent.

Besides making a great stride in protective health measures and greatly increasing State aid to rural schools, Texas has taken another significant step forward.

The creation of the Good Neighbor Commission of Texas by Governor Coke R. Stevenson in August, 1943, and its establishment, for a period of two years, as an official agency of the State by act of the 49th Legislature, effective September 4, 1945, represents an activity which cannot but be applauded. The formal acknowledgment, by the government of Texas, of the existence of the problems has not only had great political import, but has also served to bring those problems to the attention of the public.

The work of the Commission has been primarily that of fact-finding, fact-publicizing, and co-ordination. Through its activities, many persons have become aware, for the first time, that problems do exist; many others, who were conscious of the injustices and inequalities suffered by people of Mexican descent, but who were groping in the dark, so to speak, and whose approach to the problems was largely from an emotional or sentimental angle, have been enlightened as to their true nature and gravity.

Knowledge and understanding on the part of the Commission itself have also developed rapidly, with the result that the problem has been analyzed in its multiple aspects; many avenues for research hitherto overlooked have been opened; and the intellectual activity of numerous individuals and agencies has been stimulated and definitely applied in various fields, as evidenced by the instances quoted throughout this text.

At the same time, and in all fairness, it must be recognized that the activities and influence of the Commission have been limited by the lack of adequate funds and facilities. Until State funds were appropriated for its use, the Commission operated under a grant from the Office of Inter-American Affairs. House Bill No. 804, which gave the Commission official status, provides for an annual budget of only $9,470.00, and its functions are circumscribed as follows:

It shall be the duty of the Commission to devise and put into effect methods by which inter-American understanding and good will may be promoted and inter-American relations advanced, without resort to punitive measures or the application of civil or criminal sanctions.

To discharge its responsibility adequately, the Commission must be enabled to expand its staff and must be supported by an efficient network of co-workers that covers the State. The ideal situation would be one in which every *bona fide* and well-substantiated case of discrimination, whether an inequitable condition in the public schools, refusal of service, discrimination in employment, denial of civil rights, or a complaint of any other nature, could be investigated and studied immediately, in co-operation with local citizens and authorities. Upon the working out of an equitable solution to the immediate crisis, an intensive educational and organizational campaign would be developed in the community, for all its residents, in order to forestall the recurrence of any similar situation. Such procedures, however, will require ample personnel, adequate funds, and certain executive prerogatives which the Commission does not now enjoy.

The work of the Commission, however worthy, may be considered as an experiment and must be appraised, not from the viewpoint of personalities—in which too many persons, unfortunately, are prone to indulge—but from an institutional standpoint. The consideration of paramount importance is that the interest of the government of Texas in the solution of the problems of Latin Americans in the State must never wane; but, on the contrary, that each and every succeeding administration must be inspired to devote more energy, and to provide a more adequate budget, to the end that the Commission may pursue its avowed purposes to their ultimate realization.

After all, incumbents in any public office are always transitory, and subject to replacement by new officials. What is important is the survival of the institution itself, whether the same or a new, and possibly better, crew comes to administer it.

It is essential, therefore, during the 1947 session of the Texas Legislature, that the permanency of the Commission be assured, its appropriation increased, and its powers enlarged. In addition, the bill must provide for the appointment, in each county, and in each city of more than 20,000 population, of a committee composed of three prominent citizens, who will be charged with the investigation of all incidents of conflict between Latin and Anglo Americans within its jurisdiction, and the study of local matters in which the interests of Latin Americans are specifically at stake. With a statewide network of this kind, the work and effectiveness of the Good Neighbor Commission will be immeasurably strengthened and expanded.

Enlightened Journalism

There exists an urgent need for a more enlightened and impartial journalism—on both sides of the Border—when any question of things inter-American in Texas arises.

Many editors, feature writers, and news reporters in the past, intending to be of help in a better understanding of the situation, have nevertheless often acted as if they were following the injunction given in the popular song—but in reverse: "accentuate the negative, eliminate the positive." Such a policy—playing up the sensational incident and neglecting all the constructive activities—fails utterly to form intelligent public opinion.

It is sad, but true, that overt incidents of discrimination *are* sensational, and their recital guaranteed to increase circulation. With or without verification, they make good reading and, as a consequence, are generally played up out of all proportion to their real significance. For obvious reasons, this negative type of news appears most frequently in the Mexican press and the Spanish-language newspapers in Texas, but may be noted, also, from time to time, in the English-language dailies.

Thus it happens that the refusal of service to Juan Martínez in the Greasy Spoon Cafe at Raspberry Junction may make the headlines, while the fact that a group of civic-minded citizens of the same town have undertaken a serious study of means by which relations between Latin and Anglo American residents of the community may be improved is never mentioned in the news at all.

Some editorial and news writers are beginning to recognize the necessity for presenting the complete story instead of a distorted version of one phase of the story. Regardless of viewpoint, greater objectivity is being practiced. This changing philosophy is reflected in an editorial which appeared in *La Prensa* of Mexico City on December 1, 1944. Translated, the article says, in part:

The publicity that certain sensational acts receive—publicity which is undoubtedly deserved, but at the same time unfortunate—eclipses other developments which are of equal importance today, and which will be of even greater significance tomorrow. . . . It is only right that the demand for justice be accompanied by a recognition of the tenacious work of worthy persons, of whom, fortunately, there are many.

We have already treated in this column some aspects of this fraternal work. Today we should like to tell you of a magnificent report that we have received, in which the problem is discussed impartially, and very effective means are suggested to counteract harmful elements. This program is sponsored by the Good Neighbor Commission of Texas, an organization which coordinates the Good Neighbor work of that State. . . .

It may be noted that the Mexicans who have gone to the United States at a more recent date have received better treatment. This treatment is undoubtedly influenced by the conviction that the contribution of the Mexicans is an evident proof of the respect they deserve. And this also shows that acts of discrimination are more local than international in character, and are determined by economic factors. . . .

The report tells how to combat this situation "by following the teachings of Christ in human relations throughout the State of Texas, promoting education, and offering the necessary opportunities to all, at the same time obtaining a better understanding by means of a more intimate knowledge of the factors involved in the disagreement."

If we refer to this point it is in order to make it clear that there are those who are working hard, and with good criteria and therefore arbitrary judgments that affect all, good or bad, should be carefully avoided. Organizations like the Good Neighbor Commission of Texas have really known how to realize the true interests of their country and also their patriotic duty with the obligations inherent in their democratic citizenship. . . . They are legion, the men of good will in the United States, who are working . . . "to preserve the honor and prestige of their State before the nation, before their allies, and before the world." Their efforts should awaken in us an affectionate response in just correspondence to the affection they hold for all that is Mexican.

One of the Texas newspapers that has made an honest effort to present an unbiased commentary on inter-American problems is the San Antonio *Light*. In an editorial on March 9, 1945, devoted to an evaluation of the anti-discrimination bill then pending in the State Legislature, the *Light* said:

Promotion of goodwill is largely an educative process. It has got to change the hearts and minds of people who are in need of being changed. It can not be done by passing a law. It can not be speeded up beyond a certain rate. . . .

After all, what discrimination does exist is primarily economic in character and not biological. Economic discrimination can be found south, as well as north of the Rio Grande, the difference being that in the latter case owners and employes of some public places do not exercise the discrimination that is practiced among the people of Mexico themselves. That causes the trouble.

The great amount of publicity given cases of discrimination is evidence of the fact that the people of Texas have a greater awareness than ever before of this blemish on their state. It is a good sign, for the acknowledgment of an error is essential to correction. At the same time, however, it tends to give a distorted perspective of conditions as they really are.

If discrimination against Latin Americans were the prevailing rule in Texas—as most certainly it is not—then the so-called anti-discrimination bill might be needed, not to cure a situation, for that it could not do, but to relieve the more aggravated symptoms.

As it is, the bill can serve no good purpose in the promotion of a better understanding and greater goodwill in inter-American relations. If anything, it would tend to provoke new irritations.

Certainly it might force some stubborn rural cafe owner to serve a hamburger to a Latin American who may or may not be a better man than he is, but it can not keep that cafe owner from being insulting and hostile in his attitude toward his unwanted customer.

In other words, this or any other anti-discrimination bill can be enforced to the letter and still be violated in spirit.

This is not what any of us want who oppose discrimination against a people to whom we are indebted, not only for a great amount of our culture but for some of the most enlightened laws of this state.

On November 30, 1944, Pedro Gringoire, columnist on the Mexico City newspaper *Excelsior,* made the following fair and impartial comments in introducing a discussion of various educational programs under way in Texas:

> In Texas, frequent cases of social and economic discrimination occur against persons of Mexican origin, regardless of whether or not they are citizens of the United States. For example, they are denied service in restaurants and other public places. They are treated as inferior beings not only when they happen to be of the laboring class, but, sometimes, even when they are cultured persons of high social position. Among the victims of this attitude may be found Consular employees, businessmen, intellectuals, and persons on special commissions for the Mexican Government.
>
> This is an undeniable fact, well known and of no small international importance. The most well-informed and sincere citizens of the United States and of Texas recognize it and do not attempt to excuse it. Any study of our international relations brings one face to face with it. But no picture of the problems which such relations offer would be complete without equal recognition of another significant fact: that of the forces which are now operating in Texas to do away with prejudice and humiliating discrimination, and to achieve better understanding, sympathy and friendship between Anglo and Latin Americans.
>
> If inter-American relations have passed from a negative to a positive phase, it is just and right that publicity be given also to these noble efforts to do away with, once and for all, the unfortunate incidents which, until the present time, have almost monopolized public attention.

Regardless of the fact that conflicts of opinion still exist as to the *means* of achieving better intercultural and inter-group understanding and the causes lying behind the still too frequent lapses in these matters, it is increasingly obvious that the better newspapers on both sides of the Border have developed objectivity and fair-mindedness in their attitudes and expressed opinions.

Disregarding the international implications of the problems, if every local newspaper in Texas were to give free rein to an "inquiring reporter," supported by a crusading editorial writer, the inequitable conditions surrounding the State's Latin American population could be bettered immeasurably, and in short order. Substandard housing, public health hazards, unfair employment practices, low enrollment in the schools— these and many other civic blemishes urgently need the healing benefits of a planned, intelligent public airing. The presentation of facts must precede remedial action.

The Spanish-language press in Texas should strive always to be conservative, both journalistically and editorially. It should bear foremost in mind the welfare of citizens of this country, devoting as much space to matters of local concern as to affairs in Mexico. While many Texans may rightfully be considered former residents of Mexico, and therefore may logically be expected to have a normal interest in what goes on in their native country, publishers of Spanish newspapers and magazines should give primary consideration to their readers' needs as permanent residents of this country.

"Ye shall know the truth, and the truth shall make you free" is as valid today as it was when the thought was first expressed. Nothing but delay and confusion is to be gained by denying the existence of the problems in Texas, or by placing undue emphasis on the negative aspects of those problems. But a high service can be rendered by journalists in both Texas and Mexico if they will present the truth—the whole truth—to the reading public in a constructive, forward-looking manner. In order to accomplish this end, the journalists themselves must be fully cognizant of all facets of the truth.

Social Welfare

Although, because of the low economic status of so large a portion of the Latin Americans in Texas, the expenditure of public and private funds for social welfare work among them exceeds the amount spent on any other group of people, it was not until its annual conference in December, 1944, that the Texas Social Welfare Association gave specific attention to the problems of Latin Americans.

During that three-day meeting, four sessions of a round table were held, the members of which gave serious consideration to all phases of the problems, and presented the closing general assembly with fifteen recommendations.

One of the most noteworthy aspects of the conference was the almost total absence of Latin American social welfare workers. The round table recommended, therefore, that the T.S.W.A. make a special effort to interest Latin Americans in preparing themselves for a career in social welfare work among Texas people of Mexican descent. This is a "must" if the greatest possible good is to be accomplished by welfare agencies. In this field, as elsewhere, the language handicap serves as a barrier to mutual understanding, and a Spanish-speaking case worker can much more easily inspire confidence in Spanish-speaking people than one who does not speak or understand the language.

Another recommendation emphasized a great need: that all social workers dealing with Latin Americans be intelligently informed on the over-all problem in Texas and its international significance.

The round table urged that the T.S.W.A. support a revised and adequate Child Labor law in Texas; that the T.S.W.A. advocate the extension of unemployment compensation assistance to include agricultural workers; that the T.S.W.A. support legislation for more adequate health facilities, with emphasis on those for the tuberculous.

It was also recommended that each regional chairman of the T.S.W.A. encourage, in her local community, provision for pre-school training in English for non-English-speaking children; and that, in general, the regional and county organizations of T.S.W.A. give more attention in their local communities to the study of conditions relating to Latin Americans.

Other recommendations submitted included one to the effect that the T.S.W.A. should petition local housing authorities to give due consideration to adequate housing for Latin Americans in their post-war planning; and another which urged that local social welfare organizations should encourage the establishment, by local bar associations, of legal aid clinics.

All of which represents signal progress on the part of so large and influential a body as the Texas Social Welfare Association.

Health Education

Aside from the economic situation among many Texas people of Mexican descent which engenders disease and ill health, and the deplorable sanitary conditions arising from the failure of local authorities in many communities to extend sewer lines and other public services into Latin American residential districts, the chief contributing factor to the high death rates from tuberculosis, diarrhea, etc., is ignorance—ignorance of even the most rudimentary principles of personal hygiene and sanitation.

Health officials, for example, have found that quite apart from the pernicious effects of open pit privies, infant diarrhea is able to claim so many victims among Latin Americans in Texas, first, because mothers and other members of the family who handle the baby do so with unclean hands and fingernails; and second, because soiled toilet tissue, instead of being deposited in the toilet, is frequently allowed to accumulate on the floor of the outhouse where it is easily accessible to flies. The fatal results of the habit are obvious.

When we remember that a large proportion of our adult Latin American citizens in the lower economic brackets have been deprived of education of any kind, it is easy to understand that their knowledge of health and sanitation is likewise deficient. Until their economic status is materially improved, and sanitary facilities extended, it will not be possible to bring about an entirely satisfactory improvement in health conditions among them. Nevertheless, much can be accomplished through the dissemination of carefully prepared health information.

State and national organizations are now working to formulate a program of health education in Spanish, simple in content and eloquently illustrated. The American Public Health

Association, the United States-Mexico Border Public Health Association, the Good Neighbor Commission of Texas, and other agencies, are co-operating in a plan to make available, in attractive, understandable form, educational materials dealing with the basic principles of health, hygiene, nutrition, and sanitation.

A study is being made of all Spanish-language health education materials now published in the Southwest and elsewhere. In Texas, the best job has been done by the Texas Tuberculosis Association, which has more than eight booklets and leaflets available for distribution. Excellent materials on maternal health, infant and pre-school health, and adult hygiene have been prepared by several agencies in New Mexico, and Arizona and California have made valuable contributions in various phases of health education. Furthermore, the Children's Bureau of the U. S. Department of Labor and the National Tuberculosis Association have developed significant booklets, in Spanish, on tuberculosis, child care, maternal health, etc.

The problem now is to evaluate the materials already available, to develop new materials, colorful, profusely illustrated, and written in the vernacular, and to devise some means through which these new materials may be published. Also, the best of the materials already developed by private or state agencies should be reprinted for widespread distribution along with the newer information.

Inasmuch as many of the people badly in need of health education are illiterate in both English and Spanish, major emphasis will be placed on media of visual education. The most valuable instruments of this type yet developed are the Walt Disney health films, in technicolor and with Spanish sound tracks, which have been used to such great advantage in Latin America. Eight films have to date been released by the Walt Disney Studios, but so far their use has been restricted to the other American republics. As soon as certain technicalities have been worked out by the distributors of these films, they will be available for exhibition in the Southwest.

Leadership

Perhaps the most important single factor requisite to the speedy and permanent solution of problems in Texas is that of leadership—intelligent, informed, positive leadership among both Latins and Anglos. Various civic and cultural organizations in the State have made material contributions to the promotion of understanding and the dissipation of prejudices on a local and international basis. Junior Chambers of Commerce, the Rotary International, Lions and Kiwanis Clubs, Business & Professional Women's Clubs, to name only a few, have devoted part of their efforts to inter-American activities. Other groups, such as the Pan American Round Tables, the Pan American Council of Texas at Corpus Christi, the Latin-Anglo-American Council of Houston, and similar organizations throughout the State, have confined themselves exclusively to work in the inter-American field.

Unfortunately, too much attention has been paid by some of these groups to Pan Americanism on a high, international plane, rather than to work within the community and the State. Real Pan Americanism, like charity, must begin at home.

Outstanding among Latin American organizations in Texas is the League of United Latin American Citizens, popularly known as LULAC, which came into being in 1929 and which represented a coalition of several clubs and societies in Corpus Christi, San Antonio, Laredo, Brownsville, and elsewhere, not only in Texas, but also in Arizona, Colorado, New Mexico, and California. The aims and purposes of LULAC are clearly set forth in Article II of its Constitution, which reads as follows:

Section 1. As loyal citizens of the United States of America:
We believe in the democratic principle of individual political and religious freedom, in the right of equality of social and economic opportunity, and in the duty of cooperative endeavor towards the development of an American society wherein the cultural resources and integrity of every individual and group constitute basic assets of the American way of life. As citizens of Latin American descent, we assume our responsibilities and duties and claim our rights and privileges in the pursuit of a fuller and richer civilization for this, our native country.

We believe that education is the foundation for the cultural growth and development of this nation and that we are obligated to protect and promote the education of our people in accordance with the best American principles and standards. We deplore any infringement of this goal wherever it may occur and regardless of whom it may affect.

We accept that it is not only the privilege but also the obligation of every member of this organization to uphold and defend the rights and duties vested in every American citizen by the letter and the spirit of the law of the land.

Section 2. As members of a democratic society, we recognize our civic duties and responsibilities and we propose:

To use all the appropriate means at our disposal to implement with social action the principles set forth above.

To foster the acquisition and facile use of the official language of our country that we may thereby equip ourselves and our families for the fullest enjoyment of our rights and privileges and the efficient discharge of our duties and obligations to this, our country.

To establish cooperative relationships with other civic organizations and agencies in these fields of public service.

That the members of the League of United Latin American Citizens constitute themselves a service organization to actively promote suitable measures for the attainment of the highest ideals of our American society.

That, in the interests of the public welfare, we shall seek in every way possible to uphold the rights guaranteed to every individual by our state and national laws and to seek justice and equality of treatment in accordance with the law of the land. We shall courageously resist un-American tendencies that deprive citizens of these rights in educational institutions, in economic pursuits, and in social and civic activities.

During the seventeen years of its existence, LULAC has continued to gain strength and to contribute to the betterment of United States citizens of Mexican descent in the fields of education, citizenship, and civil rights.

The Good Citizens League of Houston, created in June, 1945, represents a type of Latin-Anglo co-operative effort to get at the roots of problems on a local level, and it might profitably be copied in many Texas cities. The purposes of the League are to promote good citizenship through adult education; to encourage young people to finish high school; to sponsor trades preparedness training; and to find the causes of juvenile delinquency and effect cures.

Directing its first attack toward the abatement of juvenile delinquency, the Good Citizens League set up six boys' clubs in sections of Houston that were known as hotbeds of juvenile crime. A football league was then organized, the Houston Public Schools furnishing a practice field, and enough equipment was donated by other interested parties to outfit two teams. In addition to a successful football season, supervised recreational programs were conducted in the clubs, and through public lectures and personal contacts, the League secured the co-operation of parents in furnishing healthful surroundings and occupations for their children. At the end of the year 1945, Houston's police records showed that juvenile delinquency among Latin Americans had dropped considerably.

The Mexican Government maintains in Texas some fifteen consulates, including the two Consulates General at San Antonio and El Paso. While the interests and activities of Consular officials are confined, technically, to the 200,000 Mexican nationals resident in Texas, it is as impossible for them as it is for other agencies in the field of inter-American relations to divorce themselves completely from the problems of American citizens of Mexican descent, for the problems of the two groups are identical.

The result is that the leadership of Consular officials, both directly and through the numerous Mexican societies under their jurisdiction, can exert a potent influence for good in bettering the conditions of all Latin Americans in Texas. The consuls fully recognize their official limitations; nevertheless, their concern with regard to housing and sanitation facilities among Mexican nationals, for example, embraces, at least by implication, a similar concern for housing and sanitation among all persons of Mexican extraction. Furthermore, the influence of Mexican consuls in encouraging Mexican nationals—the great majority of whom are permanent residents of Texas—to exert their best efforts to send their children to school, improve their homes, learn English, etc., inevitably overflows into the Latin American community at large.

Further comment on the functions of the excellent Mexican Consular Service is not within the writer's province. Being representatives of a foreign government, Consular officials are in the realm of international rather than domestic affairs. It is desired only to point out their importance as leaders among people of Mexican descent in Texas.

Considering the scope, diversity, and urgency of problems in Texas, and acknowledging the accomplishments of all individuals and agencies in the field, there nevertheless exists a need for additional conscientious, intelligent leadership, among both Latin and Anglo Americans. Such leadership must be based on an over-all knowledge and appreciation of the true nature of the problems. Also, in order to avoid jealousies and duplication of effort, as well as to realize the greatest possible gain in the shortest possible time, there must be better understanding and increased co-operation among the organizations and agencies actively engaged in the work.

The Churches

Reduced to their simplest form, the problems in Texas represent nothing more nor less than the failure to apply Christian principles to our everyday dealings with each other. There is certainly nothing new about the teachings of Christ, but a new day would dawn in Texas if the Christian doctrines in which we profess to believe were actually to become the philosophy by which we live seven days a week instead of one.

The Federal Council of Churches in America took a strong stand on the matter of discrimination against minority groups on March 6, 1946, when it went on record to the effect that:

The pattern of racial segregation in America is given moral sanction by the fact that churches and church institutions, as a result of social pressure, have so largely accepted the pattern of racial segregation in their own life and practice.

Segregation in America is the externally imposed separation or division of individual citizens, or groups of citizens, based on race, color, creed or national origin. . . . It is an expression of the inferiority-superiority patterns of opinions about race held tenaciously by vast numbers of Americans and also the means by which the racial attitude is transmitted from one generation to another.[4]

With regard to employment, the Council passed a resolution favoring the establishment of permanent procedures for securing the objectives of the Fair Employment Practices Committee, and a resolution favoring a minimum wage of sixty-five cents an hour now and seventy-five cents after two years. It agreed that "the nature of man and the structure of modern industrial society, have caused the right to an opportunity for employment at an equitable wage to become a basic right."[5]

If the churches, regardless of denomination, are to fulfill their responsibility in eliminating the problems in Texas, theirs must be a two-way program. Both Spanish-speaking and English-speaking congregations—so long as this separation continues to be maintained—must be brought to a realization of the full significance of Matthew XXII, 37-40:

"Thou shalt love the Lord thy God with all thy heart, and with all thy soul, and with all thy mind. This is the first and great commandment. And the second is like unto it, Thou shalt love thy neighbor as thyself."

This Christian neighborliness does not begin across imaginary state or national boundary lines. It begins here and now. It begins with an active interest in seeing city sewer lines, garbage disposal service, electric light and power lines extended to all the city's residents. It begins with a militant campaign to eliminate slum areas. It begins with a concerted attack upon discrimination of any kind because of language differences or national origin, wherever and whenever such prejudices may be encountered.

[4] *The Austin American* (Austin, Texas), March 7, 1946.
[5] *Ibid.*

The sincere Christian will be deeply concerned about the economic, health, educational, and social conditions of his fellow citizens. The true Christian will regard it not only as his Christian duty, but also as his civic duty, to work earnestly toward the alleviation of those conditions. This is not charity. It is common sense. It is democratic living.

A beginning has been made by the churches, but only a beginning. Settlement houses and charitable organizations have long been sponsored by various denominations, but this is merely scratching the surface of the problems. The main task must be accomplished within the churches themselves— the task of making Christianity so real, so vital, so compelling a force that church members will undertake, individually and collectively, as a part of their daily lives, the mitigation of the ills and evils that beset their neighbors.

One new program now under way is that decided upon by the Catholic Bishops of the four Provinces of Los Angeles, Santa Fe, Denver, and San Antonio. At a meeting in Oklahoma City on January 10-12, 1945, they organized themselves into the Bishops' Committee for the Spanish-Speaking, and chose the four Archbishops as an Executive Board.

It was agreed that an intensive program of social and spiritual welfare would be conducted in each of the four Provinces during four successive years, with funds from the Catholic Church Extension Society. At the end of the first year, the staff of trained workers will move to another Province to begin the work there, leaving a skeleton force of local people to carry on, with local funds, the activities inaugurated the preceding year.

In general terms, the program outlined by the Bishops consists of three parts. The first is a building project to include clinics, settlement houses, community centers or auditoriums, and catechetical centers. The second part pertains to the services to be made available to Spanish-speaking people, including care of migrant workers, maternal and child care, health, recreation, educational opportunities, and social insurance. The final phase of the program is to be devoted to a broad, intensive campaign of religious welfare.

In addition, there is to be created, in each succeeding Province, a Catholic Council for the Spanish-Speaking, the purpose of which is to bring together the leaders and experts, Anglo and Latin Americans, for their mutual help in the whole work.

The intermediate aims, as stated by the Executive Board, are to break down prejudices on the part of both Anglo and Latin Americans, to build up and harness the organizations of both for the welfare of the latter, to secure the assistance of private secular organizations and public agencies, and to recommend programs of action to priests and other religious.

The Most Rev. Robt. E. Lucey, D. D., Archbishop of San Antonio, was successful in negotiating for the program's initiation in his Archdiocese. A budget of $240,000.00 for the year's activities was set up, and August 1, 1945, was designated as the beginning date of the project. Of the above amount, $15,000.00 was set aside for the operation of the Regional Office of the Bishops' Committee to be located in San Antonio. The Reverend John J. Birch of Los Angeles was named executive secretary, and two assistants were employed to direct field work in the Archdiocese of San Antonio. Both of these field workers are native Texans of Mexican descent, and the Regional Office has already accomplished much in the way of leadership training in the fields of juvenile delinquency, health, and social education.

The building plans for the entire region call for the construction of fifteen parish centers or clinics. In San Antonio, two such buildings have been constructed, one a parish center and the other a maternity hospital. In each diocese where centers are built, a program embracing classes in arts and crafts, Americanization, and nutrition will be conducted. The centers will also be used for parish meetings, rallies, festivals, and entertainments.

The various city and county health departments will supply the services of a doctor and two nurses for examinations, prescriptions, and treatment at the parish center clinics. General clinics will be held weekly, in addition to the Sick Baby Clinic and Well Baby Clinic, which will provide medical care for both mother and infant.

Of special significance is the fact that, in conjunction with the foregoing program, Archbishop Lucey has acquired a fifteen-bed maternity hospital formerly operated by the Beneficencia Mexicana of San Antonio. This hospital, to be known as the Santa María Maternity Hospital, will be devoted exclusively to the care of maternity cases among low-income groups. A small fee, ranging from $15.00 to $25.00, will be charged for hospitalization; but even this nominal charge will be waived if investigation reveals that the family is unable to pay.

In return for the gift of the hospital and grounds, Archbishop Lucey will erect a six-room general clinic on the same site. The building will include two examining rooms and a laboratory.

A highly important step in the right direction was taken in 1945 by the Methodist Church in Texas. For the first time, the courses of study offered in its annual leadership training schools included one entitled "Inter-American Relations in Texas."

Taught in McAllen, San Antonio, and Austin, the ten-hour course presented to pastors, Sunday School teachers, and lay leaders a comprehensive view of the difficulties confronted by Latin American Texans in employment, education, housing, and sanitation, as well as the social barriers raised against them. The same course, which contains no denominational bias, could and should be studied by Christian leaders throughout the State.

Chapter 15

Recapitulation

It would be fatal to allow the impression to gain currency that the problems in Texas are primarily or exclusively the concern of our more than one million Latin Americans. They are, on the contrary, the problems of the State of Texas as a whole, and, from a purely selfish standpoint, if we wish to look at the matter in that light, it is not only "smart" but imperative that those problems be solved by the government and the people of Texas, for their own benefit.

In the interest of clarity and emphasis, we may summarize the inequitable conditions discussed and the remedial measures proposed in the preceding pages as follows:

I. PROBLEMS

    A. Social and Civil Inequalities

        1. Refusal of service in public places of business and amusement.

        2. Denial of right to vote in some counties.

        3. Denial of right to serve on juries in some counties.

        4. Denial of right to rent or own real estate in many cities.

        5. Terrorism on the part of law enforcement officers and others.

B. Economic Evils
   1. Unfair employment practices forcing a low economic status for the majority of Latin Americans.
   2. Discrimination exercised by both management and labor unions in the admission, grading, and upgrading of Latin Americans.
   3. Human exploitation in agriculture.
   4. Demand of growers for cheap labor carried to the extreme of favoring illegal seasonal influx of workers, thereby denying employment opportunities to resident workers.

C. Sanitary: Housing, Health, and Nutrition
   1. Substandard housing.
   2. Lack of sanitary facilities and services.
   3. Improper diet and malnutrition.
   4. Ignorance of personal hygiene.
   5. High incidence of tuberculosis, diarrhea, and other communicable diseases.

D. Inequitable Educational Opportunities
   1. Arbitrary segregation in the public schools.
   2. Inability of working children to attend school.
   3. Lack of interest of school administrators in enrolling Latin American children and encouraging their attendance.
   4. Improperly trained teachers.
   5. Inferior buildings and equipment.
   6. Inequitable method of apportioning State school funds.

E. Prejudices and General Errors of Anglo Americans
   1. Lack of knowledge and understanding of Latin Americans in Texas and the conditions under which they live.

2. Ignorance of the language, culture, and history of Latin American countries.

3. Tendency to generalize.

4. Erroneous ideas of superiority.

5. Misconceptions regarding Texas history.

6. Failure to abide by the democratic ideals and principles which are the foundation of this country.

7. Failure to appreciate fully the fact that the essential grandeur of this country comes from its power to absorb, adopt, and adapt people of all countries and races.

8. Failure to appraise properly the important cultural, social, and human contributions made by Latin Americans, especially Mexicans, to the greatness of this State and nation.

9. Failure to adhere to Christian principles.

F. Errors of Latin Americans

1. Indifference on the part of some parents regarding the education of their children.

2. Reluctance, and sometimes refusal, on part of some adults to learn or speak English.

3. Tendency toward self-pity and fatalism.

4. Exaggerated individualism and consequent lack of enthusiasm for co-operative or community work.

5. Jealousy and tendency to promote personal grievances into group divisions, leading to long-standing feuds.

6. Lack of tenacity in social enterprises.

7. Apparent incapability to develop strong, permanent, widespread, and economically powerful organizations, tending instead to numerous small, ineffectual clubs and societies.

II. REMEDIES

A. Legislative

1. Advocate a constitutional amendment prohibiting, as a matter of public policy, segregation of or discrimination against any segment of the population not specifically mentioned by the laws of the State.
2. Enact a statute prohibiting discrimination in industrial employment, including discrimination by labor unions, and imposing sanctions.
3. Enact a bill making the Good Neighbor Commission of Texas a permanent State agency, providing it with ample funds, facilities, and executive powers, and providing for the establishment of a network of county and city committees to function on a local level.
4. Revise the method of apportioning State school funds in order to provide school districts with an incentive to enroll all school-age children.
5. Abolish the fee system of remuneration for law enforcement officers.
6. Abolish the poll tax.

B. Economic

1. Assure free and equal opportunities for employment on the part of both management and labor unions.
2. Assure equal promotional opportunities based exclusively on ability to do the job.
3. Establish trades preparedness programs for adults.
4. Give full co-operation and support to program of the Farm Labor Office for the improvement of agricultural working conditions.
5. Devise some effective means of prohibiting seasonal influx of illegal agricultural workers.

C. Sanitary: Housing, Health, and Nutrition

1. Campaign, on a local level, for slum clearance and the establishment of low-cost housing projects.

2. Campaign, on a local level, for the extension of sewers, gas mains, electricity, and garbage disposal service to all the city's residents.

3. Campaign, on the State level, for the establishment of more adequate hospital facilities, particularly for the tuberculous.

4. Campaign, on all levels, for the establishment of a school lunch program in all Texas schools.

5. Demand strict enforcement of the Sanitary Code.

6. Expand local health services.

7. Inaugurate a program of health education, through the distribution of literature in Spanish and the exhibition of films with Spanish sound tracks.

D. Educational

1. In the public schools

(a) Outlaw the practice of segregation on the basis of language or national origin.

(b) Establish educational facilities for the children of seasonal agricultural workers in the form of "off-season" schools.

(c) Encourage the learning of Spanish as a second language, beginning in the elementary grades.

(d) Make the heritage of every Texas child a matter of pride to him, and a cause for respect on the part of others.

(e) Employ combination school nurse and visiting teacher to investigate and help to correct home conditions which contribute to the failure of Latin American children to attend school.

(f) Construct adequate buildings, adequately equipped.

(g) Equalize salaries for all teachers in all schools.

(h) Expand library facilities on Latin American and inter-American subjects.

(i) Inaugurate statewide program of trades preparedness training in the schools.

(j) Provide pre-school training in English for non-English-speaking children.

(k) Incorporate into the curriculum, at all grade levels, information and activities relating to the history, literature, culture, and social structure of Latin America, and inter-American relations.

(l) Stress influence of Latin American culture on Texas.

(m) Stress contributions of Latin Americans to Texas in all fields.

(n) Solicit membership of Latin American parents in Parent-Teacher organizations.

2. In the colleges and universities

(a) Require a speaking knowledge of Spanish on the part of all those who are to teach Texas children in the elementary grades.

(b) Require a knowledge of the background and problems of Texas people of Mexican descent on the part of all teachers.

(c) Require a knowledge and understanding of Latin American history, culture, inter-American relations, and the human and other contributions of Latin Americans to Texas on the part of all those who are to teach Texas children.

3. Adult education

(a) Cultivate a new attitude on the part of Anglo American adults through study groups, action groups, Spanish classes, public lectures, dissemination of information through press and radio, and civic undertakings in which Latin and Anglo Americans co-operate.

(b) Enable Latin American adults to further their own progress through the conduct of classes in English, United States history, citizenship, health and sanitation, child care, nutrition, and similar subjects, and through co-operative undertakings.

E. Enlightened Leadership

1. Civic, Cultural, Patriotic, Parent-Teacher, and Social Welfare Organizations

(a) Acquaint their members generally with the nature and scope of problems in Texas.

(b) Study and attack specific problems in their special fields of interest.

(c) Support, on a local and state level, all activities directed toward the amelioration of inequitable conditions, including public endorsement of proposed legislation.

(d) Sponsor the establishment of legal aid clinics.

(e) Demand adequate public park and playground facilities for both children and adults.

2. Latin American Organizations

(a) Study all phases of the problems from the standpoint of what Latin Americans themselves can do toward their solution.

(b) Develop positive leadership in the various fields of activity, including political action.

(c) Encourage Latin American parents to enroll their children in school.

(d) Sponsor adult education through classes in English, civil rights and responsibilities, health, etc.

(e) Co-operate with other groups and organizations in attacking the problems at their roots.

3. Mexican Consular Service

It is to be hoped that the representatives of the Mexican Government in Texas, through the clubs and societies under their jurisdiction, and in co-operation with State authorities and all other agencies in the field, will always work toward the realization of the objectives herein proposed, insofar as it is within their power to do so.

4. The Press and Radio

(a) Furnish the reading and listening public with an accurate and impartial presentation of the problems in Texas, their scope and urgency, and and their bearing upon international relations.

(b) Carry adequate news coverage of Latin America.

(c) Point out, editorially, local problems to local citizens, and publicize remedial measures undertaken.

(d) Editorialize upon the principles involved.

5. The Churches

(a) Eliminate discriminatory practices within the churches.

(b) Identify Christian doctrines with civic responsibilities.

(c) Conduct study groups on the problems in Texas, emphasizing the Christian obligation to solve them.

(d) Follow the suggestions proposed for Civic, Cultural, Patriotic, Parent-Teacher, and Social Welfare Organizations.

In view of the vast variety and serious nature of these problems, as well as the multiplicity and diversity of remedies indicated and required, there is not a citizen of Texas who can conscientiously deny or avoid a measure of responsibility for their prompt and permanent solution. Every stratum of community and state life is affected. Every individual, every legislator, every club, group, official agency, educational medium or institution, church, civic or welfare organization, has a role to enact, an influence to exert, an obligation to discharge. In the well-known words of Tennyson's "Ulysses,"

'Tis not too late to seek a newer world . . .
Tho' much is taken, much abides: and tho'
We are not now that strength which in old days
Moved earth and Heaven; that which we are, we are;

One equal temper of heroic hearts,
Made weak by time and fate, but strong in will
To strive, to seek, to find, and not to yield.

We Texans must *make social justice the way of life in Texas* —if we are not to jeopardize the hard-won gains of the inter-American system, if we are to help build a peace that will last, if we are to live as greatly as our imaginations and our hearts say to us we could.

Appendix

CITATIONS TO THE CONGRESSIONAL MEDAL OF HONOR FOR SIX LATIN AMERICANS OF THE STATE OF TEXAS

Sergeant José M. López

"Sergeant José M. López, (then Private First Class) 23rd Infantry, near Krinkelt, Belgium, on December 17, 1944, on his own initiative carried his heavy machinegun from K Company's right flank to its left, in order to protect that flank which was in danger of being overrun by advancing enemy infantry supported by tanks.

"Occupying a shallow hole offering no protection above his waist, he cut down a group of ten Germans. Ignoring enemy fire from an advancing tank, he held his position and cut down 25 more enemy infantry attempting to turn his flank. Glancing to his right he saw a large number of infantry swarming in from the front. Although dazed and shaken from enemy artillery fire which had crashed into the ground only a few yards away, he realized that his position would be soon outflanked.

"Again, alone, he carried his machinegun to a position to the right rear of the sector; enemy tanks and infantry were forcing a withdrawal. Blown over backwards by the concussion of enemy fire, he immediately reset his gun and continued his fire. Singlehanded, he held off the German horde until he was satisfied his company had effected its retirement. Again he loaded his gun on his back and in a hail of small arms fire he ran to a point where a few of his comrades were attempting to set up another defense against the onrushing enemy.

"He fired from this position until his ammunition was exhausted. Still carrying his gun, he fell back with his small group to Krinkelt. Sergeant López' gallantry and intrepidity, on seemingly suicidal missions in which he killed at least 100 of the enemy, were almost solely responsible for allowing K Company to avoid being enveloped, to withdraw successfully, and to give other forces coming up in support time to build a line which repelled the enemy drive."

283

Staff Sergeant Marcario García

"Staff Sergeant Marcario García, (then PFC), Infantry, while an acting squad leader of Company B, 22nd Infantry, on November 27, 1944, near Grosshau, Germany, singlehandedly assaulted two enemy machinegun emplacements. Attacking prepared positions on a wooded hill, which could be approached only through meager cover, his company was pinned down by intense machinegun fire and subjected to a concentrated artillery and mortar barrage. Although painfully wounded, he refused to be evacuated and on his own initiative crawled forward alone until he reached a position near an enemy emplacement. Hurling grenades, he boldly assaulted the position, destroyed the gun, and with his rifle, killed three of the enemy who attempted to escape. When he rejoined his company, a second machinegun opened fire and again the intrepid soldier went forward, utterly disregarding his own safety. He stormed the position and destroyed the gun, killed three more Germans and captured four prisoners. He fought on with his unit until the objective was taken and only then did he permit himself to be removed for medical care. Private García's conspicuous heroism, his inspiring, courageous conduct and his complete disregard for his personal safety wiped out two enemy emplacements and enabled his company to advance and secure its objective."

Private First Class Cleto L. Rodríguez

"Private First Class Cleto L. Rodríguez was an automatic rifleman with Company B, 148th Infantry, on February 9, 1945, when his unit attacked the strongly defended Paco Railroad Station during the battle for Manila, Philippine Islands.

"While making a frontal assault across an open field, his position was halted one hundred yards from the station by intense enemy fire. On his own initiative, he left the platoon, accompanied by a comrade, and continued forward to a house sixty yards from the objective.

"Although under constant enemy observation, the two men remained in this position for an hour, firing at targets of opportunity, killing more than thirty-five hostile soldiers and wounding many more. Moving closer to the station and discovering a group of Japanese replacements attempting to reach pillboxes, they opened heavy fire, killed more than forty and stopped all subsequent attempts to man the emplacements. Enemy fire became more intense as they advanced to within twenty yards of the station. Then, covered by his companion, Private Rodríguez boldly moved up to the building and threw five grenades through a doorway, killing seven Japanese, destroying a 20-millimeter gun and wrecking a heavy machinegun.

"With their ammunition running low, the two men started to return to the American lines, alternately providing covering fire for each other's withdrawal. During this movement, Private Rodríguez' companion was killed.

"In two and one-half hours of fierce fighting the intrepid team killed more than eighty-two Japanese, completely disorganized their defense and paved the way for the subsequent overwhelming defeat of the enemy at this strongpoint.

"Two days later, Private Rodríguez again enabled his comrades to advance when he singlehandedly killed six Japanese and destroyed a well-placed 20-millimeter gun. By his outstanding skill with his weapons, gallant determination to destroy the enemy and heroic courage in the face of tremendous odds, Private Rodríguez on two occasions, materially aided the advance of our troops in Manila."

Staff Sergeant Lucian Adams

"For conspicuous gallantry and intrepidity at risk of life above and beyond the call of duty on October 28, 1944, near St. Die, France. When his company was stopped in its effort to drive through the Mortagne Forest to reopen the supply line to the isolated 3d battalion, Staff Sergeant Adams braved the concentrated fire of machineguns in a lone assault on a force of German troops. Although his company had progressed less than ten yards and had lost three killed, six wounded, Sergeant Adams charged forward dodging from tree to tree firing a borrowed BAR from the hip. Despite intense machinegun fire which the enemy directed at him and rifle grenades which struck the trees over his head showering him with broken twigs and branches, Sergeant Adams made his way to within ten yards of the closest machinegun and killed the gunner with a hand grenade. An enemy soldier threw hand grenades at him from a position only ten yards distant; however, Sergeant Adams dispatched him with a single burst of BAR fire. Charging into the vortex of the enemy fire, he killed another machinegunner at 15 yards range with a hand grenade and forced the surrender of two supporting infantrymen. Although the remainder of the German group concentrated the full force of its automatic weapons fire in a desperate effort to knock him out, he proceeded through the woods to find and exterminate five more of the enemy. Finally when the third German machinegun opened up on him at a range of 20 yards, Sergeant Adams killed the gunner with BAR fire. In the course of the action he personally killed nine Germans, eliminated three enemy machineguns, vanquished a specialized force which was armed with automatic weapons and grenade launchers, cleared the woods of hostile elements and reopened the severed supply lines to the assault companies of his battalion."

Private First Class Silvestre S. Herrera

"Private First Class Silvestre S. Herrera, Company E, 142d Infantry Regiment, advanced with a platoon along a wooded road near Mertzwiller, France, on March 15, 1945, until stopped by heavy enemy machinegun fire. As the rest of the unit took cover, he made a one-man, frontal assault on a strongpoint and captured eight enemy soldiers.

"When the platoon resumed its advance and was subjected to fire from a second emplacement beyond an extensive minefield, Private Herrera again moved forward, disregarding the danger of exploding mines, to attack the position. He stepped on a mine and had both feet severed; but, despite intense pain and unchecked loss of blood, he pinned down the enemy with accurate rifle fire while a friendly squad captured the enemy gun by skirting the minefield and rushing in from the flank.

"The magnificent courage, extraordinary heroism and willing self-sacrifice displayed by Private Herrera resulted in the capture of two enemy strongpoints and the taking of eight prisoners."

Private First Class Alejandro R. Ruiz

"Private First Class Alejandro Rentería Ruiz, Company A, 165th Infantry, on April 28, 1945, on Okinawa, when his unit was stopped by a skillfully camouflaged enemy pillbox, displayed conspicuous gallantry and intrepidity above and beyond the call of duty. His squad, suddenly brought under a hail of machinegun fire and a vicious grenade attack, was pinned down. Jumping to his feet, Private Ruiz seized an automatic rifle and lunged through the flying grenades and rifle and automatic fire for the top of the emplacement. When an enemy soldier charged him, his rifle jammed. Undaunted, Private Ruiz whirled on his assailant and clubbed him down. Then he ran back through bullets and grenades, seized more ammunition and another automatic rifle, and again made for the pillbox. Enemy fire now was concentrated on him, but he charged on, miraculously reaching the position, and in plain view he climbed to the top. Leaping from one opening to another, he sent burst after burst into the pillbox, killing 12 of the enemy and completely destroying the position. Private Ruiz' heroic conduct, in the face of overwhelming odds, saved the lives of many comrades and eliminated an obstacle that long would have checked his unit's advance."

BIBLIOGRAPHY

"Activities for Latin-American Children in Elementary Grades."
Southwest Texas State Teachers College, San Marcos, July, 1944.
A series of four bulletins:
No. I —Health and Physical Education. 35 pp.
No. II —Art Activities. 12 pp.
No. III —Building Better School-Community Relations. 20 pp.
No. IV —Music Activities. 27 pp.

Aikman, Duncan. *All American Front.* Doubleday, Doran & Co., New York, 1940. 344 pp.

Allen, Ruth A. "Mexican Peon Women in Texas." *Sociology and Social Research,* XV (Nov.-Dec., 1931), 131-142.

"Annual Report." Bexar County Tuberculosis Association, San Antonio, 1943. 10 pp.

"Annual Report 1944." Housing Authority of the City of San Antonio, 1945. 16 pp.

Austin American, The, Austin, April 3, 1945.

———March 7, 1946.

Baker, Nina Brown. *Juárez, Hero of Mexico.* The Vanguard Press, New York, 1942. 316 pp.

Baldwin, Leland Dewitt. *The Story of the Americas.* Simon and Schuster, New York, 1943. 720 pp.

Beals, Carleton. *Mexican Maze.* J. B. Lippincott Co., Philadelphia, 1931. 370 pp.

———*Porfirio Díaz, Dictator of Mexico.* J. B. Lippincott Co., Philadelphia, 1932. 463 pp.

Berle, Adolf A. *New Directions in the New World.* Harper and Brothers, New York, 1940. 141 pp.

Blasio, José Luis. *Maximilian, Emperor of Mexico.* Yale University Press, New Haven, 1934. 235 pp.

Bogardus, Emory S. "Current Problems of Mexican Immigrants." *Sociology and Social Research,* XXV (Nov.-Dec., 1940), 166-174.

———"The Mexican Immigrant and Segregation." *American Journal of Sociology.* XXXVI (July, 1930), 74-80.

———*The Mexican in the United States.* The University of Southern California Press, Los Angeles, 1934. 126 pp.

Brenner, Anita. *Idols Behind Altars.* Harcourt, Brace & Co., New York, 1929. 359 pp.

——— *The Wind That Swept Mexico.* Harper and Brothers, New York, 1943. 302 pp.

287

288   LATIN AMERICANS IN TEXAS

Calderón de la Barca, Mme. *Life in Mexico.* E. P. Dutton & Co., Inc., New York, 1940. 542 pp.

Callahan, James Morton. *American Foreign Policy in Mexican Relations.* The Macmillan Company, New York, 1932. 644 pp.

Callcott, Wilfrid Hardy. *Church and State in Mexico.* Duke University Press, Durham, N. C., 1926. 357 pp.

Castañeda, Carlos E. "Some Facts on Our Racial Minority." *The Pan-American,* I (October, 1944), 4-5.

"Centros de Recepción para Obreros Ambulantes." Extension Service, Agricultural and Mechanical College of Texas, College Station, 1946. 84 pp.

"Community Organization for Inter-American Understanding." Good Neighbor Commission of Texas, Austin, August, 1944. 22 pp.

"Comparison of Family Income and Expenditures for Five Principal Budget Items in Twenty Texas Cities." The University of Texas, Bureau of Business Research, Austin, April, 1943. 77 pp.

Cook, Katherine M., and Florence E. Reynolds. "The Education of Native and Minority Groups; a Bibliography." United States Department of Interior, Office of Education, Bulletin 12, Washington, D. C., 1933.

Cotterill, R. S. *A Short History of the Americas.* Prentice-Hall, Inc., New York, 1939. 459 pp.

Dann, W. J., and William J. Darby. "The Appraisal of Nutritional Status (Nutriture) in Humans." *Physiological Reviews.* XXV (April, 1945).

Diario del Norte, Ciudad Juárez, Chihuahua, México, April 24, 1946.

Díaz del Castillo, Bernal. *True History of the Conquest of Mexico.* Robert M. McBride & Co., New York, 1927. 562 pp.

Eckhardt, Robert C. "State Aid and School Attendance in Texas." Report to the Office of Inter-American Affairs, Washington, D. C., October, 1945. (Processed).

Enciso, F. B. "Rights and Duties of a Mexican Child." *School and Society,* XLIII (April 18, 1936), 547-548.

Excelsior, México, D. F., November 30, 1944.

———— January 18, 1946.

Feldman, Herman. "Mexicans and Indians." *Racial Factors in American Industry,* Harper and Brothers, New York, 1931. 104-118.

"Final Report of the Fair Employment Practice Committee." Fair Employment Practice Committee, Washington, D. C., June, 1946. 11 pp. (Processed).

Fisher, Lillian Estelle. *The Background of the Revolution for Mexican Independence.* The Christopher Publishing House, Boston, 1934. 512 pp.

Foerster, Robert F. "The Racial Problems Involved in Immigration from Latin America and the West Indies to the United States." United States Department of Labor, Washington, D. C., 1925. 62 pp.

Galarza, Ernesto. "Life in the United States for Mexican People. Out of the Experience of a Mexican." National Conference of Social Work, *Proceedings,* 1929. The University of Chicago Press, Chicago, 1930. 399-404.

Gamio, Manuel. *The Mexican Immigrant—His Life Story.* The University of Chicago Press, Chicago, 1931. 288 pp.

Gammel's *Laws of Texas*, I, 110.

Gessler, Clifford. *Pattern of Mexico*. D. Appleton-Century Co., Inc., New York, 1941. 441 pp.

Gonzales, Manuel C. "Latin Cultural Contributions to Texas." Address delivered to and published by the San Antonio Rotary Club, San Antonio, 1944. 5 pp.

González Peña, Carlos. *History of Mexican Literature*. University Press in Dallas, Southern Methodist University, Dallas, 1943. 398 pp.

Goodwyn, Frank. *The Magic of Limping John*. Farrar & Rinehart, New York, 1944. 275 pp.

Gould, David M. "Mass X-Ray Survey in San Antonio." *Public Health Reports*, LX (February 2, 1945), 117-126.

Griggs, Joseph R., and Myrtle L. Tanner. "Suggested Course of Study in Spanish for Texas High Schools 1945." State Department of Education, Bulletin 452, Austin, 1945. 206 pp.

Gruening, Ernest. *Mexico and Its Heritage*. The Century Company, New York, 1928. 728 pp.

Handman, Max S. "Economic Reasons for the Coming of the Mexican Immigrant." *American Journal of Sociology*, XXXV (January, 1930), 601-611.

Hawley, Florence, Michel Pijoan, and C. A. Elkin. "An Inquiry Into Food Economy in Zia Pueblo." *American Anthropologist*, XLV (Oct.-Dec., 1943).

Helm, Mackinley. *Modern Mexican Painters*. Harper and Brothers, New York, 1941. 205 pp.

Herring & Weinstock. *Renascent Mexico*. Covici-Friede, New York, 1935. 322 pp.

Hidalgo, Ernesto. *La Protección de Mexicanos en los Estados Unidos*. Secretaría de Relaciones Exteriores, México, D. F., 1940.

Holley, William C. "The Farm Situation in Texas." United States Department of Agriculture, Bureau of Agricultural Economics, Division of Farm Population and Rural Welfare, Washington, D. C., May, 1940.

Howard, Graeme K. *America and a New World Order*. Chas. Scribner's Sons, New York, 1940. 121 pp.

"Informe de Labores." Secretaría de la Asistencia Pública, México, D. F., 1942-1943. 323 pp.

Inman, Samuel Guy. *Latin America, Its Place in World Life*. Harcourt, Brace & Co., New York, 1942. 466 pp.

Johnston, Edgar G. "Michigan's Step-Children." The University of Michigan *School of Education Bulletin*, XV (October, 1943), 1-6.

Jones, Robert C. "Mexicans in the United States—A Bibliography." Pan American Union, Division of Labor and Social Information, Bibliographic Series 27, Washington, D. C., September, 1942.

Juárez, Benito. *Exposiciones*.

Kermack, W. O., A. G. McKendrick, and P. L. Finlay. *The Lancet*, I (1934), 698.

Kirk, Betty. *Covering the Mexican Front*. The University of Oklahoma Press, Norman, 1942. 367 pp.

Lansing, Marion. *Liberators and Heroes of Mexico and Central America*. L. C. Page & Co., Boston, 1941. 299 pp.

La Prensa, México, D. F., December 1, 1944.

290   LATIN AMERICANS IN TEXAS

"Latin-American Health Problem in Texas, The." Texas State Department of Health, Division of Maternal and Child Health, Austin, 1940. 13 pp.

"Like a Sore Thumb." Bexar County Tuberculosis Association, San Antonio, 1945. 16 pp.

Lillingston, Claude. "The House Fly." Hygeia, XIII (March, 1935), 242-245.

Little, Wilson. "Spanish-Speaking Children in Texas." The University of Texas Press, Austin, 1944. 73 pp.

Longmore, T. Wilson, and Homer L. Hitt. "A Demographic Analysis of First and Second Generation Mexican Population of the United States: 1930." Southwestern Social Science Quarterly, XXIV (September, 1943), 138-149.

Lowery, Woodbury. The Spanish Settlements Within the Present Limits of the United States. G. P. Putnams' Sons, New York, 1901. 515 pp.

Lozano, Rubén Rendón. Viva Tejas. Southern Literary Institute, San Antonio, 1936. 50 pp.

MacLeish, Archibald. "Victory Without Peace." The Saturday Review of Literature, XXIX (February 9, 1946), 5.

Mann, Horace. Life and Works of Horace Mann. Lothrop, Lee & Shepard Co., New York, 1891. IV, 115-116.

Manuel, Herschel T. The Education of Mexican and Spanish-Speaking Children in Texas. The Fund for Research in the Social Sciences, The University of Texas, Austin, 1930. 173 pp.

———— "The Educational Problem Presented by the Spanish-Speaking Child of the Southwest." School and Society, XL (1934), 692-695.

———— "The Mexican Population of Texas." Southwestern Political and Social Science Quarterly, XV (June, 1934), 29-51.

McLean, Robert N. "Mexican Workers in the United States." National Conference of Social Work, Proceedings, 1929. The University of Chicago Press, Chicago, 1930. 531-538.

McWilliams, Carey. Brothers Under the Skin. Little, Brown & Company, Boston, 1943. 325 pp.

———— Ill Fares the Land. Little, Brown & Company, Boston, 1944. 419 pp.

Menefee, Selden C. "Mexican Migratory Workers of South Texas." Federal Works Agency, Work Projects Administration, Division of Research, Washington, D. C., 1941. 67 pp.

———— and Orin C. Cassmore. "The Pecan Shellers of San Antonio." Federal Works Agency, Work Projects Administration, Division of Research, Washington, D. C., 1940. 82 pp.

"Mexico: Life Reports on a Social Revolution in Progress." Life, VI (January 23, 1939), 29.

"Mexico's Role in International Intellectual Co-operation." Proceedings of a Conference held in Albuquerque, February 24-25, 1944. The University of New Mexico Press, Albuquerque, Inter-Americana Short Papers VI, 1945.

Millan, Verna C. Mexico Reborn. Houghton-Mifflin Company, New York, 1939. 312 pp.

"Minutes of Professional Workshop." State Department of Education, Austin, March 19-24, 1945. 30 pp. (Processed).

BIBLIOGRAPHY 291

Munro, Dana Gardner. *The Latin American Republics.* D. Appleton-Century Co., Inc., New York, 1942. 650 pp.

"Need, A Study of Basic Social Needs." The Texas Social Welfare Association, Austin, November, 1940. 32 pp.

"Origins and Problems of Texas Migratory Farm Labor." Texas State Employment Service, Austin, 1940. 93 pp.

Ortega, Joaquín. "New Mexico's Opportunity." The School of Inter-American Affairs, The University of New Mexico, Albuquerque, 1942. 21 pp.

Padilla, Ezequiel. *Free Men of America.* Ziff-Davis Publishing Co., Chicago, 1943. 173 pp.

Pan-American, The. I (April, 1945), 16.

Parkes, Henry Bamford. *A History of Mexico.* Houghton-Mifflin Company, Boston, 1938. 432 pp.

Pijoan, Michel. "Certain Factors Involved in the Struggle against Malnutrition and Disease, with Special Reference to the Southwest of the United States and Latin America." The University of New Mexico Press, Albuquerque, 1943. Inter-Americana, Short Papers VII.

—— and A. Drexler. "Comments on the Taos Report." United States Indian Service, Washington, D. C., 1943.

—— and C. A. Elkin. "Secondary Anemia Due to Prolonged and Exclusive Milk Feeding among Shoshone Indian Infants." *The Journal of Nutrition,* XXVII (January, 1944).

—— and Eugene L. Lozner. "The Physiologic Significance of Vitamin C in Man." *New England Journal of Medicine,* CCXXXI (July 6, 1944), 14-21.

—— and Eugene L. Lozner. "Vitamin C Economy in the Human Subject." *Bulletin of the Johns Hopkins Hospital,* LXXV (November, 1944), 303-314.

Pinchon, Edgcumb. *Viva Villa.* Grosset & Dunlap, New York, 1933. 383 pp.

—— *Zapata, the Unconquerable.* Doubleday, Doran & Co., Inc., New York, 1941. 332 pp.

Prado, E. L. "Sinarquism in the United States." *New Republic,* CIX (July 26, 1943), 97-102.

Prewett, Virginia. *The Americas and Tomorrow.* E. P. Dutton & Co., Inc., New York, 1944. 292 pp.

Priestley, Herbert I. *The Mexican Nation.* The Macmillan Company, New York, 1923. 507 pp.

"Proceedings of an Inter-American Conference." Baylor University, Waco, January, 1945. 72 pp.

Quintanilla, Luis. *A Latin American Speaks.* The Macmillan Company, Dallas, 1943. 268 pp.

"Report on Migratory Farm Labor in Texas." Good Neighbor Commission of Texas, Austin, December 29, 1944. 12 pp. (Processed).

Reynolds, Anne E. "The Education of Spanish-Speaking Children in Five Southwestern States." United States Department of Interior, Office of Education, Bulletin 11, Washington, D. C., 1933. 64 pp.

San Antonio Light, The, San Antonio, March 9, 1945.

Sánchez, George I. *Mexico: A Revolution by Education.* The Viking Press, New York, 1936. 211 pp.

Saunders, Lyle. "A Guide to the Literature of the Southwest." Regular feature in *New Mexico Quarterly Review* since January 1, 1942. Reprints available at School of Inter-American Affairs, The University of New Mexico, Albuquerque.

"Seis Años de Gobierno al Servicio de México, 1934-1940." La Nacional Impresora, S. A., México, D. F., November, 1940. 459 pp.

Simpson, Eyler N. *The Ejido: Mexico's Way Out.* The University of North Carolina Press, Chapel Hill, 1937. 849 pp.

Soule, George, David Efron and Norman T. Ness. *Latin America in the Future World.* Farrar & Rinehart, Inc., New York, 1945. 372 pp.

"Spanish-Speaking of the Southwest and West, The." A Report of the Conference held at San Antonio, Texas, July 20-23, 1943. National Catholic Welfare Conference, Washington, D. C., 1943.

——— A Report of the Conference held at Denver, October 17-20, 1944. National Catholic Welfare Conference, Washington, D. C., 1944.

"Statewide Survey of Enumeration, Enrollment, Attendance, and Progress of Latin American Children in Texas Public Schools." State Department of Education, Austin, 1943-1944. 8 pp. (Processed).

Stegner, Wallace Earle. *One Nation.* Houghton-Mifflin Company, Boston, 1945. 340 pp.

Stewart, Watt. *Builders of Latin America.* Harper and Brothers, New York, 1942. 343 pp.

Stilwell, Hart. *Border City.* Doubleday, Doran & Co., Inc., Garden City, N. Y., 1945. 276 pp.

Stowell, Jay S. *The Near Side of the Mexican Question.* George H. Doran Company, New York, 1921. 123 pp.

Strode, Hudson. *Timeless Mexico.* Harcourt, Brace & Company, New York, 1944. 436 pp.

Sullivan, Mary Loretta, and Bertha Blair. "Women in Texas Industries: Hours, Wages, Working Conditions, and Home Work." United States Department of Labor, Women's Bureau Bulletin 126, Washington, D. C., 1936. 81 pp.

"Summary Report of the College and University Conference on Inter-American Education." The University of Texas, Austin, February 9-10, 1944. 22 pp. (Processed).

"Summary Report of the Conference of Co-operating Colleges in Inter-American Education." The University of Texas, Austin, January 5, 1944. 11 pp. (Processed).

"Summary Report, Professional Conference, Inter-American Relations Education." State Department of Education, Austin, October 5-7, 1944. (Processed).

"Summary Report, Teacher Training Workshop, Inter-American Relations Education." The University of Texas, Austin, April 17-22, 1944. 35 pp. (Processed).

Tannenbaum, Frank. *Peace by Revolution.* Columbia University Press, New York, 1933. 317 pp.

Taylor, Paul Schuster. *An American-Mexican Frontier.* The University of North Carolina Press, Chapel Hill, 1934, 337 pp.

"T. E. F. L. 20 Migratory Labor." Co-operative Extension Work, Agricultural and Mechanical College of Texas, College Station, January 5, 1945. 15 pp. (Processed).

"Texas Almanac and State Industrial Guide." A. H. Belo Corporation, Dallas, 1944. 138-139.

"Texas' Children." Texas Child Welfare Survey, The University of Texas, Bureau of Research in the Social Sciences, Austin, 1938. 885 pp.

"Texas: Summary of Vital Statistics, 1942." Department of Commerce, Bureau of the Census, Washington, D. C., XX (March 11, 1944). 15 pp.

Thomson, Charles A. "Mexicans—An Interpretation." National Conference of Social Work, *Proceedings,* 1928, The University of Chicago Press, Chicago, 1929. 499-503.

Torres-Rioseco, Arturo. *The Epic of Latin American Literature.* Oxford University Press, New York, 1942. 279 pp.

"United Nations Dumbarton Oaks Proposals for a General International Organization." Department of State Publication 2297, Conference Series 66, Washington, D. C., 1945. 8 pp.

Vaillant, George C. *Aztecs of Mexico.* Doubleday, Doran & Co., Garden City, N. Y., 1941. 340 pp.

Valley Evening Monitor, The, McAllen, Texas, March 30, 1944.

Velázquez Chávez, Agustín, *Contemporary Mexican Artists.* Covici-Friede, New York, 1937. 304 pp.

Warburton, Amber Arthun, Helen Wood and Marian M. Crane, M. D. "The Work and Welfare of Children of Agricultural Laborers in Hidalgo County, Texas." United States Department of Labor, Children's Bureau, Publication 298, Washington, D. C., 1943. 74 pp.

Watson, Walter T. "Mexicans in Dallas." In Myers, S. D., Jr., Ed., *Mexico and the United States.* Institute of Public Affairs, Southern Methodist University, Dallas, 1938. 231-250.

Wertenbaker, Charles. *A New Doctrine for the Americas.* The Viking Press, New York, 1941. 211 pp.

Weyl, Nathaniel and Sylvia. *The Reconquest of Mexico.* Oxford University Press, New York, 1939. 394 pp.

Winters, Jet C. "A Report on the Health and Nutrition of Mexicans Living in Texas." The University of Texas Bulletin No. 3127, Austin, July 15, 1931. 99 pp.

Zavala, Silvio. *New Viewpoints on the Spanish Colonization of America.* The University of Pennsylvania Press, Philadelphia, 1943. 118 pp.

INDEX

Act of Chapultepec, 9, 12-13
Adams, Lucian, 224
Adult education, 119-121, 276-277
Aircraft industry, 162
Alamo, 32
Alemán, Miguel, 74
Alonso, Ernesto, 225
Alvarado, Pedro de, 48
American Public Health Association, 261
Americanization, 97, 98, 269
Aoy Elementary School, El Paso, 142
Argentina, 9, 12, 13, 18
Atlantic Charter, 9, 245
Austin, Stephen F., 32
Avila Camacho, Manuel, 44, 61, 65-66, 69, 71 74, 82

Bailey, Dr. Charles A., 58
Baz, Dr. Gustavo, 70
Benavides, Captain Plácido, 33
Beneficencia Mexicana, 270
Beteta, Ramón, 75
"Big Depression," 17
Big Spring, 179-180, 184
"Big Stick" Policy, 15
Birch, Rev. John J., 269
Bishops' Committee for the Spanish-Speaking, 268-270
Blue Moon Night Club, 213-214
Bolívar, Simón, 15, 20
Bonilla y Segura, Professor Guillermo, 67
Brazil:
airports built in, 23
government, violent change in, 18
membership on Security Council, 13
military assistance of, 26
reciprocal trade agreement with, 20
United States flying instructors in, 23
Brenner, Anita, 43, 53
Brockette, Connie Garza, 114
Brownsville *Herald,* 223
Bureau of Business Research, 165
Bureau of Census, 125

CIO International, 161
Cabeza de Vaca, 31
Calles, Plutarco Elías, 53
Cantinflas, 207
Cárdenas, Colonel Antonio, 30
Cárdenas, Lázaro, 20, 44, 59, 61-64, 65, 74
Carranza, Venustiano, 53, 54
Castañeda, Carlos E., 157, 162
Castillo, Henry, 226
Castillo Nájera, Francisco, 75
Catholic Church:
Bishops' Committee for the Spanish-Speaking, 268-270
colonial education in Mexico, 50
parochial schools in Texas, 86
role in Mexican history, 51-52
Catholic Church Extension Society, 268
"Centros de Recepción para Obreros Ambulantes," 187
Chamberlain, Neville, 21
Chancery Office, San Antonio, 86
Chapultepec, Act of, 9, 12-13
Children's Bureau, United States Department of Labor, 89-91, 93, 124, 192, 262
Chile, 17, 18, 23, 25
Churches, 266-270, 278
Civil rights, 220, 227-230, 234, 271
Cockrell, Lloyd, 224
Colombia, 20, 23, 24, 25
"Colossus of the North," 17, 19
Compulsory school attendance law:
ineffectual under present system, 94
law enforcement, 93
Conferences of American Foreign Ministers:
Havana (1940), 22
Panama (1939), 22
Rio de Janeiro (1942), 25
Connally, Senator Tom, 12
Constitution of 1917, 17, 20, 54
Coordinator of Inter-American Affairs, Office of, 23, 81, 84, 108, 110, 112, 113, 140, 253

THE AUTHOR

Pauline Rochester Kibbe: born, Pueblo, Colorado, 1909; began work in inter-American field, San Antonio, Texas, 1939; bilingual secretarial service and purchasing service for Mexican business firms, 1940-1941; script writer and producer, series of twenty weekly radio programs on Latin America, entitled "Americans All," broadcast over KTSA, San Antonio, 1942; chairman, city-wide Central Planning Committee for Inter-American Understanding, under sponsorship of Business and Professional Women's Club, San Antonio, 1942-43; columnist, San Antonio *Light*, weekly column entitled "Looking South," 1942-43; lecturer on history and literature of Latin America, inter-American relations, and problems of Latin Americans in Texas, since 1941; Field Associate for Executive Committee on Inter-American Relations in Texas, The University of Texas, Austin, 1943; Executive Secretary, Good Neighbor Commission of Texas, Austin, since September 1, 1943. Author: two-year *Educational Program Outline on Latin America,* published first by Phi Eta National Sorority, St. Louis, Mo., and reprinted by Office of Inter-American Affairs, Washington, D. C., 1943; *Community Organization for Inter-American Understanding,* Good Neighbor Commission of Texas, 1944.

The Mexican American

An Arno Press Collection

Castañeda, Alfredo, et al, eds. **Mexican Americans and Educational Change.** 1974
Church Views of the Mexican American. 1974
Clinchy, Everett Ross, Jr. **Equality of Opportunity for Latin-Americans in Texas.** 1974
Crichton, Kyle S. **Law and Order Ltd.** 1928
Education and the Mexican American. 1974
Fincher, E. B. **Spanish-Americans as a Political Factor in New Mexico, 1912-1950.** 1974
Greenwood, Robert. **The California Outlaw:** Tiburcio Vasquez. 1960
Juan N. Cortina: Two Interpretations. 1974
Kibbe, Pauline R. **Latin Americans in Texas.** 1946
The Mexican American and the Law. 1974
Mexican American Bibliographies. 1974
Mexican Labor in the United States. 1974
The New Mexican Hispano. 1974
Otero, Miguel Antonio. **Otero:** An Autobiographical Trilogy. 1935/39/40
The Penitentes of New Mexico. 1974
Perales, Alonso S. **Are We Good Neighbors?** 1948
Perspectives on Mexican-American Life. 1974
Simmons, Ozzie G. **Anglo-Americans and Mexican Americans in South Texas.** 1974
Spanish and Mexican Land Grants. 1974
Tuck, Ruth D. **Not With the Fist.** 1946
Zeleny, Carolyn. **Relations Between the Spanish-Americans and Anglo-Americans in New Mexico.** 1974